VISUALISING THE
BEATLES

VISUALISING THE BEATLES

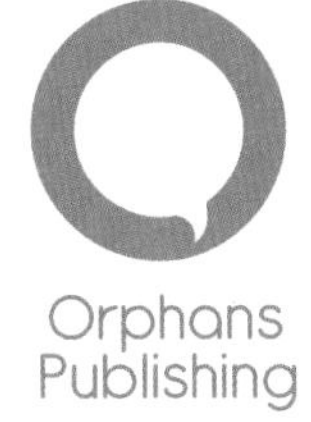

Orphans Publishing

Published by Orphans Publishing 2016

First published in Great Britain in 2016 by
Orphans Publishing

orphanspublishing.co.uk

ISBN 978-1-903360-16-3 (Paperback Edition)

Orphans Publishing supports the Forest Stewardship Council® (FSC®), the leading international forest-certification organisation. Our books carrying the FSC label are printed on FSC®- certified paper.

Cover illustration by Orphans Publishing

Typeset in Gotham Narrow 8pt / 15pt

Designed, printed and bound in Great Britain by Orphans Press Ltd, Enterprise Park, Herefordshire HR6 0LD

CONTENTS

FOREWORD

As a young bass player, I remember constantly borrowing my mum's Beatles records in an attempt to learn every single Paul McCartney bassline that I could. With each tune I played, Mum would pop her head around the door to tell me, 'I was there when they played that one!'

Ever since, in all my years of supporting, advising and encouraging musicians and bands, I have referenced the Beatles a million times. Quite simply because they set the rules for rock and pop music. While fashion and musicianship has changed and improved, it remains clear that, from start to finish, the Beatles stuck to certain key principles.

The evolution of the Fab Four – not only as a band but individually as musicians and people – has never before been documented in such a concise and exciting way. John and Rob have researched a huge number of details that explain the Beatles' development into one of the greatest bands ever and why this title is so deserved.

Using a captivating array of infographics this book takes us on an exhilarating ride through the Beatles years. Even the most avid fan will learn something and everyone will enjoy the beautiful graphics. It perfectly depicts how the early songwriting partnership of Lennon and McCartney developed into a melting pot of ideas and creativity from everyone, including the 'fifth Beatle' George Martin. From documenting instrumentation to songwriting splits, fashion to tours and even song keys and waveforms, this book has it all. It will inspire you to dust off your *Rubber Soul* vinyl or Spotify *Sgt. Pepper*.

Damian Keyes
Bass Player & Founder of Brighton Institute of Modern Music

INTRODUCTION

1960-1962

A NOTE FROM THE AUTHORS

Even now, nearly fifty years since the Beatles released their final album and performed one last time on the rooftop of the Apple Corps building, the world's love for this, perhaps ultimate, band shows no signs of cooling. Each generation jubilantly passes the Fab Four's music onto the next, hoping to inspire a budding songwriter or groundbreaking guitarist, or simply to share the magic of the first notes of 'All You Need Is Love'.

The Beatles have become ingrained in modern popular culture, as much shaped by it as they were instrumental in shaping it. The pair of us - two friends who played, wrote songs, sketched and photographed through our youth in noughties Brighton (not quite the incredible live music scene of post-war Liverpool the Beatles thrived in but as near as our generation will ever get) - grew up enthralled to their creativity, experimentation and originality.

As designers, we wondered what it would look like to visualise the Beatles and chart their story - the evolution of their music, style and characters - through a series of graphics. What might presenting the information in a totally different way never done before on this scale, tell us that we hadn't noticed or appreciated previously? With the help of an incredible bunch of Beatles and infographic fans on Kickstarter, we began to find out. This book is a product of their generosity and encouragement, and was made possible by one of the biggest sources of our generation's creativity: the internet.

The book is organised by album (in order of the dates the albums were released rather than recorded). It is by no means a definitive history of the Beatles. Instead it is an attempt to create something beautiful, vibrant and original from the data their music left behind. It is an attempt to present the facts in a way you haven't seen them before, so you can spot, in an instant, the patterns, anomalies and changes. And finally, it is an attempt to capture the spirit of the Beatles and the sixties, a decade we're almost as unwilling to let go of as the band themselves, visually.

John Pring & Rob Thomas

MEET THE BEATLES

Known in their formative years as Blackjacks, The Quarrymen, Johnny and the Moondogs, Beatals, Silver Beetles, Silver Beatles and finally the Beatles, John Lennon, Paul McCartney and George Harrison were joined by Richard Starkey in 1962 to form the group we know and love today.

The Beatles' first ever 'professional' performance was on Friday 20th May 1960 in Scotland, as Johnny Gentle's backing group. Their first break came not long afterwards when their manager Allan Williams secured a deal for the group to go and play at Indra bar in Hamburg, Germany for two months, famously driving them and a host of other acts all the way there in his van.

Once there, the Beatles performed for a staggering 205 hours over seven weeks and it transformed them. It was also where they first got to know Ringo Starr, playing with his band the Hurricanes at *Tanzpalast der Jugend* 'dance palace of the youth'. By the time the Beatles got back to Liverpool, their new audiences were transfixed by them. The effect was explosive...

John Winston (later Ono) Lennon	James Paul McCartney	George Harrison	Richard Starkey (professional name Ringo Starr)
Parents: Alfred Lennon, Julia Stanley	**Parents:** James McCartney, Mary Mohan	**Parents:** Harold Harrison, Louise French	**Parents:** Richard Starkey, Elsie Gleave
Favourite childhood book: Alice in Wonderland	**Alternative career:** Paul's mother wanted him to become a doctor	**School:** Liverpool Institute (with Paul) on the same street as John's art college	**Pre-Beatles:** 'Ritchie' was an apprentice at manufacturing company H. Hunt & Son
Date of Birth: 9 October 1940	**Date of Birth:** 18 June 1942	**Date of Birth:** 25 February 1943	**Date of Birth:** 7 July 1940

LIVERPOOL: WHERE IT ALL BEGAN

The Beatles spent much of their later years in London, but Liverpool is their spiritual home. All four band members were born here, met here and honed their talents here before hitting the big time.

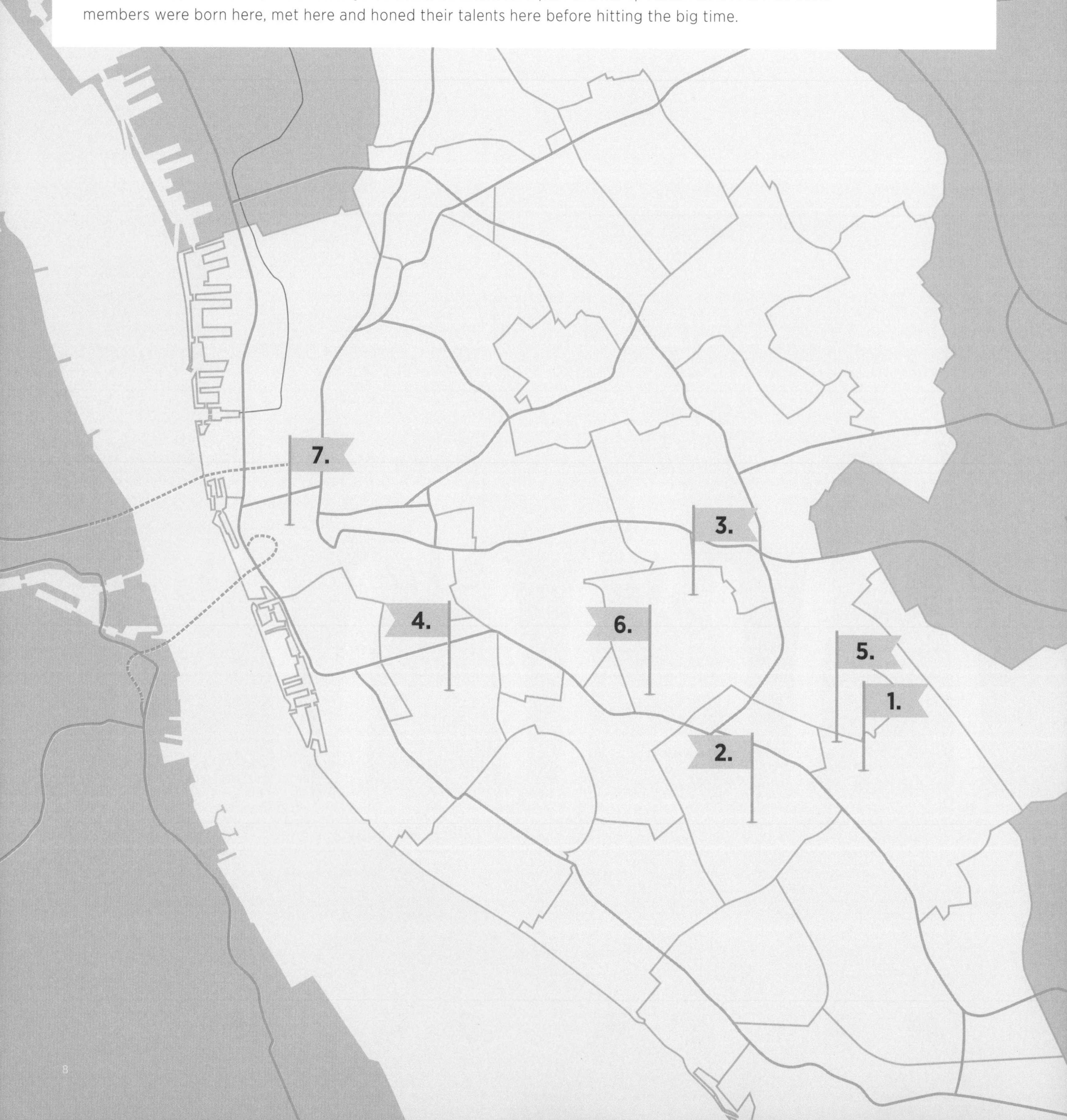

Mendips, 251 Menlove Avenue

The childhood home of John Lennon. He moved to this address aged five after his mother was persuaded that his Aunt Mimi and Uncle George were better suited to looking after him. He lived there until he was 22.

20 Forthlin Road, Allerton

The childhood home of Paul McCartney. Known by many as 'the birthplace of the Beatles', it's not only where the McCartney family lived and Paul was born, it's also where the Beatles wrote and recorded some of their earliest songs.

12 Arnold Grove

The childhood home of George Harrison. Harrison was born in this tiny house, and lived there for six years with his mother, father and three older siblings – Louise, Harry and Peter.

10 Admiral Grove, Dingle

The childhood home of Ringo Starr. Ringo was born close by at 9 Madryn Street, but his parents separated when he was three, and he and his mother moved to Admiral Grove. Starr lived there for 20 years, until 1963, when he became famous.

Strawberry Field, Beaconsfield Road

A former Salvation Army children's home near to where John Lennon grew up, it became famous as the title of one of the Beatles' best known hits. As a child, Lennon would look forward to the summer garden party held there each year.

Penny Lane

A street near to where John Lennon was born, and believed to have been named after an affluent slave trader in the 18th century, James Penny. Lennon and McCartney would often meet here to catch a bus in to the centre of Liverpool together.

The Cavern Club, 10 Mathew Street

Originally opened in 1957 as a jazz club, the Cavern Club later became the centre of the rock and roll scene in Liverpool. It was instrumental in the Beatles' success.

The Beatles First Ever Tour

After arriving back in Liverpool from Hamburg in December 1960, the Beatles embarked on their first (unofficial) tour, playing 25 dates in their home city between 5 January and 9 February 1961.

The last date of this tour was the start of a new era: their first ever performance at the now legendary Cavern Club. Reportedly, they were paid £5 for their appearance and George Harrison was nearly denied admission because he was wearing jeans! Their nearly 300 performances at the club between then and 1963 would be instrumental in amassing their fanbase – and sparking 'Beatlemania'.

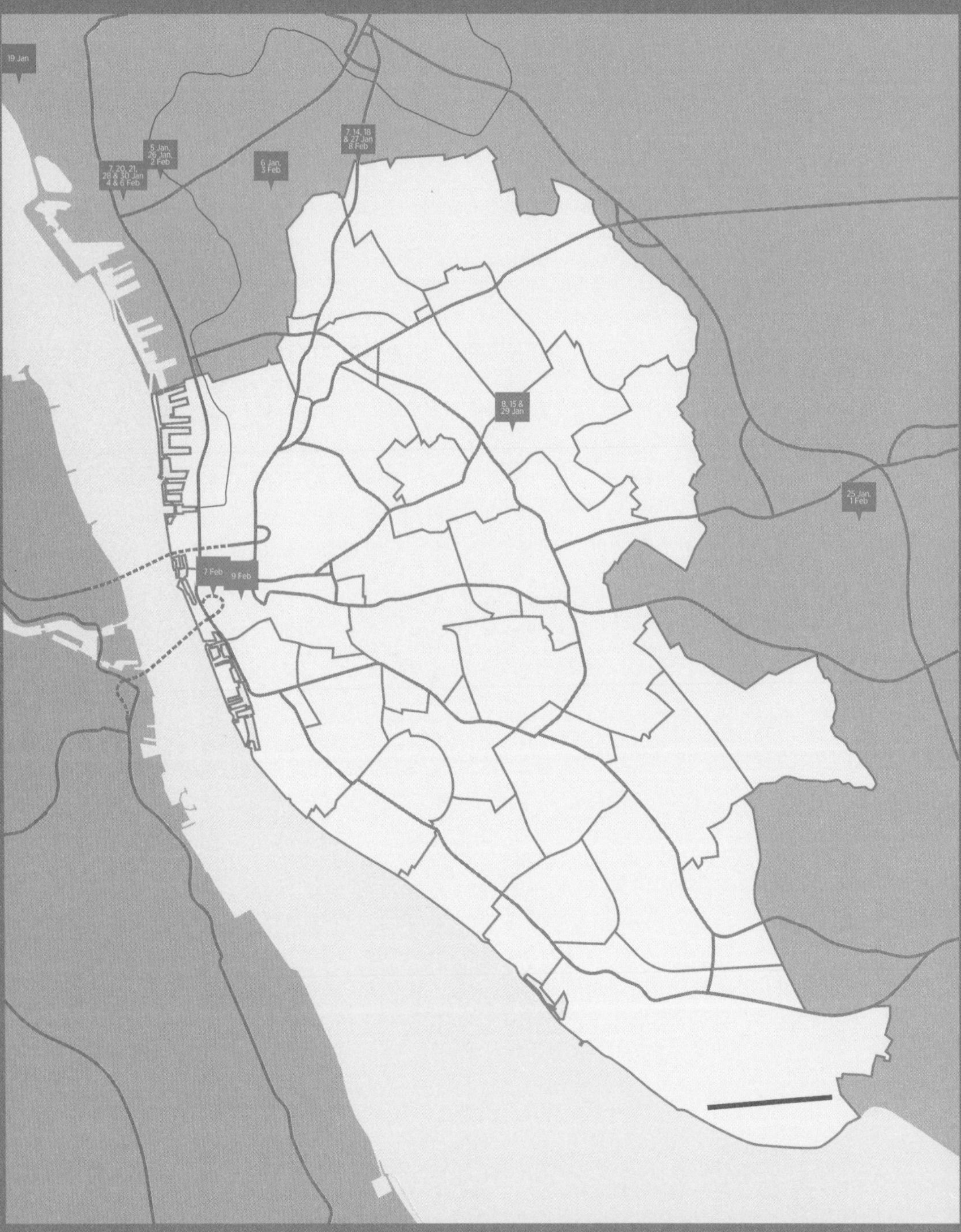

All with Pete Best as drummer instead of Ringo Starr

5 January 1961
Litherland - Town Hall
6 January 1961
Bootle - St John's Hall
7 January 1961
Aintree - Aintree Institute
Seaforth - Lathom Hall
8 January 1961
Liverpool - The Casbah Coffee Club
14 January 1961
Aintree - Aintree Institute
15 January 1961
Liverpool - The Casbah Coffee Club
18 January 1961
Aintree - Aintree Institute
19 January 1961
Crosby - Alexandra Hall
20 & 21 January 1961
Seaforth - Lathom Hall
25 January 1961
Huyton - Hambleton Hall
26 January 1961
Litherland - Town Hall
27 January 1961
Aintree - Aintree Institute
28 January 1961
Seaforth - Lathom Hall
29 January 1961
Liverpool - The Casbah Coffee Club
30 January 1961
Seaforth - Lathom Hall
1 February 1961
Huyton - Hambleton Hall
2 February 1961
Litherland - Town Hall
3 February 1961
Bootle - St John's Hall
4 February 1961
Seaforth - Lathom Hall
5 February 1961
Walton - Blair Hall
6 February 1961
Seaforth - Lathom Hall
7 February 1961
Liverpool - Merseyside Civil Service Club
8 February 1961
Aintree - Aintree Institute
9 February 1961
Liverpool - The Cavern Club

Hamburg: The Top Ten Club

The Beatles returned to Hamburg in March 1961. This time, they were performing at the Top Ten Club. They played even longer hours here than they had at the Indra: seven nights a week, till 4am at weekends, for three months. Their confidence leaped again and it was during this stint that Germany's best-known producer Bert Kaempfert spotted them. The band did their first ever recording session for him and it was this single that would, eventually, on 9 November 1961, lead Brian Epstein to watch one of their performances at the Cavern Club. On 24 January 1962 the band (with Pete Best as drummer) would sign a management contract with Epstein. It wouldn't be long before they'd be signing a recording contract with EMI...

ALBUM OVERVIEW

Released: 22 March 1963
Producers: George Martin, Ron Richards
Engineers: Norman Smith, Stuart Eltham

The Beatles' very first single 'Love Me Do' was recorded over three days in June and September 1962 at Abbey Road studios, shortly after the band signed with EMI. It was released in the UK on 5 October, reaching no. 17. But it was the band's second single 'Please Please Me' that attracted the attention of the record industry when it was released in January 1963. It reached no. 2 and left the people clamouring for more. To ride on this success, the band needed to produce an album sharpish, so *Please Please Me* was released just two months later, on 22 March.

The norm for British 12" vinyl pop albums in 1963 was to have seven songs on each side. These would include the four sides of the two singles 'Love Me Do'/'PS I Love You' and 'Please Please Me'/'Ask Me Why'. But this still left the Beatles' producer George Martin with ten tracks to fill. George asked the band what they could record quickly and the answer was their stage act. So the album is essentially a straightforward performance of their live repertoire at the time.

MARCH

1963

PLEASE PLEASE ME

TIMELINE: MARCH–OCTOBER 1963

March 21, 1963
The Alcatraz Federal Penitentiary on Alcatraz Island in San Francisco Bay closes

May 1, 1963
The Coca-Cola Company introduces its first diet drink

July 1, 1963
ZIP codes are introduced by the United States Postal Service

March 28, 1963
Alfred Hitchcock's film The Birds is released in the United States

June 3, 1963
Pope John XXIII dies

March 22, 1963
Please Please Me album released

May 8, 1963
Dr. No, the first James Bond film, is shown in U.S. theatres

March 5, 1963
Country music superstar Patsy Cline is killed in a plane crash

April 8, 1963
Julian Lennon is born in Liverpool to John and Cynthia Lennon

June 16, 1963
Vostok 6 carries the first woman into space, Soviet cosmonaut Valentina Tereshkova

September 16, 1963
Malaysia is formed through the merging of the Federation of Malaya and the British crown colony of Singapore, North Borneo and Sarawak

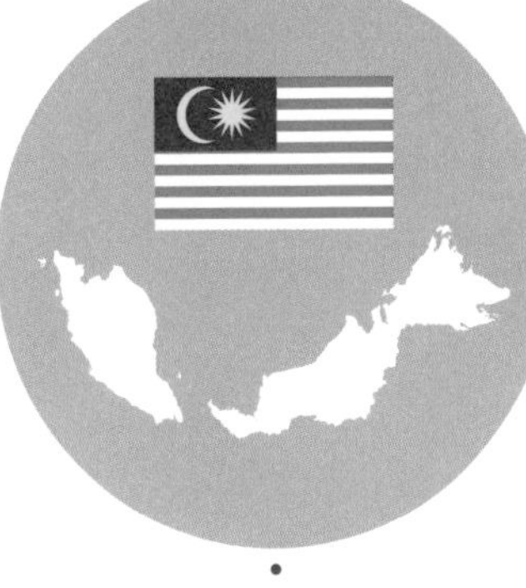

July 26, 1963
NASA launches Syncom 2, the world's first geostationary satellite

October 16, 1963
The thousandth day of John F. Kennedy's presidency

August 8, 1963
The Great Train Robbery takes place in Buckinghamshire, England

September 16, 1963
'She Loves You' released

August 28, 1963
Martin Luther King Jr. delivers his "I Have a Dream" speech

July 12, 1963
Twist and Shout released

August 3, 1963
The Beatles perform at the Cavern Club for the final time

October 13, 1963
The Beatles' performance on ITV's weekly musical variety show, Val Parnell's Sunday Night at the London Palladium, launches Beatlemania

ALBUM COVER DESIGN

The now iconic image of the Beatles that graces the album cover of *Please Please Me* was taken in the atrium of EMI's headquarters in London (illustrated here) by Angus McBean.

"IT WAS A DAY THAT LASTED THREE WEEKS... WE DID 11 SONGS IN 11 HOURS!"

— GEORGE MARTIN —

(PRODUCER) ON RECORDING PLEASE PLEASE ME

HEY
LIPS
BOP
THINGS
C'MON
PS
AIN'T
SHAKE
MUCH
WANT
LOVE
REMEMBER
THINKING
KIND
SHUOP
NEVER
OH
CHAINS
WORDS
MISERY
LITTLE
TWIST
WELL
CRY
ALONE
LONG
SWEETER
BOYS
KISS
SHOUT
LET
SOMEONE
PLEASE
ALWAYS
BABY
WINE
SECRET
REALLY
LOCKED
NOW
WHOA
LISTEN
TRUE
MINE
NOBODY
SEE
FINE
GIRL
KNOW
HEART
RETURN
LIKE
BELIEVE
PROMISE
HOLD
EAR
STANDING
LA
GONNA
HONEY
THERE
ANOTHER
ANNA
BLUE
YEAH
PLACE
CLOSER
SAD
BACK
NIGHT

VOCALS: WHICH BEATLE TOOK THE LEAD?

Where band members shared lead vocals both are listed as singing lead vocals (as a result numbers may add up to more than the total number of tracks on the album).

6 COVERS
VS
8 ORIGINALS
I Saw Her Standing There
Misery
Please Please Me
Love Me Do
P.S. I Love You
Do You Want to Know a Secret
There's a Place
Ask Me Why
Twist and Shout (originally written by Phil Medley & Bert Berns)
A Taste of Honey (originally written by Bobby Scott and Ric Marlow)
Baby It's You (originally written by Burt Bacharach, Barney Williams and Mark David)
Boys (originally written by Luther Dixon and Wes Farrell)
Chains (originally written by Gerry Goffin & Carole King)
Anna (Go to Him) (originally written by Arthur Alexander)

SONGWRITING: WHO WROTE WHAT?

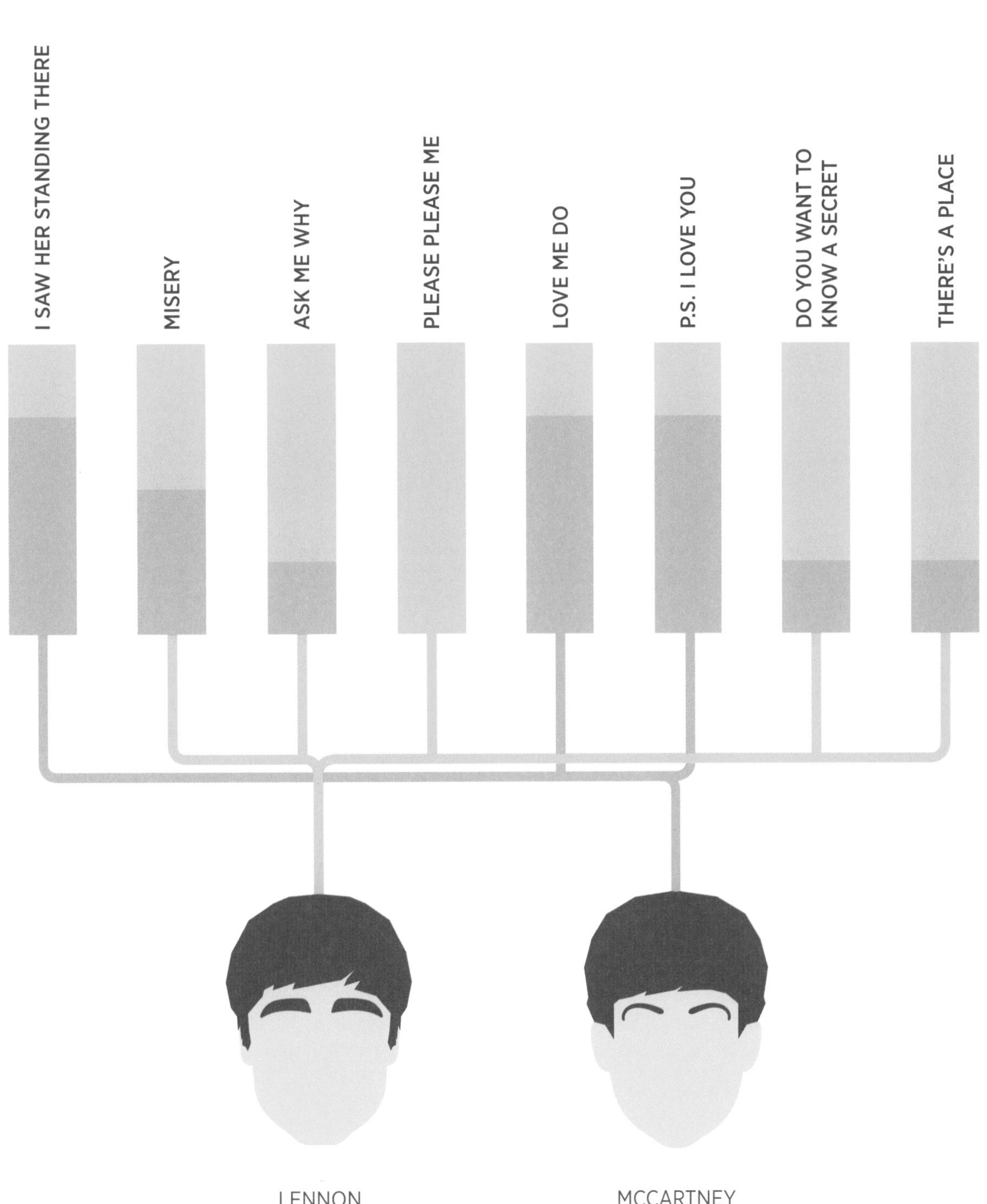

LENGTH: TRACKS AND ALBUM

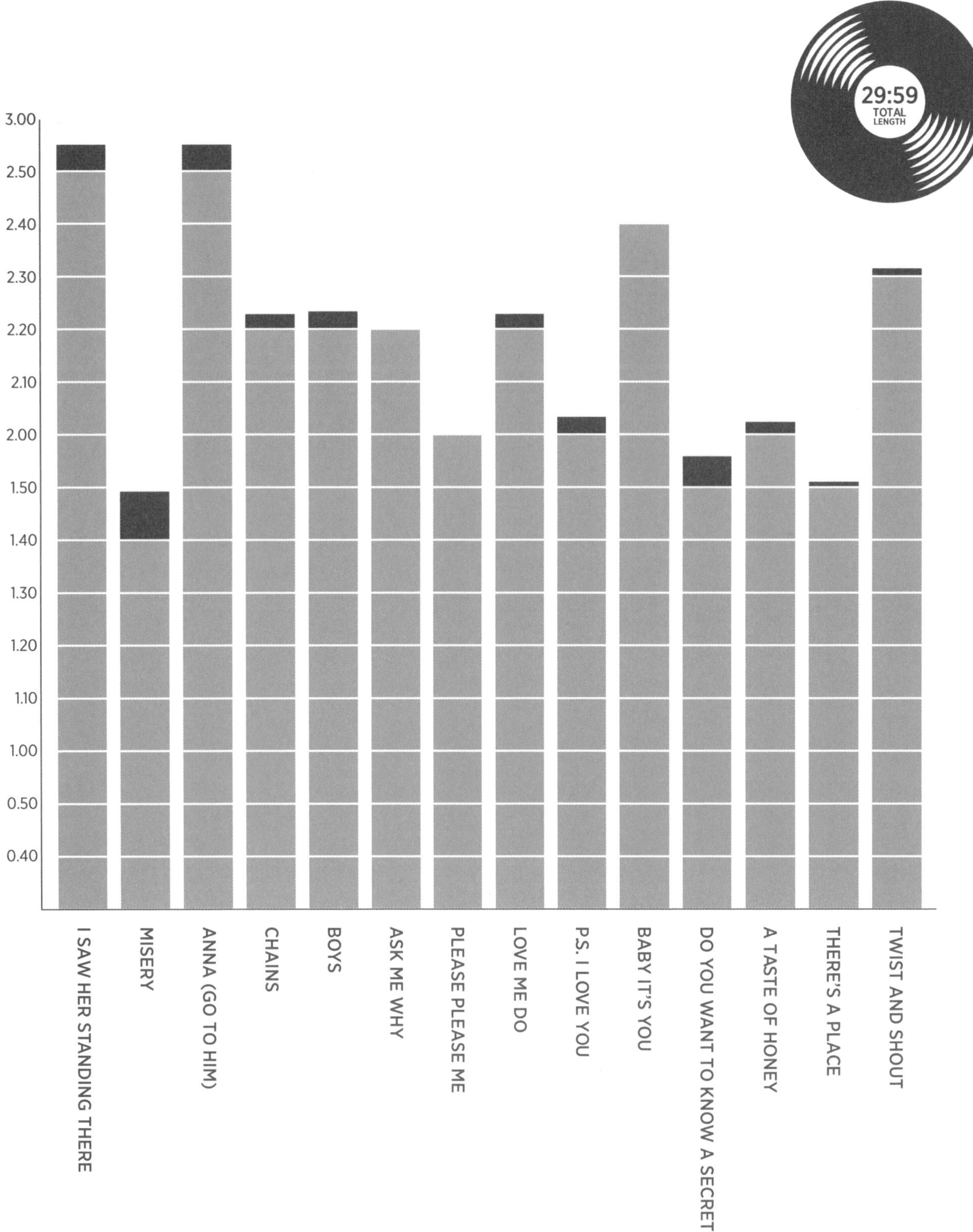

SONG KEYS

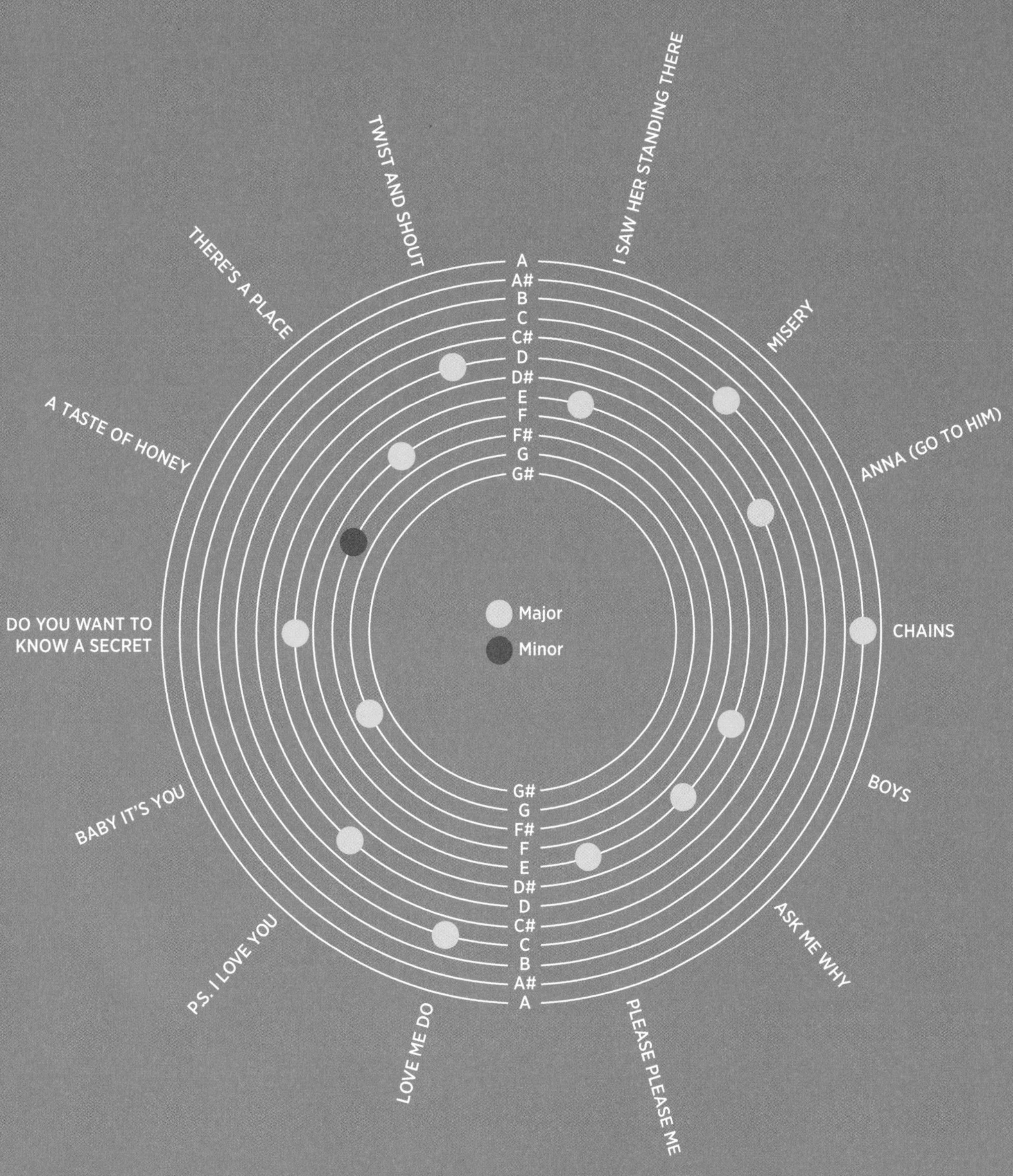

I SAW HER STANDING THERE
MISERY
ANNA (GO TO HIM)
CHAINS
BOYS
ASK ME WHY
PLEASE PLEASE ME
LOVE ME DO
P.S. I LOVE YOU
BABY IT'S YOU
DO YOU WANT TO KNOW A SECRET
A TASTE OF HONEY
THERE'S A PLACE
TWIST AND SHOUT
A
A#
B
C
C#
D
D#
E
F
F#
G
G#
Major
Minor

UK SINGLE RELEASES

I SAW HER STANDING THERE
MISERY
ANNA
CHAINS
BOYS
ASK ME WHY
PLEASE PLEASE ME
LOVE ME DO
P.S. I LOVE YOU
BABY IT'S YOU
DO YOU WANT TO KNOW A SECRET
A TASTE OF HONEY
THERE'S A PLACE
TWIST AND SHOUT

17 17

2 2

NOT RELEASED
TOP 20
TOP 10

'Love Me Do' was the first single the Beatles ever released (with 'P.S. I Love You' as the B-side), closely followed by 'Please Please Me' (B-side: 'Ask Me Why'), which was much more successful, reaching number 2 in the main Record Retailer chart, but number 1 in the NME charts.

Non-album singles that reached number 1 around this time include 'From Me To You'/'Thank You Girl' (11/4/63), 'She Loves You'/'I'll Get You' (23/8/63) and 'I Want To Hold Your Hand'/'This Boy' (29/11/63)

ALBUM CHART POSITIONS

UNITED KINGDOM
Number One

UNITED STATES
Number Two

FRANCE
Number Five

GERMANY
Number Five

VOLUME AND INTENSITY

A VISUAL REPRESENTATION OF THE VOLUME
AND INTENSITY OF EACH TRACK ON THE ALBUM

INSTRUMENTS: WHAT CAN YOU HEAR?

LENNON

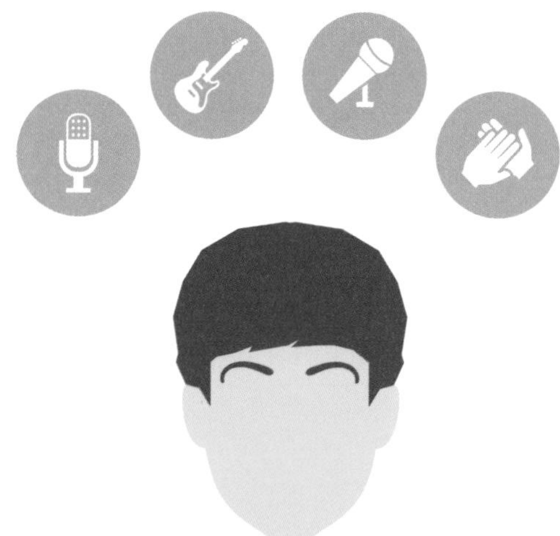

MCCARTNEY

HARRISON

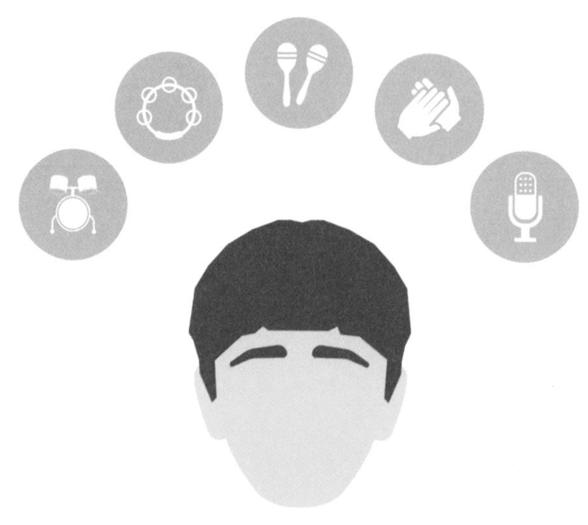

STARR

 **INSTRUMENT KEY**

 BACKGROUND VOCALS

 LEAD VOCALS

 RHYTHM GUITAR

 ACOUSTIC GUITAR

 BASS GUITAR

 LEAD GUITAR

 HARMONICA

 HAND CLAPS

 DRUMS

 TAMBOURINE

 MARACAS

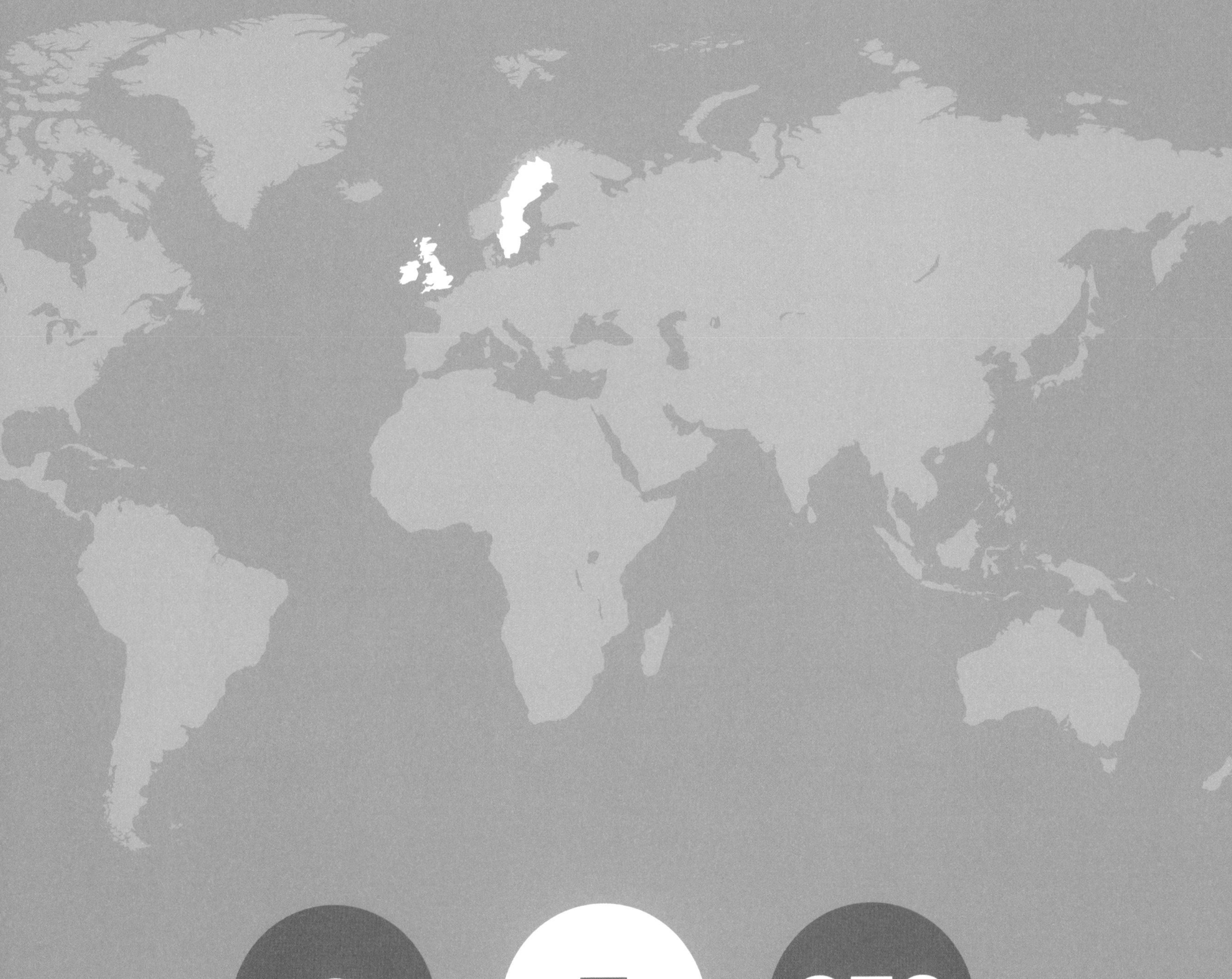

2

COUNTRIES

7

TOURS

259

LIVE SHOWS

STYLE

1963

late 1963
mid 1964
late 1964
mid 1965
late 1965

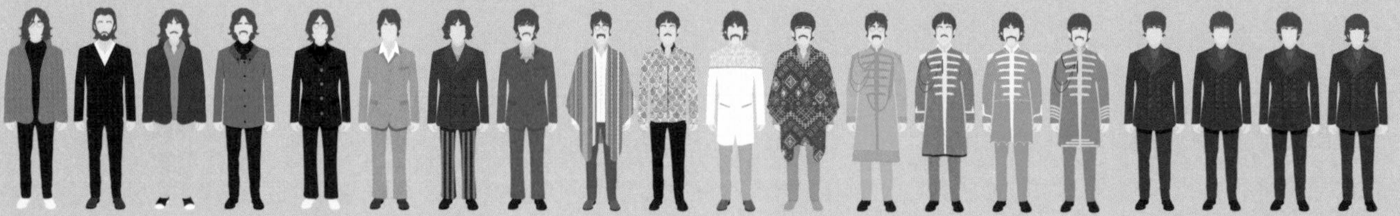
early 1969
late 1968
late 1967
mid 1967
mid 1966

1969
1970
1970

The classic collarless suits of the Beatles' early years were an immediate hit. Whilst many people credit the design to Pierre Cardin, they were designed by the Beatles' stylist, Douglas Millings. They differ slightly to the Cardin design, but it is likely that Millings took his inspiration from the slim, sleek and revolutionary cut of his suits.

ALBUM OVERVIEW

Released: 22 November 1963
Producer: George Martin
Engineer: Norman Smith

With the Beatles was recorded in just seven (non-consecutive) days. Released exactly eight months after *Please Please Me*, it was an immediate hit and cemented the band's new-found stardom. In fact, the album's release had to be delayed because of the sensational success of *Please Please Me*, which was still at the top of the UK album chart.

It took the release of the Beatles' second album to topple it to number two. *With the Beatles* was at no. 1 for 21 weeks, giving the band a spectacular continuous run of 51 weeks in the top spot.

NOVEMBER
1963
WITH THE BEATLES

TIMELINE: NOVEMBER 1963–JUNE 1964

November 22, 1963
Assassination of U.S. president
John F. Kennedy by Lee Harvey Oswald

November 23, 1963
The first episode of the
BBC television series
Doctor Who is broadcast

January 15, 1964
'I Want To Hold Your Hand'
becomes the Beatles' first US no. 1

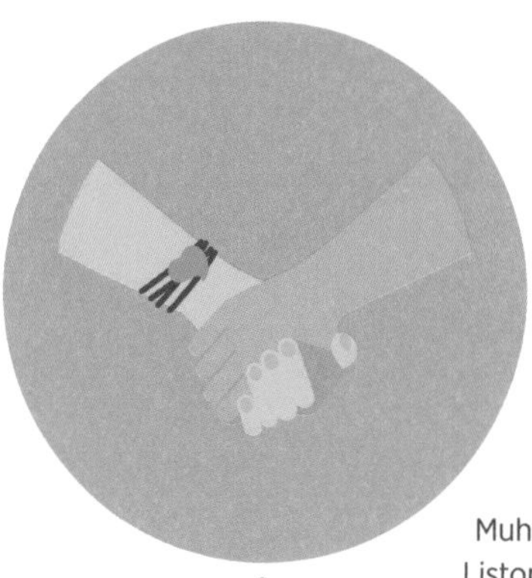

February 25, 1964
Muhammad Ali beats Sonny
Liston in Miami Beach, Florida

March 9, 1964
The first Ford Mustang rolls off the
assembly line at Ford Motor Company

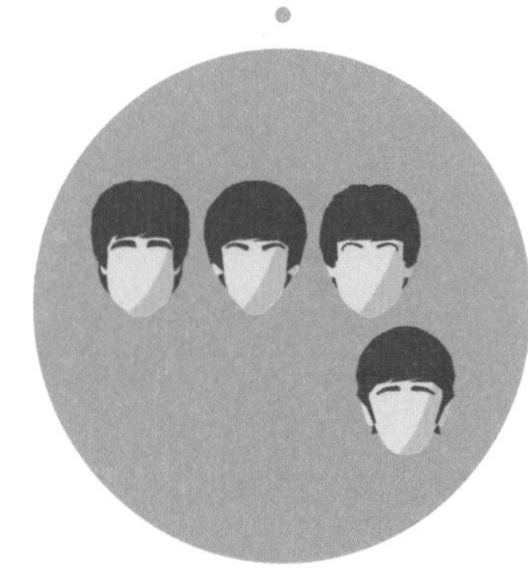

November 22, 1963
With The Beatles
is released

December 24, 1963
The Beatles' Christmas Show
opens at the Astoria Theatre,
Finsbury Park, London for 3 weeks

February 9, 1964
The Beatles appear on *The
Ed Sullivan Show*, their first
live performance on
American television

March 6, 1964
Malcolm X says in New York City that
he is forming a black nationalist party

November 18, 1963
The first push-button telephone
is made available to AT&T customers

April 16, 1964
The Rolling Stones release their debut album, The Rolling Stones

April 26, 1964
Tanganyika and Zanzibar merge to form Tanzania

May 12, 1964
Twelve young men in New York City publicly burn their draft cards to protest the Vietnam War; the first such act of war resistance.

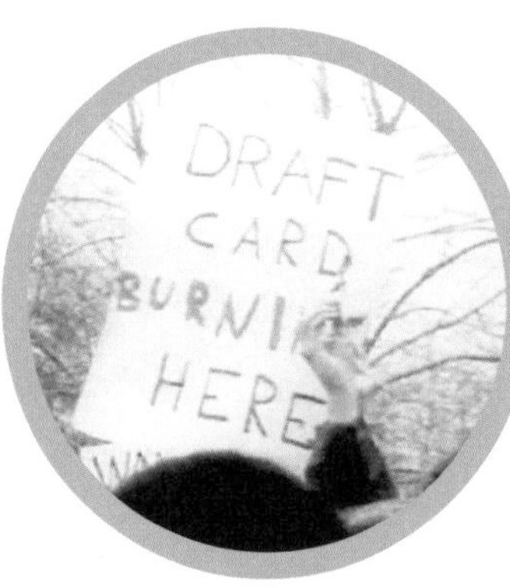

June 12, 1964
Nelson Mandela and 7 others are sentenced to life imprisonment on Robben Island, South Africa

TOP
5

April 4, 1964
The Beatles hold the top 5 positions on the US singles chart

April 20, 1964
Nelson Mandela makes his "I Am Prepared to Die" speech at the opening of the Rivonia Trial, a key event for the anti-apartheid movement

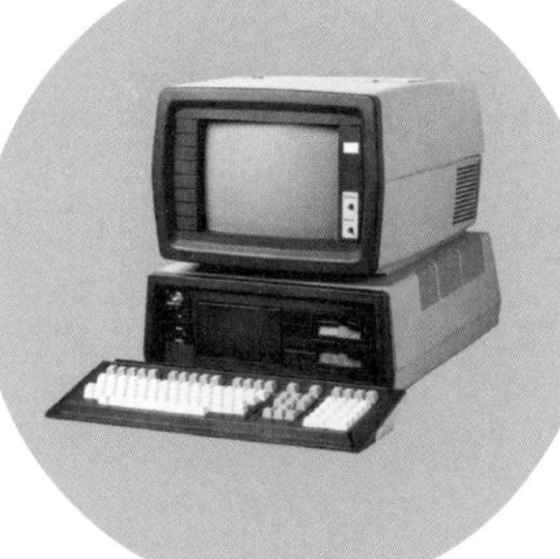

May 1, 1964
John George Kemeny and Thomas Eugene Kurtz run the first computer program written in BASIC

July 2, 1964
President Lyndon Johnson signs the Civil Rights Act of 1964 into law, officially abolishing racial segregation in the United States

ALBUM COVER DESIGN

The photograph for *With the Beatles*' cover was taken by Robert Freeman in a corridor of the Palace Court Hotel, Bournemouth. The Beatles wanted a treatment similar to the iconic images of Astrid Kirchherr, which they had shown to Freeman. Ringo (as he was the shortest) was placed in the bottom right, rather than in a line with the others, in order to fit the square format of the cover. We've visualised the band members standing ready in position here.

EMI were reluctant to use the photo at first because it was black and white but George Martin and Brian Epstein convinced them.

WE LIKE DOING STAGE SHOWS, BUT THE THING WE LIKE BEST IS GOING INTO THE RECORDING STUDIO TO MAKE NEW RECORDS

—PAUL MCCARTNEY—

1963, AROUND 'WITH THE BEATLES'

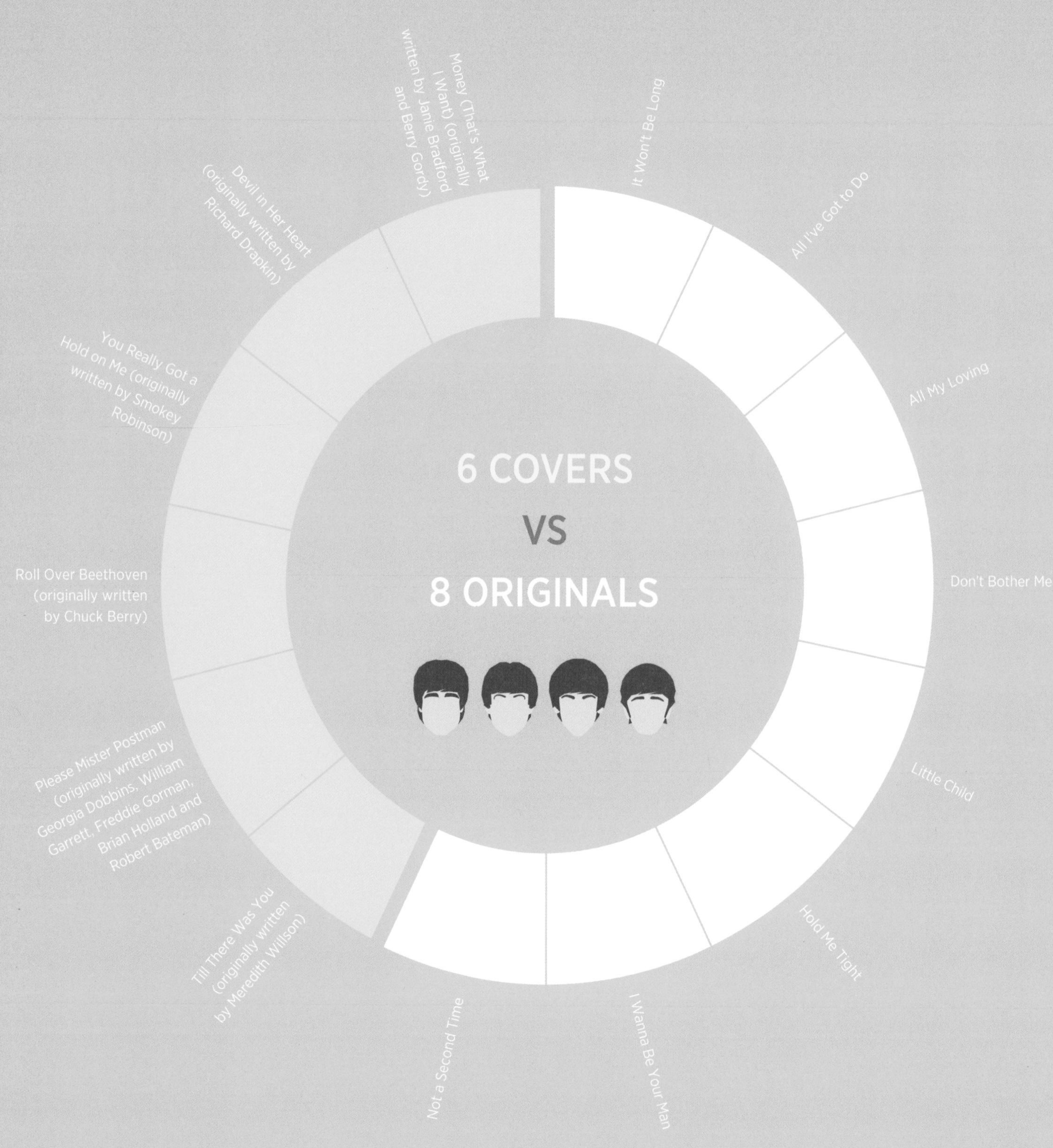
6 COVERS
VS
8 ORIGINALS
It Won't Be Long
All I've Got to Do
All My Loving
Don't Bother Me
Little Child
Hold Me Tight
I Wanna Be Your Man
Not a Second Time
Till There Was You (originally written by Meredith Willson)
Please Mister Postman (originally written by Georgia Dobbins, William Garrett, Freddie Gorman, Brian Holland and Robert Bateman)
Roll Over Beethoven (originally written by Chuck Berry)
You Really Got a Hold on Me (originally written by Smokey Robinson)
Devil in Her Heart (originally written by Richard Drapkin)
Money (That's What I Want) (originally written by Janie Bradford and Berry Gordy)

SONGWRITING: WHO WROTE WHAT?

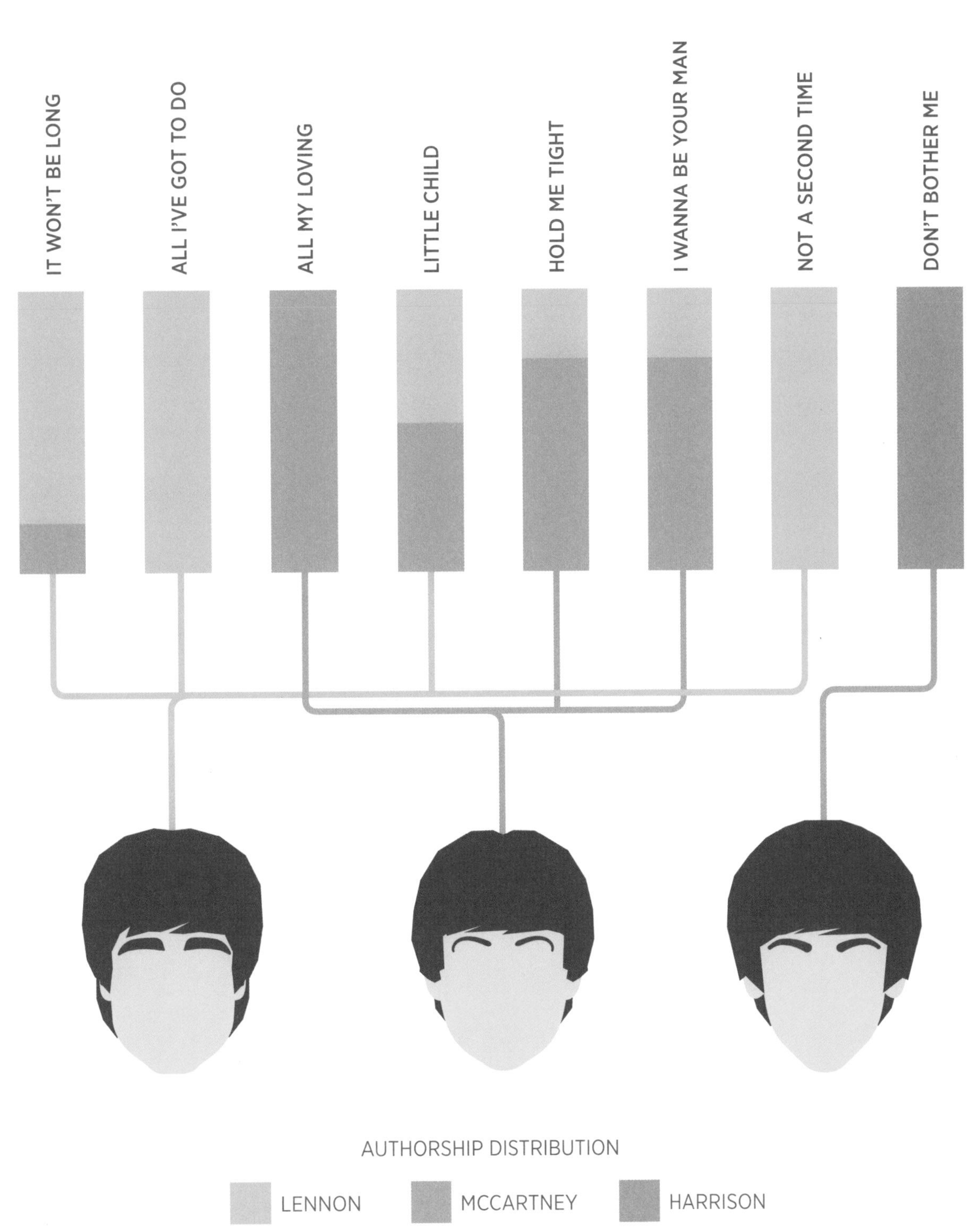

AUTHORSHIP DISTRIBUTION

LENNON MCCARTNEY HARRISON

LENGTH: TRACKS AND ALBUM

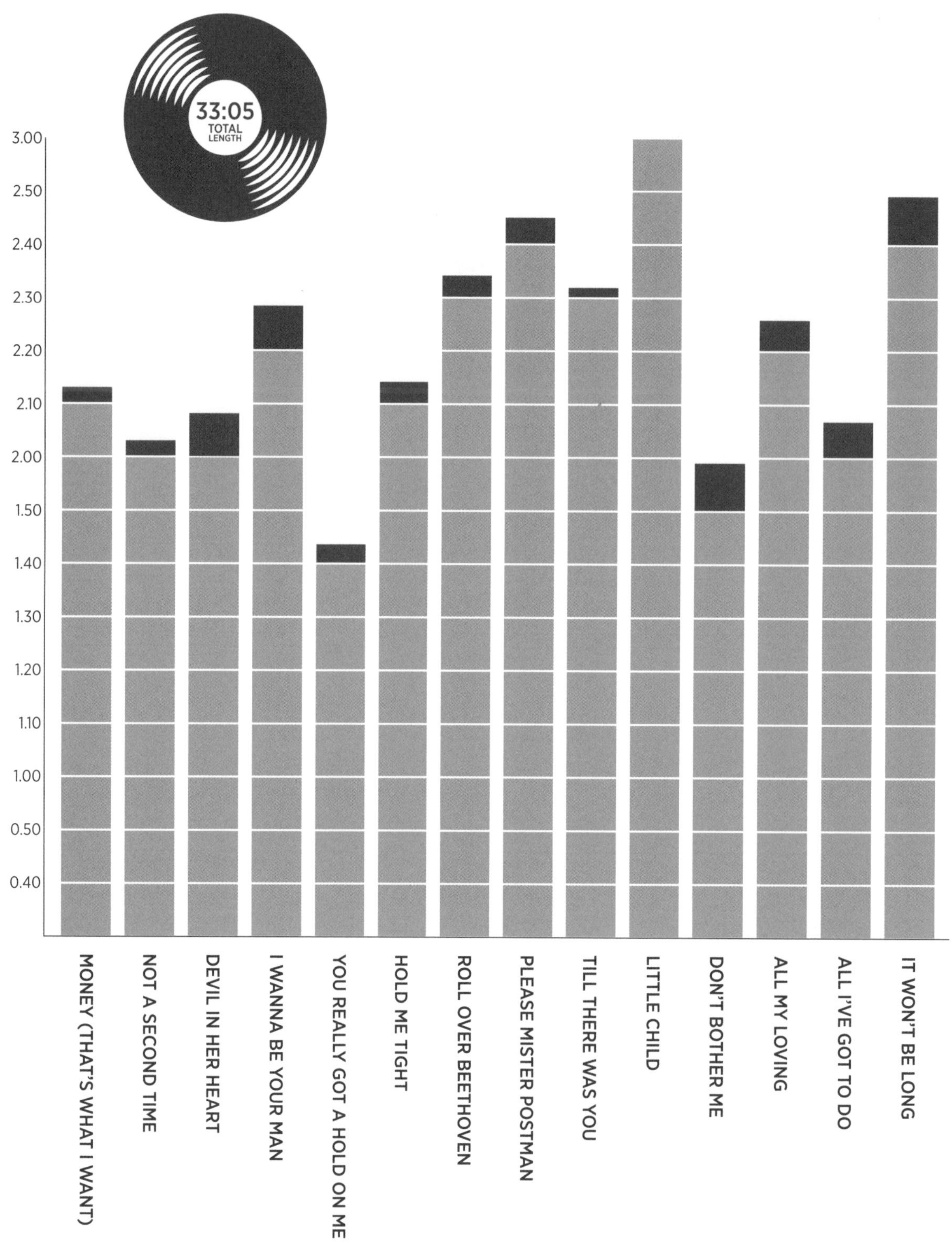

SONG KEYS

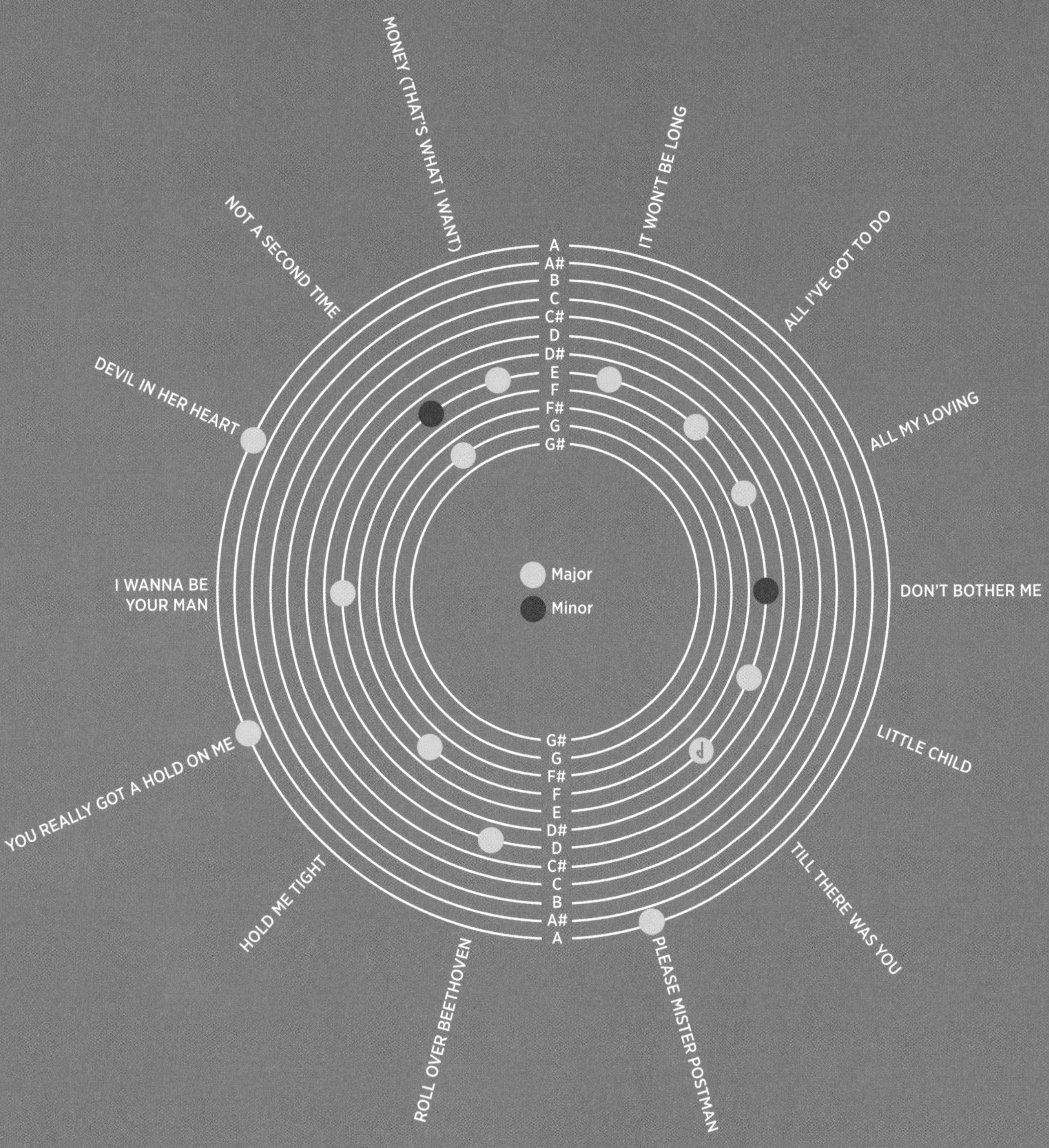

MONEY (THAT'S WHAT I WANT)
IT WON'T BE LONG
ALL I'VE GOT TO DO
ALL MY LOVING
DON'T BOTHER ME
LITTLE CHILD
TILL THERE WAS YOU
PLEASE MISTER POSTMAN
ROLL OVER BEETHOVEN
HOLD ME TIGHT
YOU REALLY GOT A HOLD ON ME
I WANNA BE YOUR MAN
DEVIL IN HER HEART
NOT A SECOND TIME
A
A#
B
C
C#
D
D#
E
F
F#
G
G#
Major
Minor

VOCALS: WHICH BEATLE TOOK THE LEAD?

Where band members shared lead vocals both are listed as singing lead vocals (as a result numbers may add up to more than the total number of tracks on the album).

UK SINGLE RELEASES

IT WON'T BE LONG
ALL I'VE GOT TO DO
ALL MY LOVING
DON'T BOTHER ME
LITTLE CHILD
TILL THERE WAS YOU
PLEASE MISTER POSTMAN
ROLL OVER BEETHOVEN
HOLD ME TIGHT
YOU REALLY GOT A HOLD ON ME
I WANNA BE YOUR MAN
DEVIL IN HER HEART
NOT A SECOND TIME
MONEY (THAT'S WHAT I WANT)

NOT RELEASED
TOP 20
TOP 10

No songs from *With the Beatles* were released as singles but in the interim between *Please Please Me* and this album, the single 'She Loves You' was released and went to number one in both the UK and the US. Then, one week after *With the Beatles* came out, the band had another runaway hit with 'I Want To Hold Your Hand'.

ALBUM CHART POSITIONS

UNITED KINGDOM
Number One

GERMANY
Number One

INSTRUMENTS: WHAT CAN YOU HEAR?

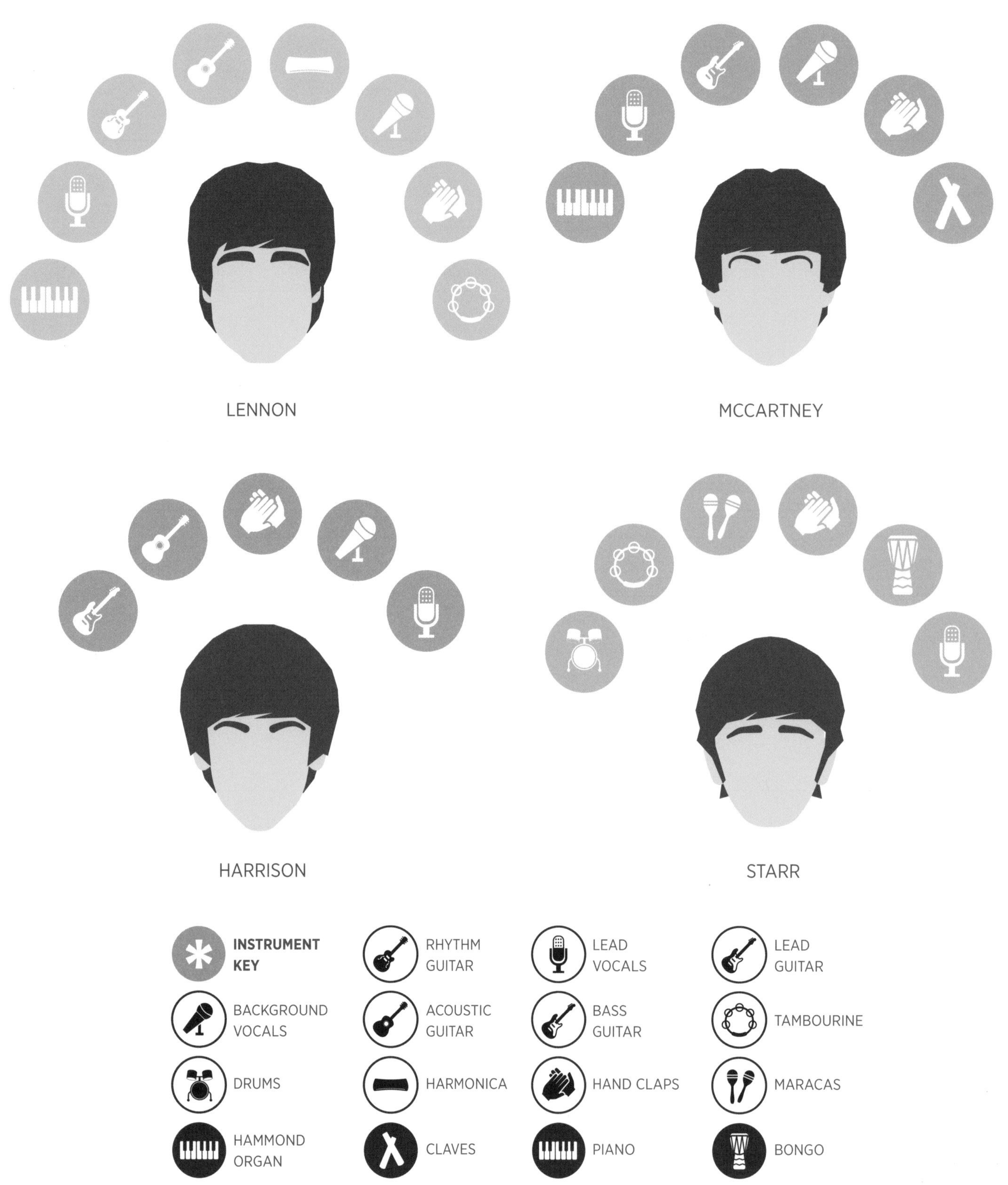

Black circle indicates instruments used for the first time in a Beatles' album

PERFORMANCES

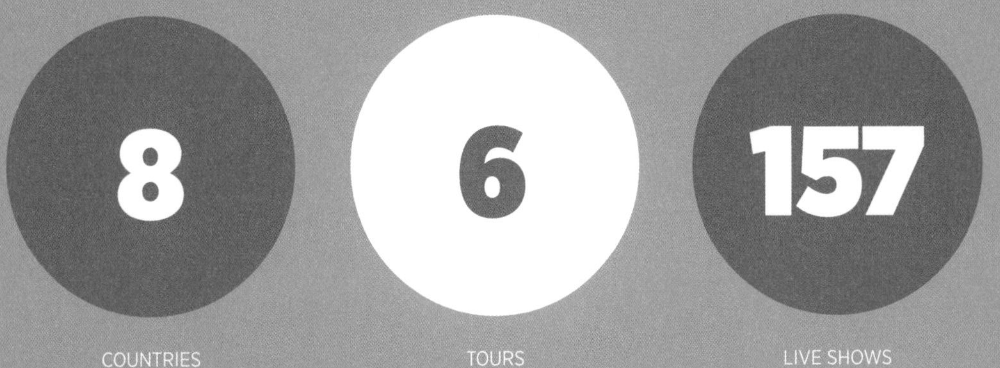

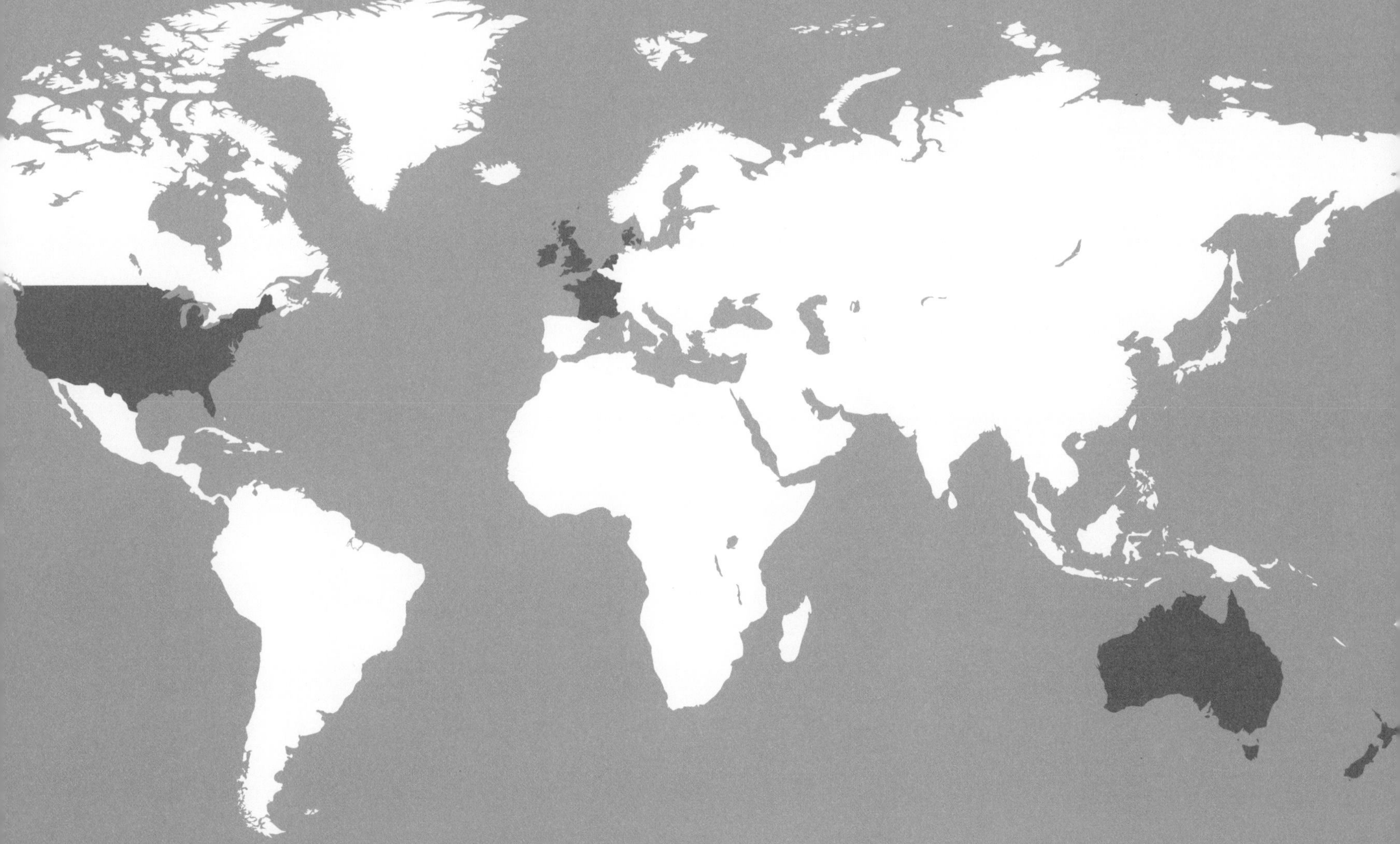

8

COUNTRIES

6

TOURS

157

LIVE SHOWS

STYLE

The classic English Chesterfield suit was another favourite of the Beatles during their early years. Characterised by the velvet lapels and high buttoning, they are also known as 'Sullivan suits' as they were worn by the band for their historic first appearance on *The Ed Sullivan Show* in the US.

Press Conference Humour

The Beatles' dry sense of humour led to some classic press conference retorts showcasing true British wit.

How do you feel about teenagers imitating you with Beatles wigs?

They're not imitating us because we don't wear Beatles wigs!

How did you find America?

Turned left at Greenland

Do you speak French?

Non.

Does it bother you that you can't hear what you sing during concerts?

No, we don't mind. We've got the records at home.

What do you do when you're cooped up in a hotel room between shows?

We ice skate

What would you do if the fans got past the police lines?

We'd die laughing!

Are you a mod or a rocker?

I'm a mocker

What do you call that hairstyle?

Arthur

Were you worried about the oversized roughnecks who tried to infiltrate the airport crowd on your arrival?

That was us...

The US Top Five

In the week of 4 April 1964, the Beatles achieved a feat that's unlikely to ever be repeated: they occupied the top five positions of the Billboard Hot 100 chart.

Not only did the band hold the top five positions, but they also had a further seven records in the top 100, giving them twelve places in total on the US chart.

1 Can't Buy Me Love
The Beatles

2 Twist And Shout
The Beatles

3 She Loves You
The Beatles

4 I Want To Hold Your Hand
The Beatles

5 Please Please Me
The Beatles

6 Suspicion
Terry Stafford

7 Hello, Dolly!
Louis Armstrong And The All Stars

8 The Shoop Shoop Song (It's In His Kiss)
Betty Everett

9 My Heart Belongs To Only You
Bobby Vinton

10 Glad All Over
The Dave Clark Five

11 Dawn (Go Away)
The Four Seasons

12 The Way You Do The Things You Do
The Temptations

13 Fun, Fun, Fun
The Beach Boys

14 Don't Let The Rain Come Down (Crooked Little Man)
The Serendipity Singers

15 Needles And Pins
The Searchers

16 Stay
The Four Seasons

17 Kissin' Cousins
Elvis Presley With The Jordanaires

18 You're A Wonderful One
Marvin Gaye

19 Java
Al (He's the King) Hirt

20 Hi-Heel Sneakers
Tommy Tucker

21 Ain't Nothing You Can Do
Bobby Bland

22 Money
The Kingsmen

23 I Love You More And More Every Day
Al Martino

24 Hippy Hippy Shake
The Swinging Blue Jeans

25 Dead Man's Curve
Jan & Dean

26 Think
Brenda Lee

27 Navy Blue
Diane Renay

28 Blue Winter
Connie Francis

29 It Hurts Me
Elvis Presley With The Jordanaires

30 Nadine (Is It You?)
Chuck Berry

31 I Saw Her Standing There
The Beatles

32 Hey Jean, Hey Dean
Dean And Jean

33 Tell It On The Mountain
Peter, Paul & Mary

34 White On White
Danny Williams

35 Hey, Bobba Needle
Chubby Checker

36 Rip Van Winkle
The Devotions

37 See The Funny Little Clown
Bobby Goldsboro

38 My Heart Cries For You
Ray Charles

39 That's The Way Boys Are
Lesley Gore

40 The New Girl In School
Jan & Dean

41 From Me To You
The Beatles

42 We Love You Beatles
The Carefrees

43 Understand Your Man
Johnny Cash

44 Forever
Pete Drake And His Talking Steel Guitar

45 Penetration
The Pyramids

46 Do You Want To Know A Secret
The Beatles

47 Ebb Tide
Lenny Welch

48 Bits And Pieces
The Dave Clark Five

49 Baby, Don't You Cry
(The New Swingova Rhythm)
Ray Charles and his Orchestra

50 My Guy
Mary Wells

51 The Matador
Major Lance

52 I'll Make You Mine
Bobby Vee With The Eligibles

53 I Can't Stand It
Soul Sisters

54 Worried Guy
Johnny Tillotson

55 He's A Good Guy (Yes He Is)
The Marvelettes

56 Castles In The Sand
Little Stevie Wonder

57 Ain't Gonna Tell Anybody
Jimmy Gilmer And The Fireballs

58 All My Loving The Beatles

59 (You Can't Let The Boy Overpower)
The Man In You
The Miracles

60 Shangri-La
Robert Maxwell His
Harp And Orchestra

61 I'm So Proud
The Impressions

62 Love With The Proper Stranger
Jack Jones

63 Congratulations
Rick Nelson

64 Book Of Love
The Raindrops

65 You Can't Do That The Beatles

66 Look Homeward Angel
The Monarchs

67 Make Me Forget
Bobby Rydell

68 Roll Over Beethoven The Beatles

69 Sha-La-La
The Shirelles

70 Shangri-La
Vic Dana

71 My Girl Sloopy
The Vibrations

72 Baby Baby Baby
Anna King-Bobby Byrd

73 Wish Someone Would Care
Irma Thomas

74 Giving Up On Love
Jerry Butler

75 Stay Awhile
Dusty Springfield

76 Our Everlasting Love
Ruby And The Romantics

77 T'ain't Nothin' To Me
The Coasters

78 To Each His Own
The Tymes

79 Thank You Girl The Beatles

80 The Pink Panther Theme
Henry Mancini And His Orchestra

81 You Lied To Your Daddy
The Tams

82 I Should Care
Gloria Lynne

83 Where Does Love Go
Freddie Scott

84 Can You Do It
The Contours

85 A Letter To The Beatles
The Four Preps

86 Soul Serenade
King Curtis

87 It's All Right (You're Just In Love)
The Tams

88 That's When It Hurts
Ben E. King

89 Charade
Sammy Kaye And His Orchestra

90 Kiss Me Sailor
Diane Renay

91 Mexican Drummer Man
Herb Alpert's Tijuana Brass

92 Come To Me
Otis Redding

93 I Can't Wait Until I See My Baby
Justine Washington

94 Be Anything (But Be Mine)
Gloria Lynne

95 Hand It Over
Chuck Jackson

96 Vanishing Point
The Marketts

97 How Blue Can You Get
B.B. King And His Orchestra

98 (The Best Part Of) Breakin' Up
The Ronettes

99 Hey, Mr. Sax Man
Boots Randolph

100 People
Barbra Streisand

ALBUM OVERVIEW

Released: 10 July 1964
Producer: George Martin
Engineer: Norman Smith

1964 was the year Beatlemania began to spread from the UK and infect the rest of the world. A US record deal was signed late in 1963, shortly before the band appeared on American TV's *The Ed Sullivan Show*, which was broadcast to more than 70 million people. A world tour followed, along with the band's debut feature film and innumerable interviews and recordings.

The title of the album was born out of a comment Ringo Starr made about working hard in the studio. It took nine days to record the fourteen songs, which were solely written by Lennon and McCartney (the only album on which this is the case). By now the band had advanced to four-track recording and the memorable chord that opens the album remains one of the most iconic moments in the band's music. Many years later, George Martin revealed that the chord was Fadd9, played on a 12-string guitar.

JULY

1964

A HARD DAY'S NIGHT

TIMELINE: JULY–NOVEMBER 1964

July 10, 1964
The people of Liverpool line the Beatles' childhood streets for the premiere of the Hard Day's Night film and release of the album

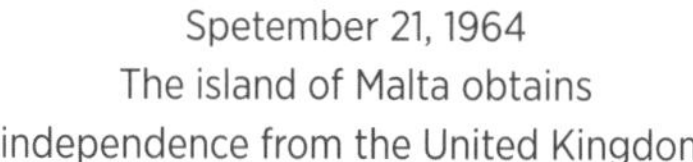

Spetember 21, 1964
The island of Malta obtains independence from the United Kingdom

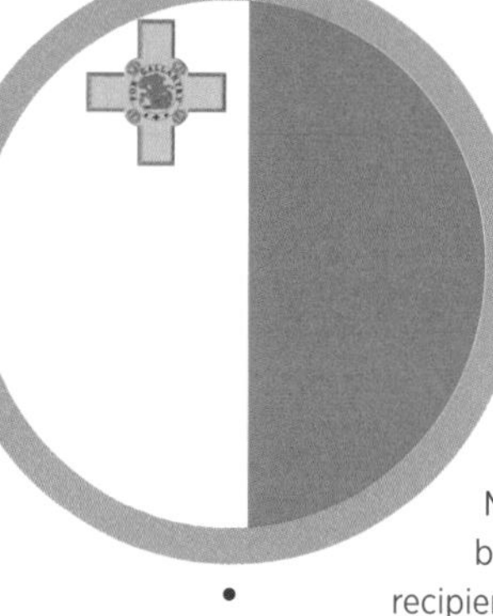

November 28, 1964
NASA launches the Mariner 4 space probe from Cape Kennedy toward Mars

August 27, 1964
Walt Disney's Mary Poppins has its world premiere in Los Angeles

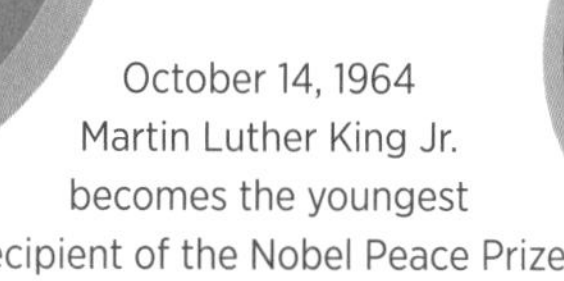

October 14, 1964
Martin Luther King Jr. becomes the youngest recipient of the Nobel Peace Prize

August 19, 1964
The Beatles begin their first US tour, visiting 24 cities in 34 days

October 2, 1964
The Kinks release their first album, Kinks

September 18, 1964
King Constantine II of Greece marries Princess Anne-Marie of Denmark, who becomes Europe's youngest Queen at age 18 years, 19 days

November 9, 1964
The House of Commons of the United Kingdom votes to abolish the death penalty for murder in Britain

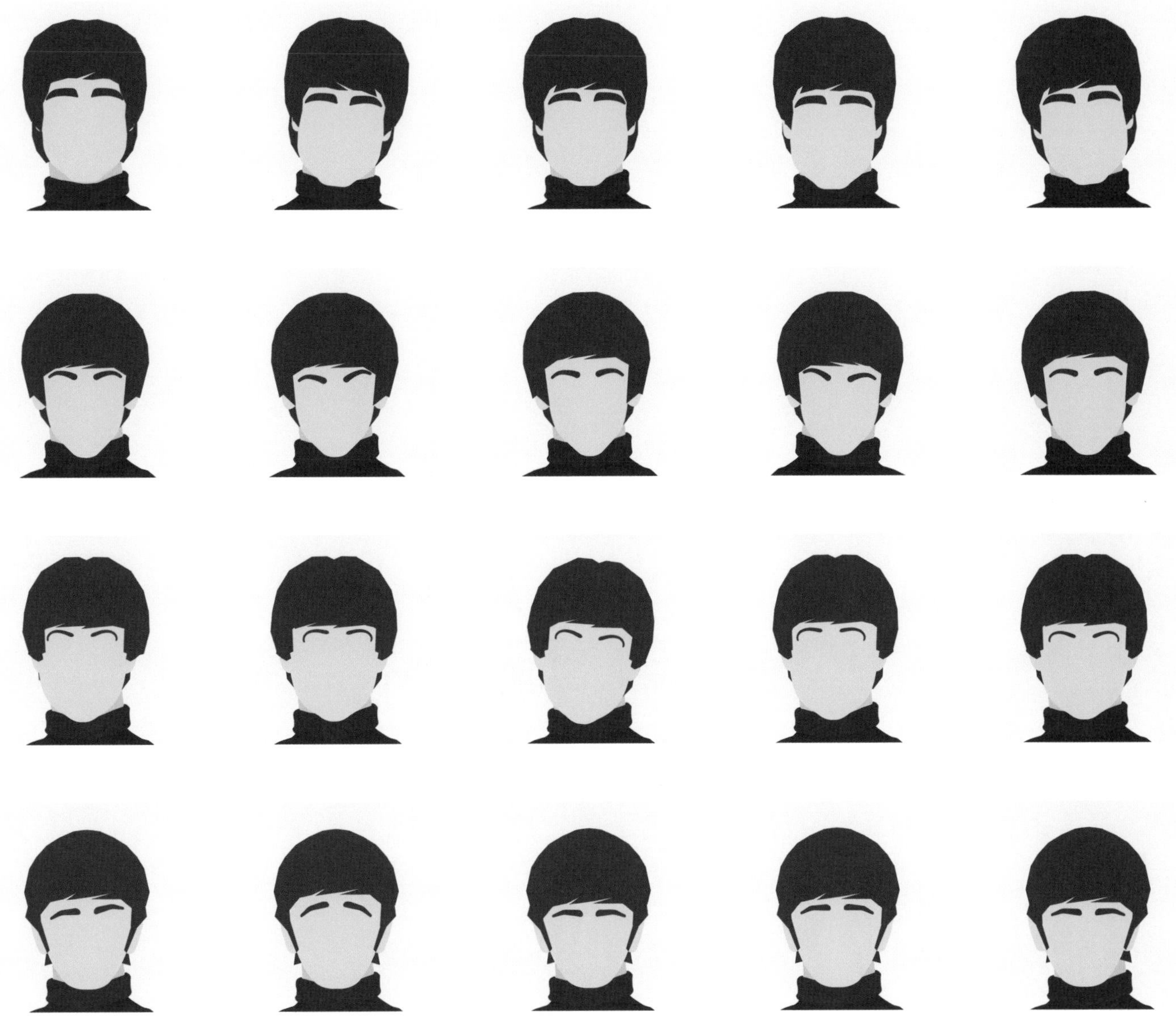

ALBUM COVER DESIGN

The original album cover was again designed and photographed by Robert Freeman. Just as with *With the Beatles*, Freeman used black and white photography of the band, this time featuring multiple images of each member. The concept is similar to that of a photography contact sheet, which was used by photographers at the time to allow them to view a mini-preview of a roll of film. Here we've visualised what a contact sheet from this shoot could have looked like.

The idea was totally unique in its day but in the years since has become iconic and often imitated.

LYRICS: THE WORDS THEY SANG THE MOST

VOCALS: WHICH BEATLE TOOK THE LEAD?

Where band members shared lead vocals both are listed as singing lead vocals (as a result numbers may add up to more than the total number of tracks on the album).

A Hard Day's Night
I Should Have Known Better
If I Fell
I'm Happy Just to Dance with You
And I Love Her
Tell Me Why
Can't Buy Me Love
Any Time at All
I'll Cry Instead
Things We Said Today
When I Get Home
You Can't Do That
I'll Be Back
0 COVERS
VS
13 ORIGINALS

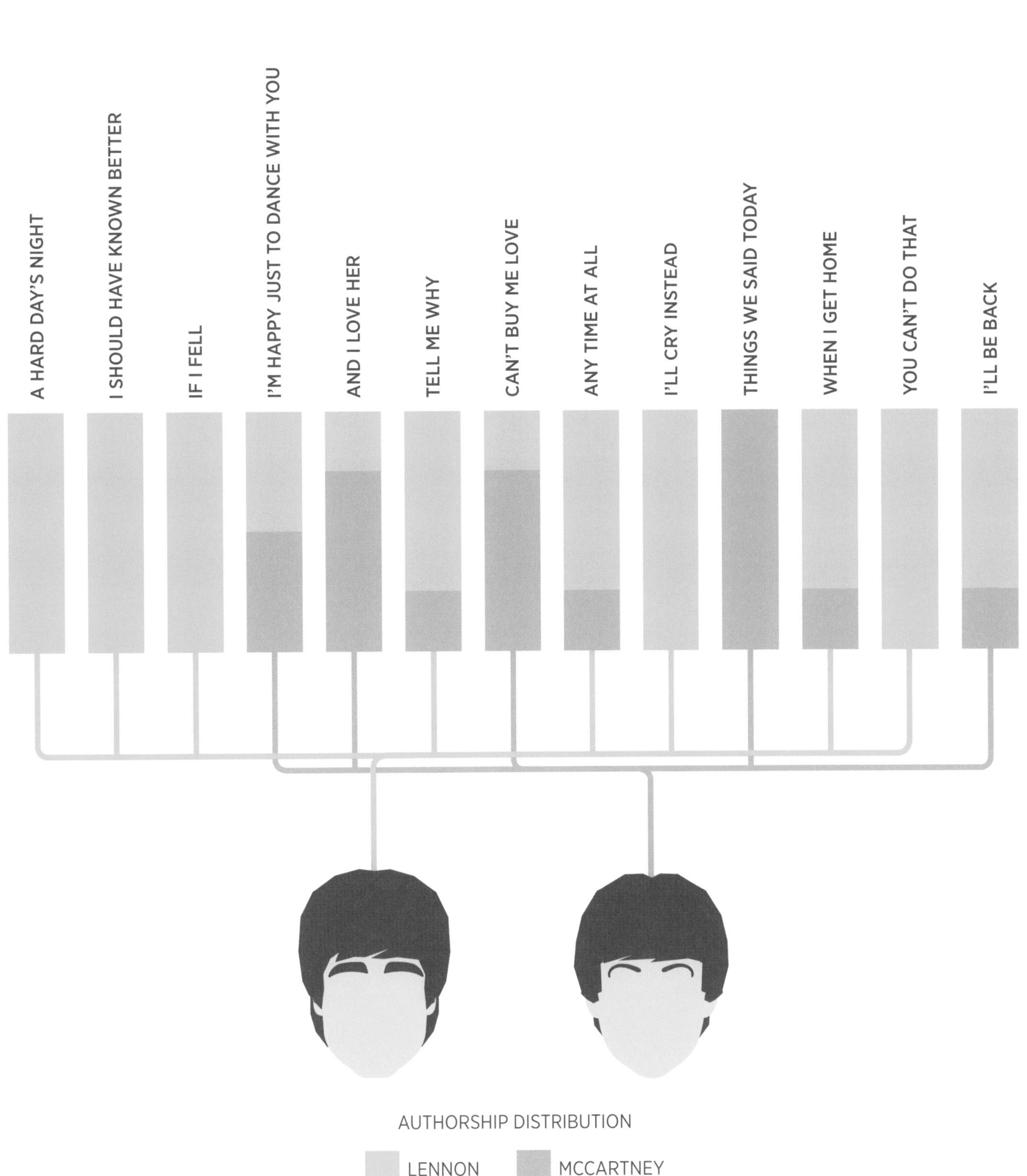
A HARD DAY'S NIGHT
I SHOULD HAVE KNOWN BETTER
IF I FELL
I'M HAPPY JUST TO DANCE WITH YOU
AND I LOVE HER
TELL ME WHY
CAN'T BUY ME LOVE
ANY TIME AT ALL
I'LL CRY INSTEAD
THINGS WE SAID TODAY
WHEN I GET HOME
YOU CAN'T DO THAT
I'LL BE BACK
AUTHORSHIP DISTRIBUTION
LENNON
MCCARTNEY

LENGTHS: TRACKS AND ALBUM

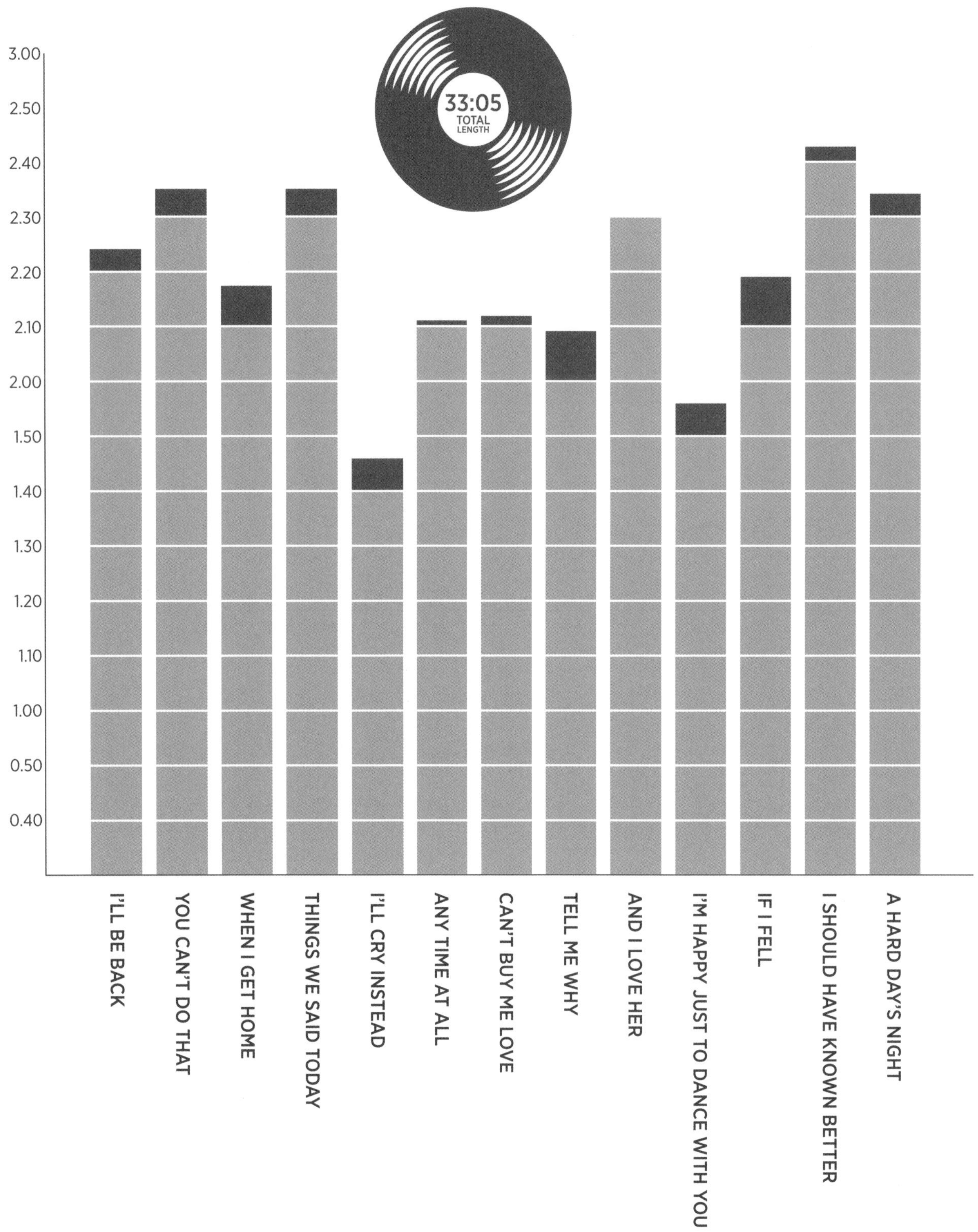

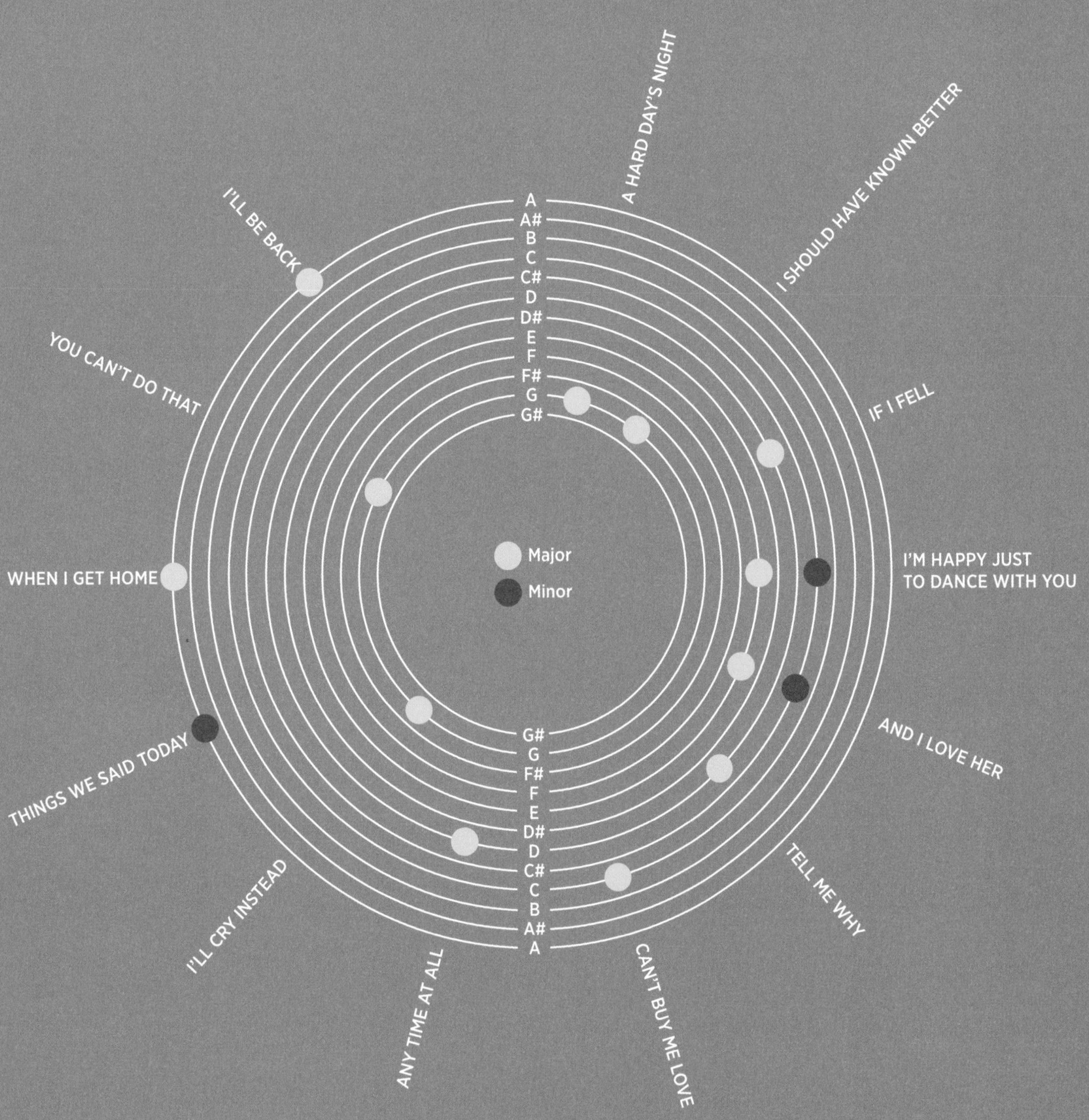
A HARD DAY'S NIGHT
I SHOULD HAVE KNOWN BETTER
IF I FELL
I'M HAPPY JUST
TO DANCE WITH YOU
AND I LOVE HER
TELL ME WHY
CAN'T BUY ME LOVE
ANY TIME AT ALL
I'LL CRY INSTEAD
THINGS WE SAID TODAY
WHEN I GET HOME
YOU CAN'T DO THAT
I'LL BE BACK
A
A#
B
C
C#
D
D#
E
F
F#
G
G#
Major
Minor

A VISUAL REPRESENTATION OF THE VOLUME AND INTENSITY OF EACH TRACK ON THE ALBUM

SUCCESS

UK SINGLE RELEASES

A HARD DAY'S NIGHT
I SHOULD HAVE KNOWN BETTER
IF I FELL
I'M HAPPY JUST TO DANCE WITH YOU
AND I LOVE HER
TELL ME WHY
CAN'T BUY ME LOVE
ANY TIME AT ALL
I'LL CRY INSTEAD
THINGS WE SAID TODAY
WHEN I GET HOME
YOU CAN'T DO THAT
I'LL BE BACK

1 1

NOT RELEASED
TOP 20
TOP 10

By the end of 1964, *A Hard Day's Night* had sold 600,000 copies and spent 21 consecutive weeks at the top of the UK album chart. It sold over a million advanced copies in the US and then another million within 3 months of its release, topping the US Billboard album chart for 14 weeks. It remains one of the fastest-selling albums of all time.

ALBUM CHART POSITIONS

UNITED KINGDOM
Number One

GERMANY
Number One

AUSTRALIA
Number Five

INSTRUMENTS: WHAT CAN YOU HEAR?

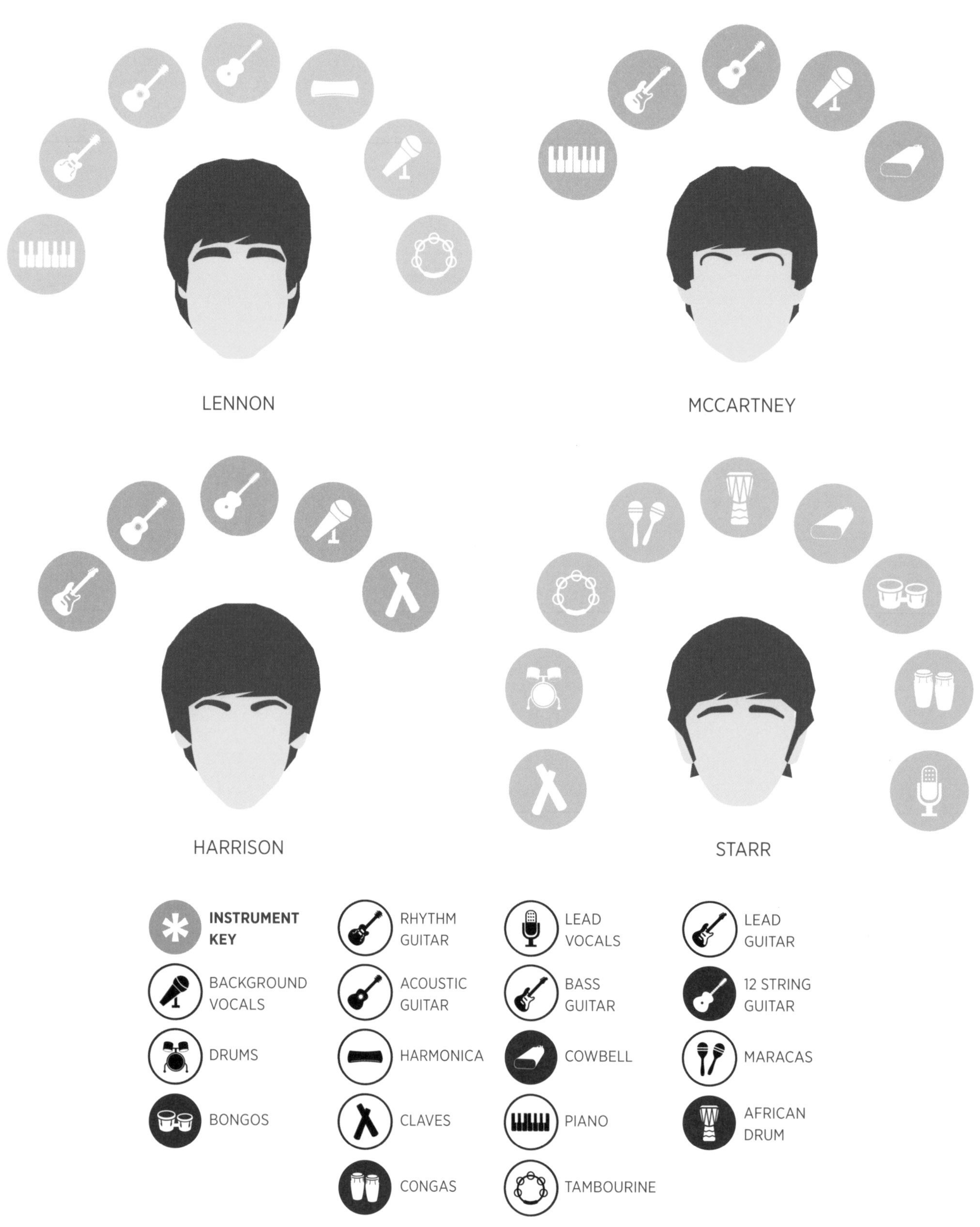

Black circle indicates instruments used for the first time in a Beatles' album

4 COUNTRIES

3 TOURS

101 LIVE SHOWS

1963
late 1963

mid
1964
late 1964
mid 1965

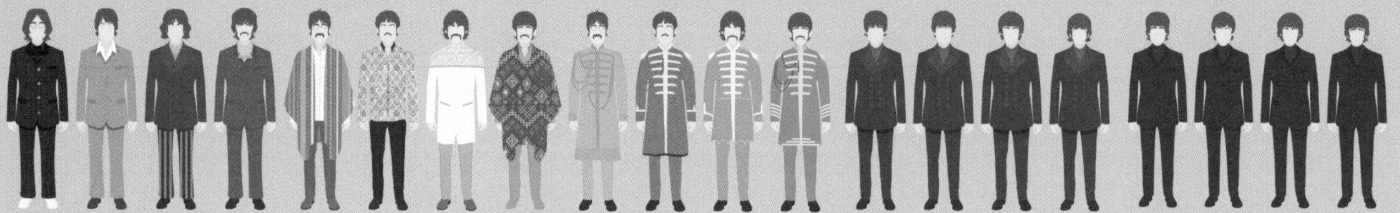
late 1968
late 1967
mid 1967
mid 1966
late 1965

early 1969
1969
1970

1970

Similar in style to the classic English Chesterfield suits worn throughout 1963, this newer model still has the black lapels but is now a Harrier grey.

ALBUM OVERVIEW

Release: 4 December 1964
Producer: George Martin
Engineer: Norman Smith

Beatlemania was at its height when *Beatles For Sale* was made. Recording sessions had to be fitted in around the band's hectic schedule and it has been documented that they were absolutely exhausted. As a result, George Martin has said the album isn't particularly memorable.

Indeed, the band lacked some of the creative drive showcased in the previous album, demonstrated by the band's use of old cover versions and early Lennon-McCartney compositions, along with only a few new songs. It has also been suggested that the more downbeat tone of the album in comparison to *A Hard Day's Night* is a further reflection of their depleted energy levels. The growing influence of Bob Dylan on the band, particularly on John Lennon, was also becoming evident.

'Eight Days A Week' was the first pop music recording to feature a fade-in introduction and 'Every Little Thing' was one of the first recorded songs to feature multi-tracked bass guitar.

DECEMBER

1964

BEATLES FOR SALE

TIMELINE: DECEMBER 1964–JULY 1965

December 24, 1964
The Beatles perform *Another Beatles Christmas Show* at the Hammersmith Odeon, London for 3 weeks

January 20, 1965
Lyndon B. Johnson is sworn in as U.S. President for his second term

February 11, 1965
Ringo Starr marries his long-term girlfriend Maureen Cox

February 21, 1965
African-American Muslim minister and human rights activist Malcolm X is assassinated in New York City

March 8, 1965
United States Marines arrive in Da Nang, South Vietnam, becoming the first American ground combat troops in Vietnam

March 18, 1965
Cosmonaut Alexey Leonov, leaving his spacecraft Voskhod 2 for 12 minutes, becoming the first person to walk in space

April 23, 1965
The Pennine Way officially opens

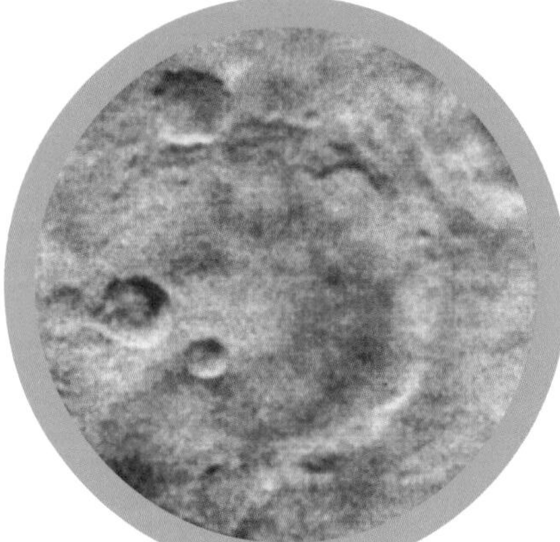

July 14, 1965
U.S. spacecraft Mariner 4 flies by Mars, becoming the first spacecraft to return images from the Red Planet

July 29, 1965
The Beatles' second movie *Help!* premieres

JOHN AND I WOULD SIT DOWN
AND BY THEN IT MIGHT BE ONE OR TWO 'CLOCK
BY FOUR OR FIVE O'CLOCK
WE'D BE DONE

—PAUL MCCARTNEY—

ON WRITING FOR 'BEATLES FOR SALE'

ALBUM COVER DESIGN

This was Robert Freeman's third Beatles' album cover. The photograph was taken in Hyde Park, London and the band look noticeably tired in it – another reflection of their intense schedule at the time. Here we've illustrated the band members wrapped up against the cold ready for the shoot. The album was packaged in a gatefold sleeve, which was a first for the Beatles.

LYRICS: THE WORDS THEY SANG THE MOST

LET COME
BLACK
WELL EIGHT
OH
BABE
ROCKIN FEEL BLUE
LOVE LONG DANCE
WAITING REAL TELL HONEY EVERYBODY'S
BABY SEE
I'M DAYS
MUSIC HOLD DAY TRYING AW
SOFT HELL YEAH LYING CRYING
GONE HEY TREE WHISPER KNOW BYE
ROCK LATE WONDERING
GIRL DON'T
YOU'RE ENOUGH ANOTHER BACK LOSER GO
ROLL PLACE CARE YOU'LL
LIKE NEED USE THING TIME
WEEK NOW
OLD DIDN'T WANNA PLEASE PAST
LOOK I'LL ONE
LOSE CAUSE GOT
WAY

VOCALS: WHICH BEATLE TOOK THE LEAD?

Beatles For Sale was the first album where the band members attended the mixing sessions – previously they had been happy to let George Martin conduct the sessions with his engineers.

Where band members shared lead vocals both are listed as singing lead vocals (as a result numbers may add up to more than the total number of tracks on the album).

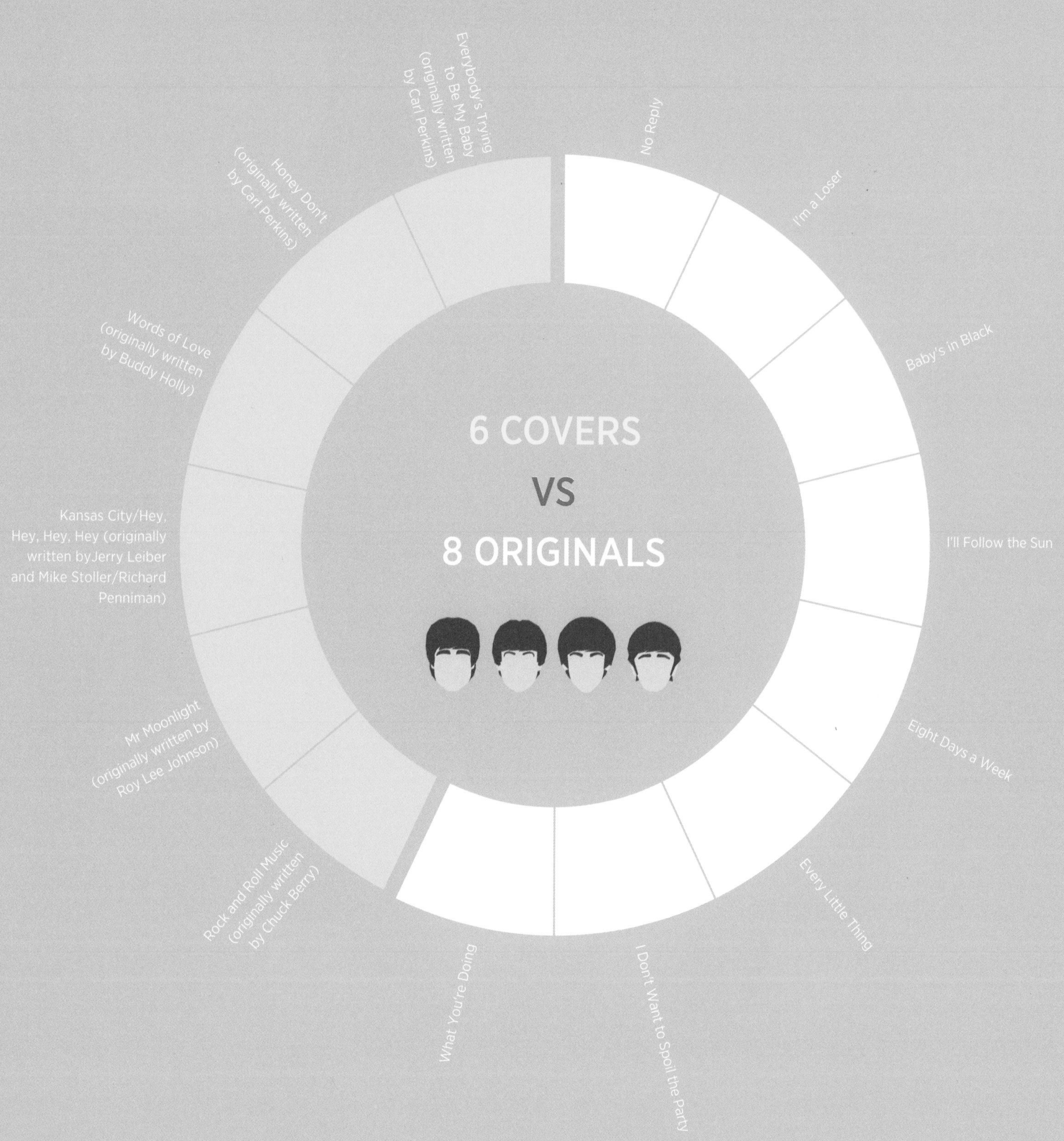
6 COVERS
VS
8 ORIGINALS
No Reply
I'm a Loser
Baby's in Black
I'll Follow the Sun
Eight Days a Week
Every Little Thing
I Don't Want to Spoil the Party
What You're Doing
Rock and Roll Music (originally written by Chuck Berry)
Mr Moonlight (originally written by Roy Lee Johnson)
Kansas City/Hey, Hey, Hey, Hey (originally written byJerry Leiber and Mike Stoller/Richard Penniman)
Words of Love (originally written by Buddy Holly)
Honey Don't (originally written by Carl Perkins)
Everybody's Trying to Be My Baby (originally written by Carl Perkins)

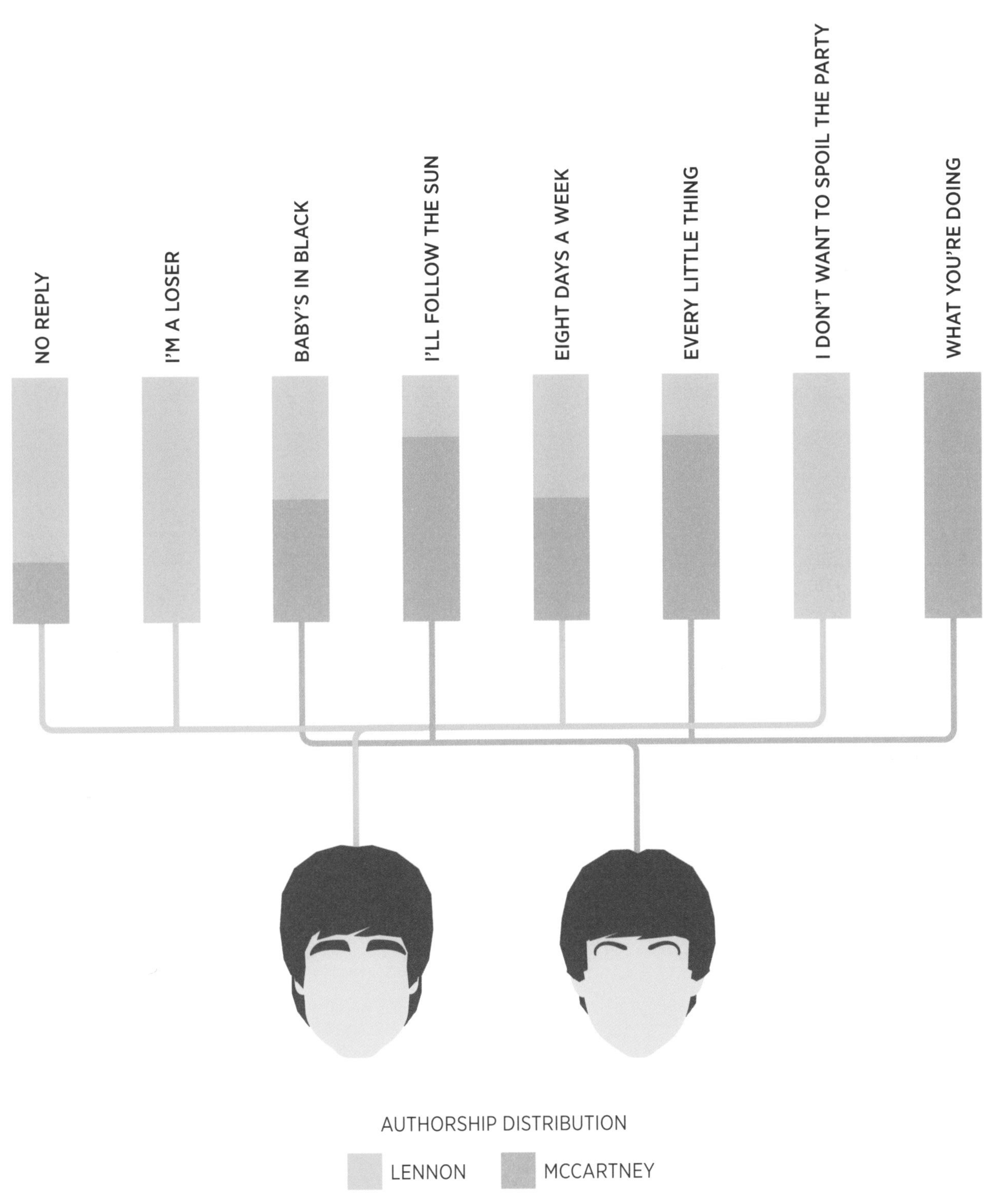
NO REPLY
I'M A LOSER
BABY'S IN BLACK
I'LL FOLLOW THE SUN
EIGHT DAYS A WEEK
EVERY LITTLE THING
I DON'T WANT TO SPOIL THE PARTY
WHAT YOU'RE DOING
AUTHORSHIP DISTRIBUTION
LENNON
MCCARTNEY

LENGTH: TRACKS AND ALBUM

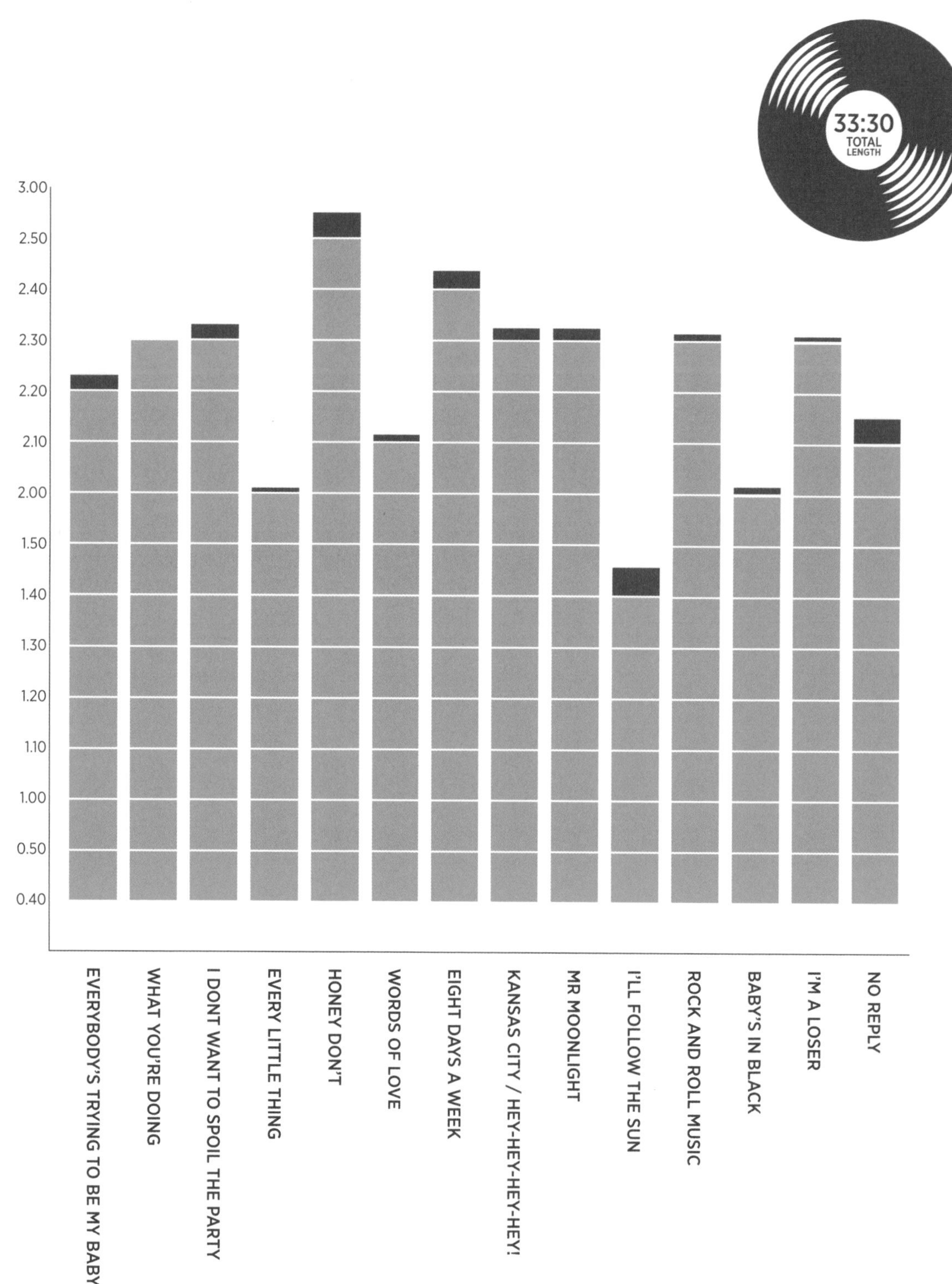

SONG KEYS

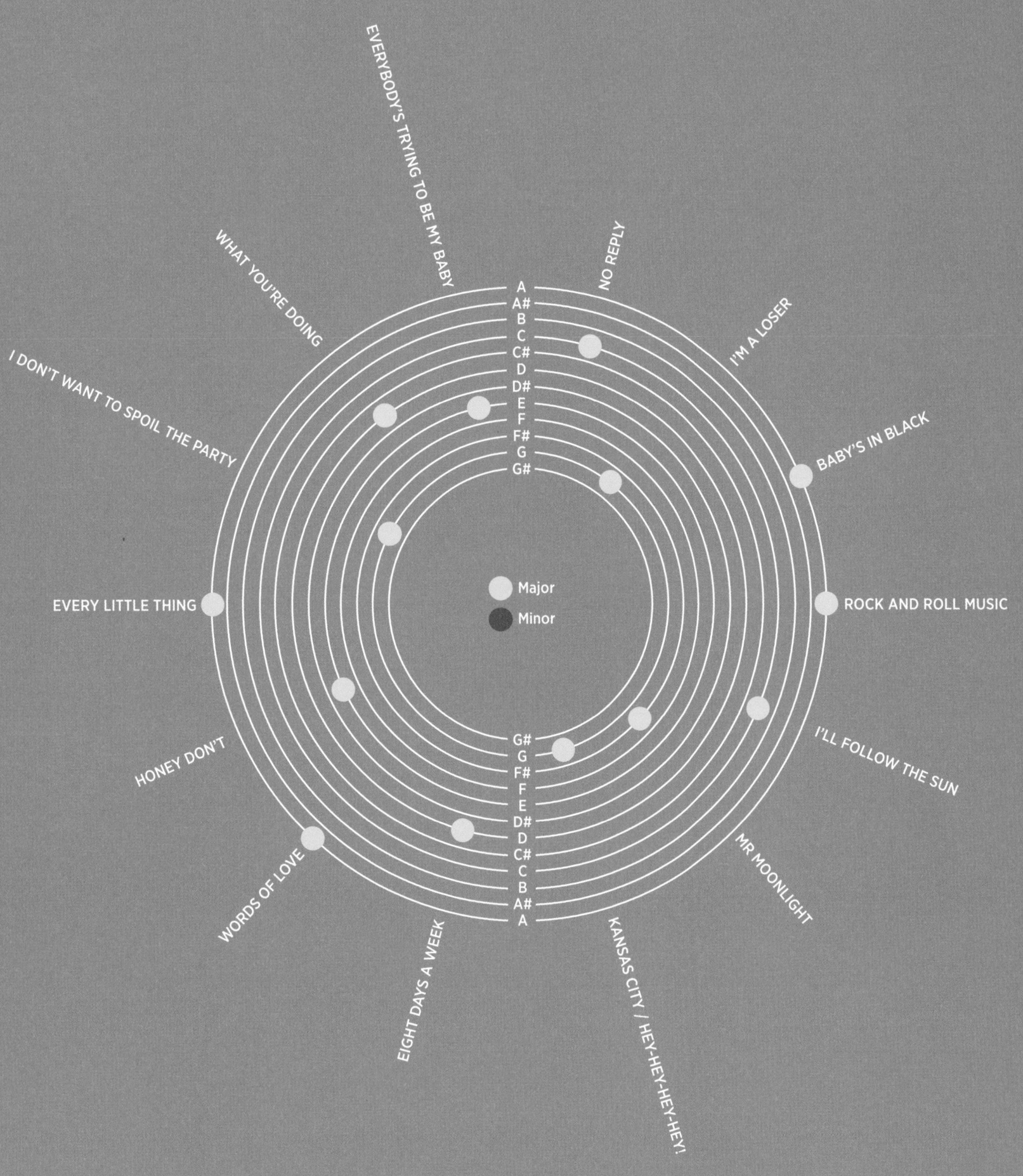

EVERYBODY'S TRYING TO BE MY BABY
NO REPLY
WHAT YOU'RE DOING
I'M A LOSER
I DON'T WANT TO SPOIL THE PARTY
BABY'S IN BLACK
EVERY LITTLE THING
ROCK AND ROLL MUSIC
HONEY DON'T
I'LL FOLLOW THE SUN
WORDS OF LOVE
MR MOONLIGHT
EIGHT DAYS A WEEK
KANSAS CITY / HEY-HEY-HEY-HEY!
A
A#
B
C
C#
D
D#
E
F
F#
G
G#
Major
Minor

A VISUAL REPRESENTATION OF THE VOLUME AND INTENSITY OF EACH TRACK ON THE ALBUM

SUCCESS

UK SINGLE RELEASES

NO REPLY
I'M A LOSER
BABY'S IN BLACK
ROCK AND ROLL MUSIC
I'LL FOLLOW THE SUN
MR. MOONLIGHT
KANSAS CITY / HEY-HEY-HEY-HEY!
EIGHT DAYS A WEEK
WORDS OF LOVE
HONEY DON'T
EVERY LITTLE THING
I DON'T WANT TO SPOIL THE PARTY
WHAT YOU'RE DOING
EVERYBODY'S TRYING TO BE MY BABY

NOT RELEASED
TOP 20
TOP 10

Beatles for Sale topped the UK album charts as soon as it was released, knocking *A Hard Day's Night* off the top spot. The album spent seven consecutive weeks at number one. None of the songs from this album were released as singles.

ALBUM CHART POSITIONS

UNITED KINGDOM
Number One

GERMANY
Number One

AUSTRALIA
Number Five

INSTRUMENTS: WHAT CAN YOU HEAR?

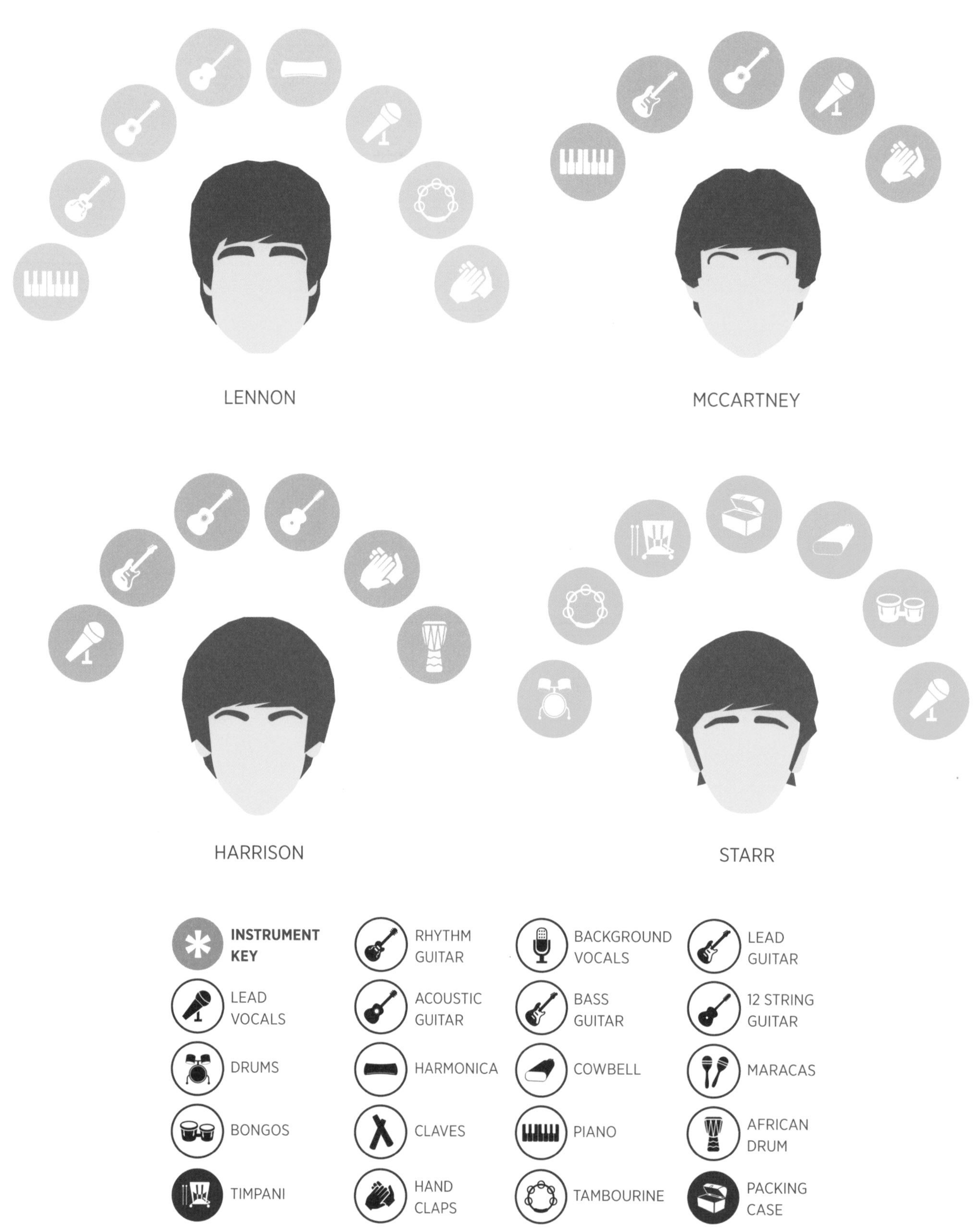

Black circle indicates instruments used for the first time in a Beatles' album

PERFORMANCES

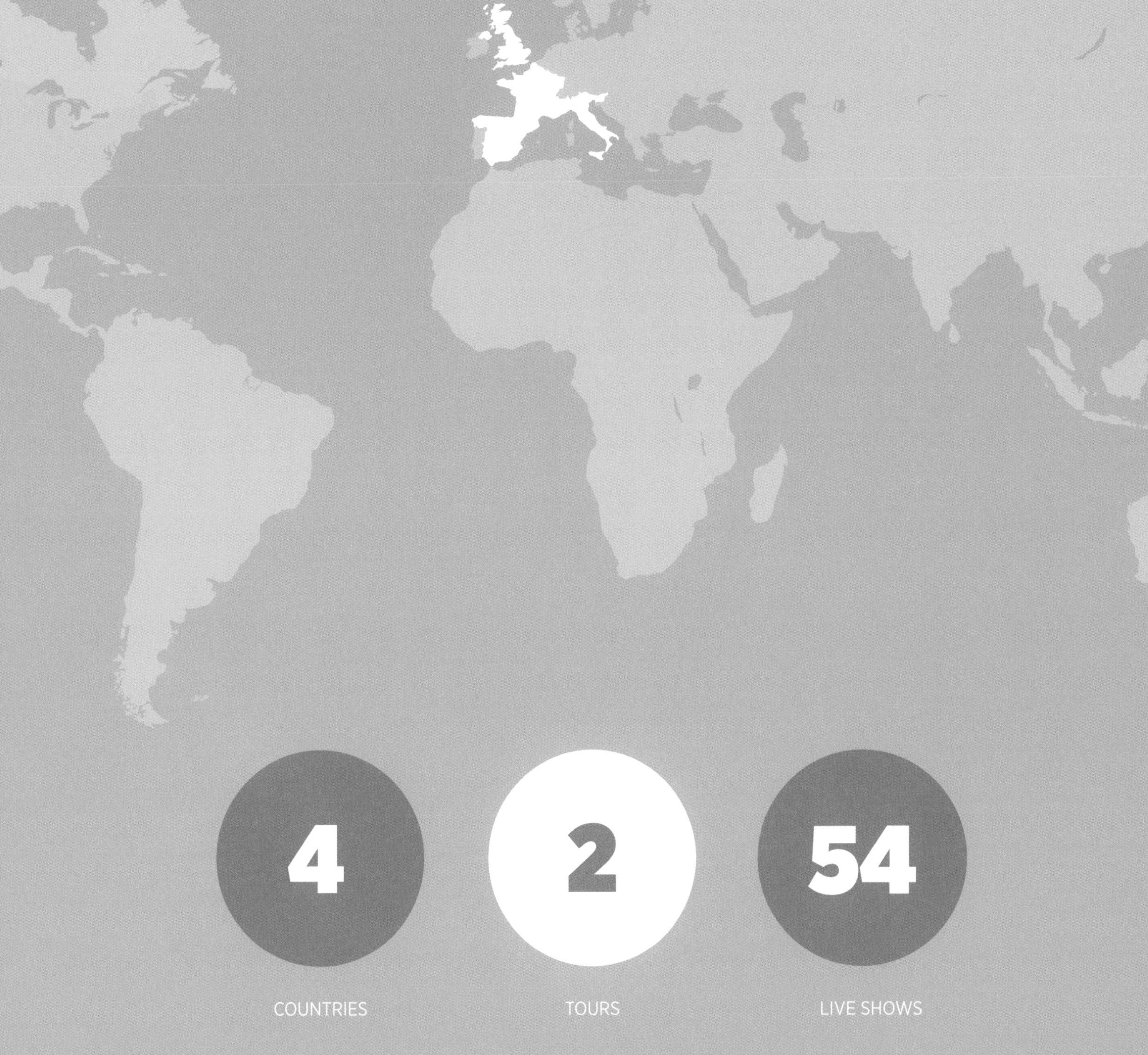

1963
late 1963
mid 1964

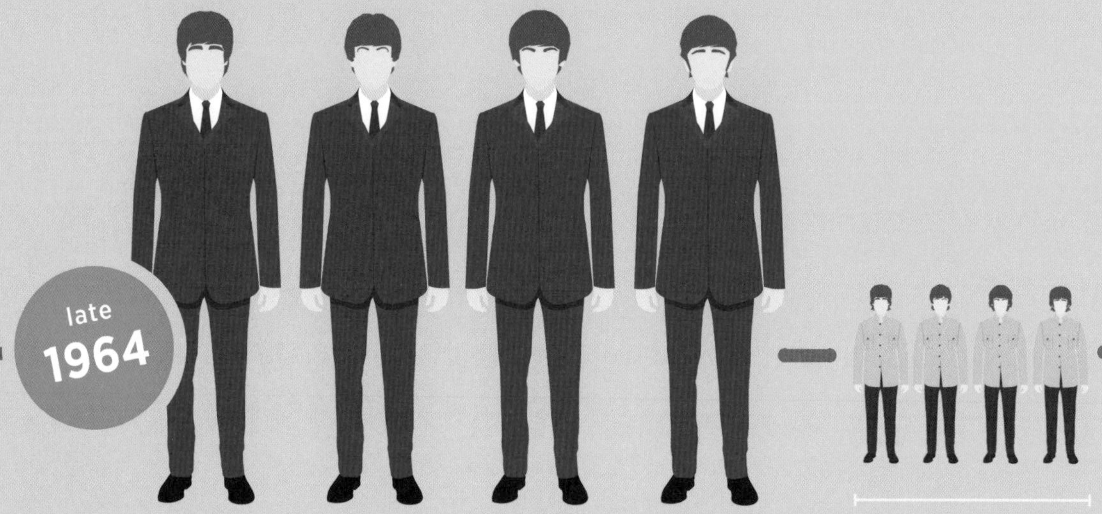
late
1964
mid 1965

late 1968
late 1967
mid 1967
mid 1966
late 1965

early 1969
1969
1970

1970

Again, similar in style to the outfits worn over the past few years, the classic sharp black suit, white shirt, black tie and, of course, 'Beatle boots' were a favourite.

ALBUM OVERVIEW

Released: 6 August 1965
Producer: George Martin
Engineer: Norman Smith

Originally set to be called Beatles II, and then Eight Arms To Hold You, *Help!* was the Beatles' fifth UK album release and the soundtrack to their second feature film. It is considered to be one of the band's most diverse albums, featuring elements of folk, rock, country and western, classical and bluegrass. Bob Dylan also played a part in it, not least through the inspiration the Beatles took from his music but also through his introducing the band to marijuana the previous year. The drug greatly influenced *Help!*

John Lennon wrote the title track during a period of inward reflection. He suggested that he was dissatisfied with himself and was subconsciously crying for help. Technology-wise, from this point onwards, reduction mixes played a crucial role in their albums (until the introduction of eight-track recording in 1968).

AUGUST

1965

HELP!

TIMELINE: AUGUST–NOVEMBER 1965

August 1, 1965
Cigarette advertising is banned on British television

August 15, 1965
The Beatles begin their 1965 US Tour

August 27, 1965
The Beatles meet their hero Elvis Presley

September 25, 1965
The Tom & Jerry cartoon series makes its world broadcast premiere on CBS

October 26, 1965
The Beatles are awarded MBEs by Queen Elizabeth II at Buckingham Palace

November 15, 1965
U.S. racer Craig Breedlove sets a new land speed record of 600.601 mph (966.574 km/h)

November 16, 1965
The Soviet Union launches the Venera 3 space probe from Baikonur, Kazakhstan toward Venus

ALBUM COVER DESIGN

You guessed it, the cover photograph was yet another Robert Freeman original. This time it features the band members standing in their ski outfits from the film *Help!*, spelling out letters in semaphore.

Originally, they intended to spell the word 'HELP', but Freeman decided the arrangement of their arms didn't look good that way. In the end they settled on the letters NUJV, as it worked better visually. For the US version, the order was amended and they spelt NVUJ. Here we've visualised how the album might have looked if the band spelt 'HELP' as originally intended.

NEVER
FALLING
DIZZY
TRY
NOW
WITHOUT
BIG
TRUE
YOU'RE
CHANGE
ONE
PA
TICKET
GIRL
GONE
LIKE
CAUSE
GO
EYES
HEY
LOOK
LOSE
SEE
WELL
RIDE
NEW
MEAN
LOSE
GONNA
KNOW
RUN
LET
TELL
DON'T
I'M
CRY
DA
AWAY
SING
TREAT
MM
AIN'T
NOBODY
WANT
PIE
ACT
OOO
LOVE
COME
OH
GIRLS
MON
BACK
AH
MAKE
NEED
PART
GET
I'VE
STAR
HELP
RIGHT
FEEL
KIND
I'LL
TAKE
SHE'S
JUST
CARE
WRONG
YES
FOOL
MAN
WAY
NEAR

VOCALS: WHICH BEATLE TOOK THE LEAD?

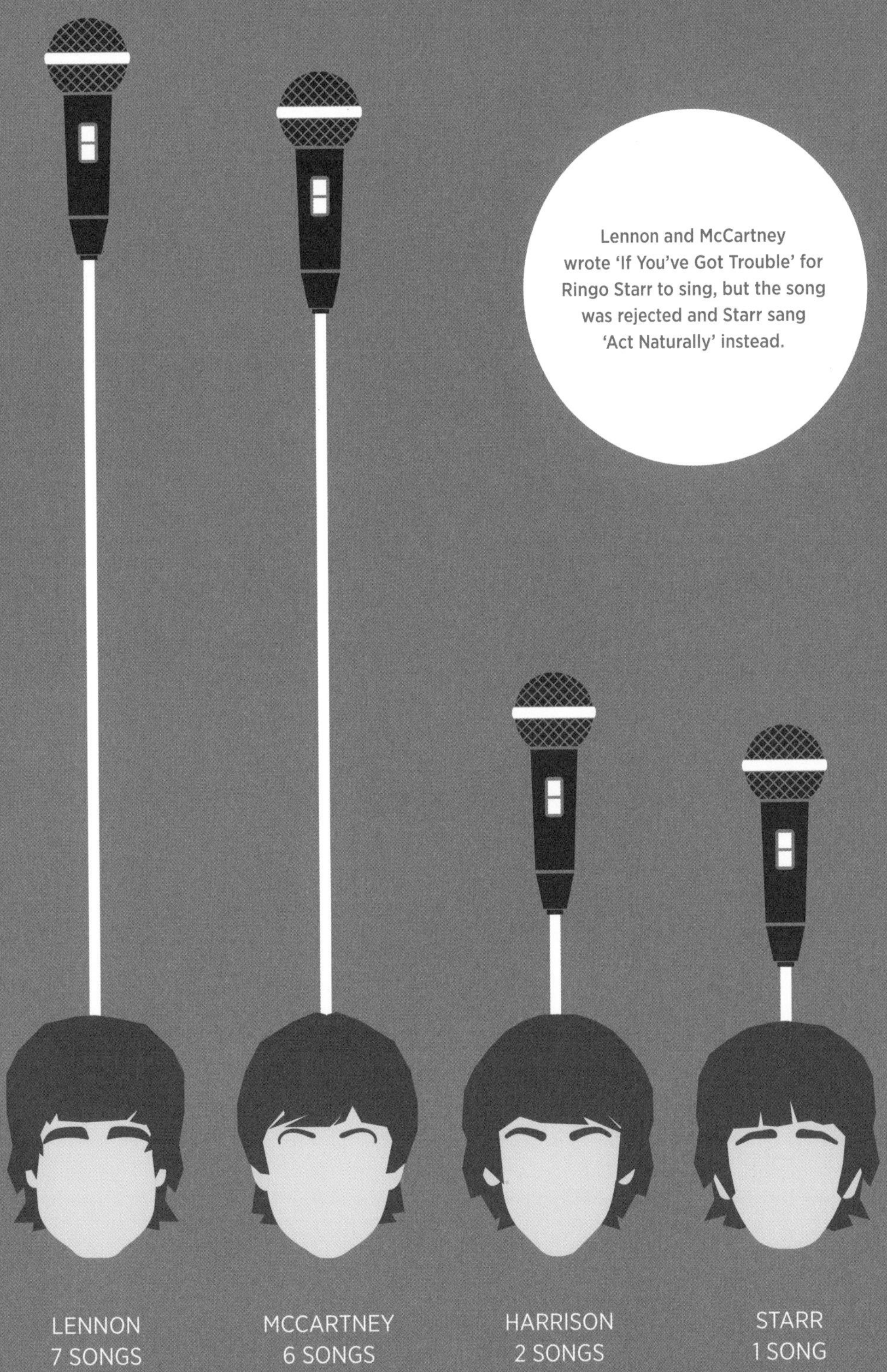

Where band members shared lead vocals both are listed as singing lead vocals (as a result numbers may add up to more than the total number of tracks on the album).

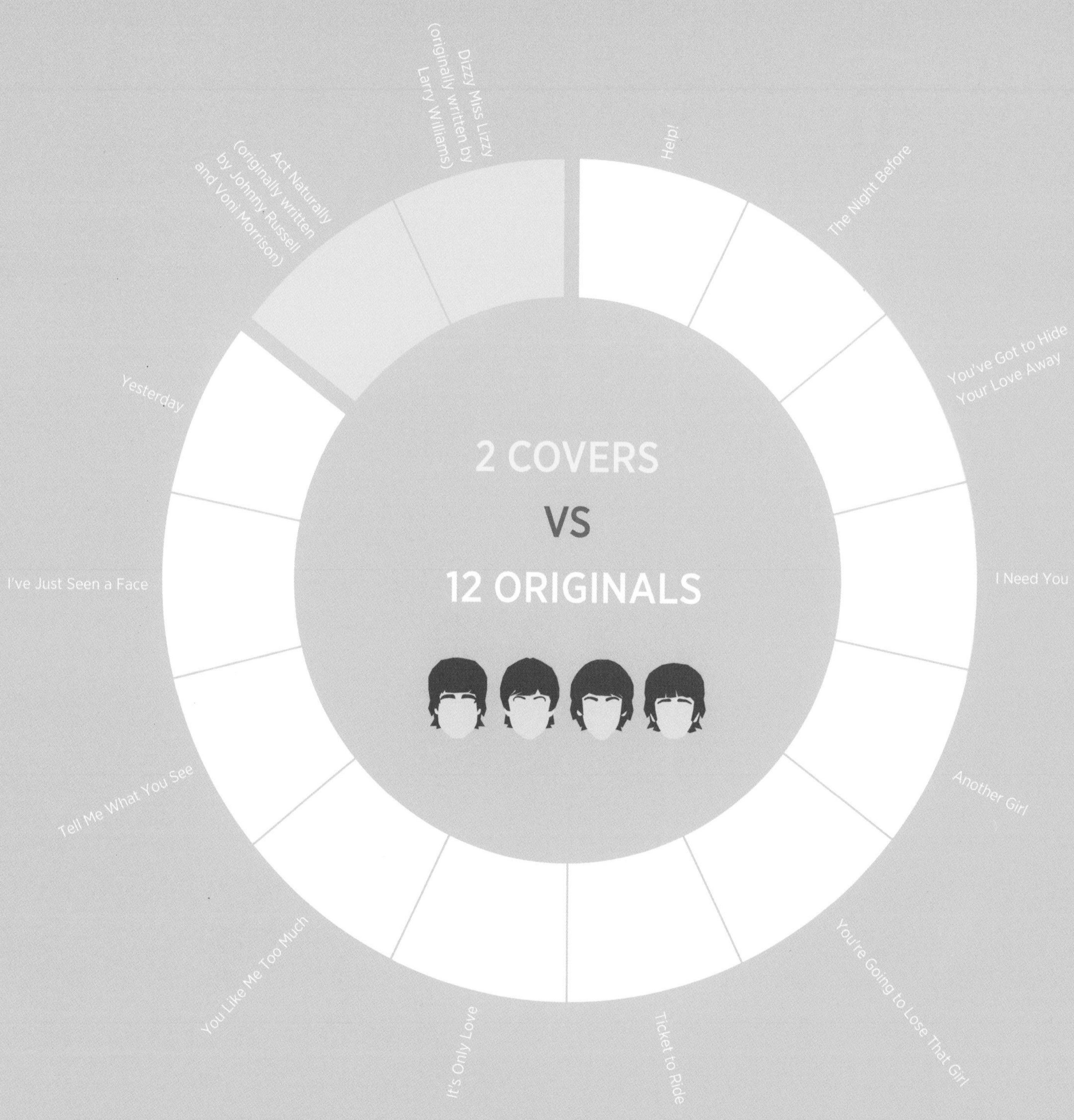
2 COVERS
VS
12 ORIGINALS
Help!
The Night Before
You've Got to Hide Your Love Away
I Need You
Another Girl
You're Going to Lose That Girl
Ticket to Ride
It's Only Love
You Like Me Too Much
Tell Me What You See
I've Just Seen a Face
Yesterday
Act Naturally (originally written by Johnny Russell and Voni Morrison)
Dizzy Miss Lizzy (originally written by Larry Williams)

SONGWRITING: WHO WROTE WHAT?

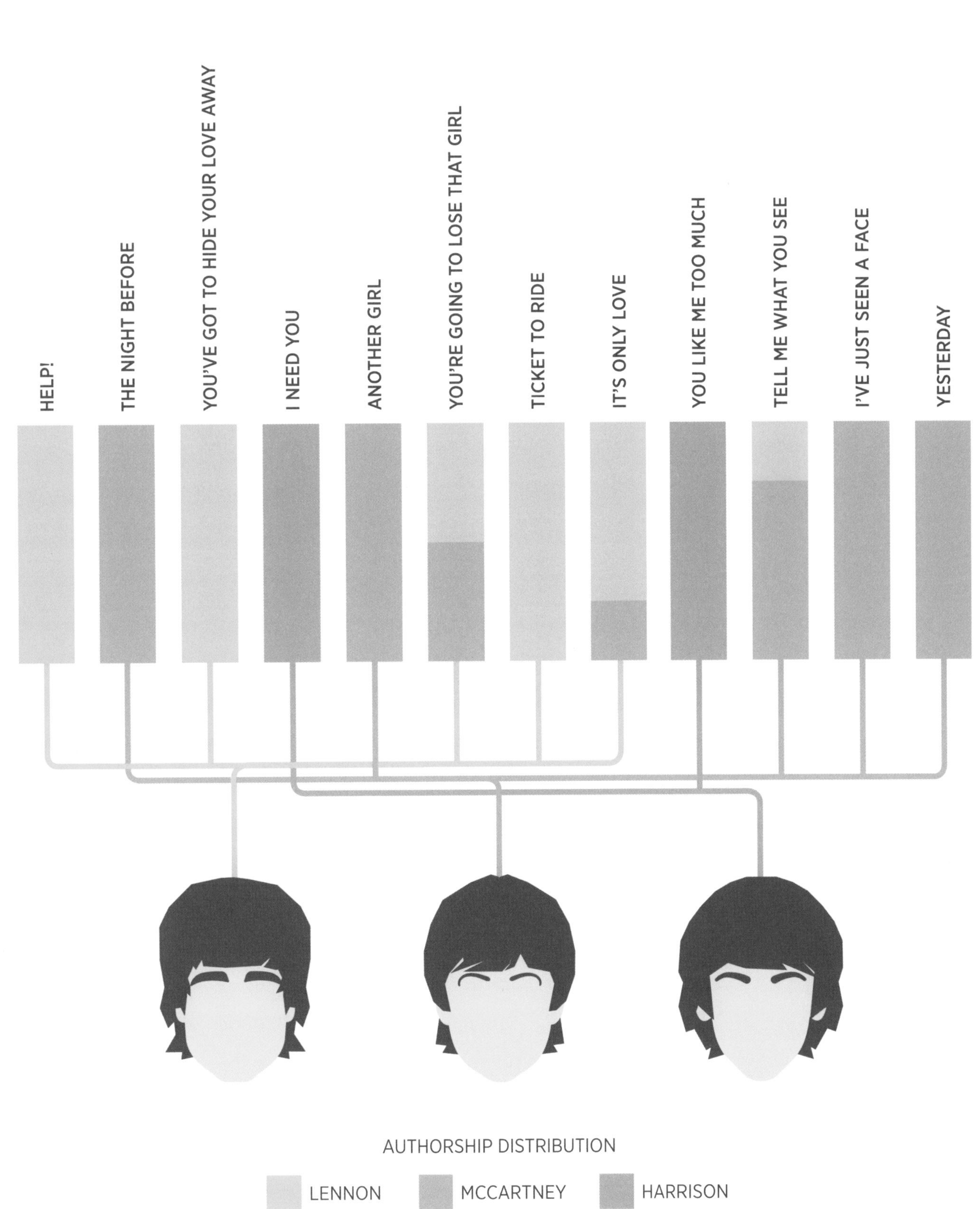

LENGTH: TRACKS AND ALBUM

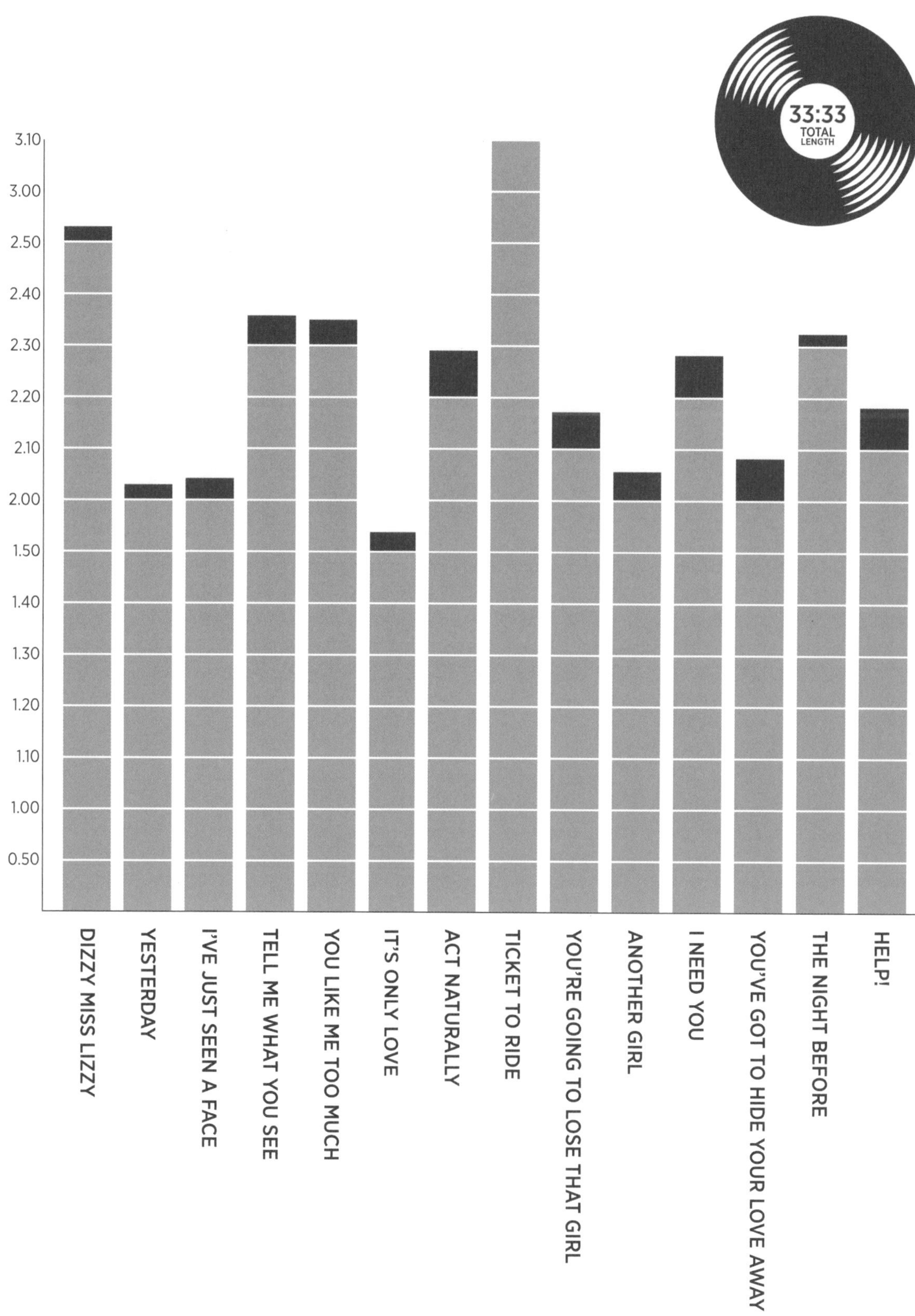

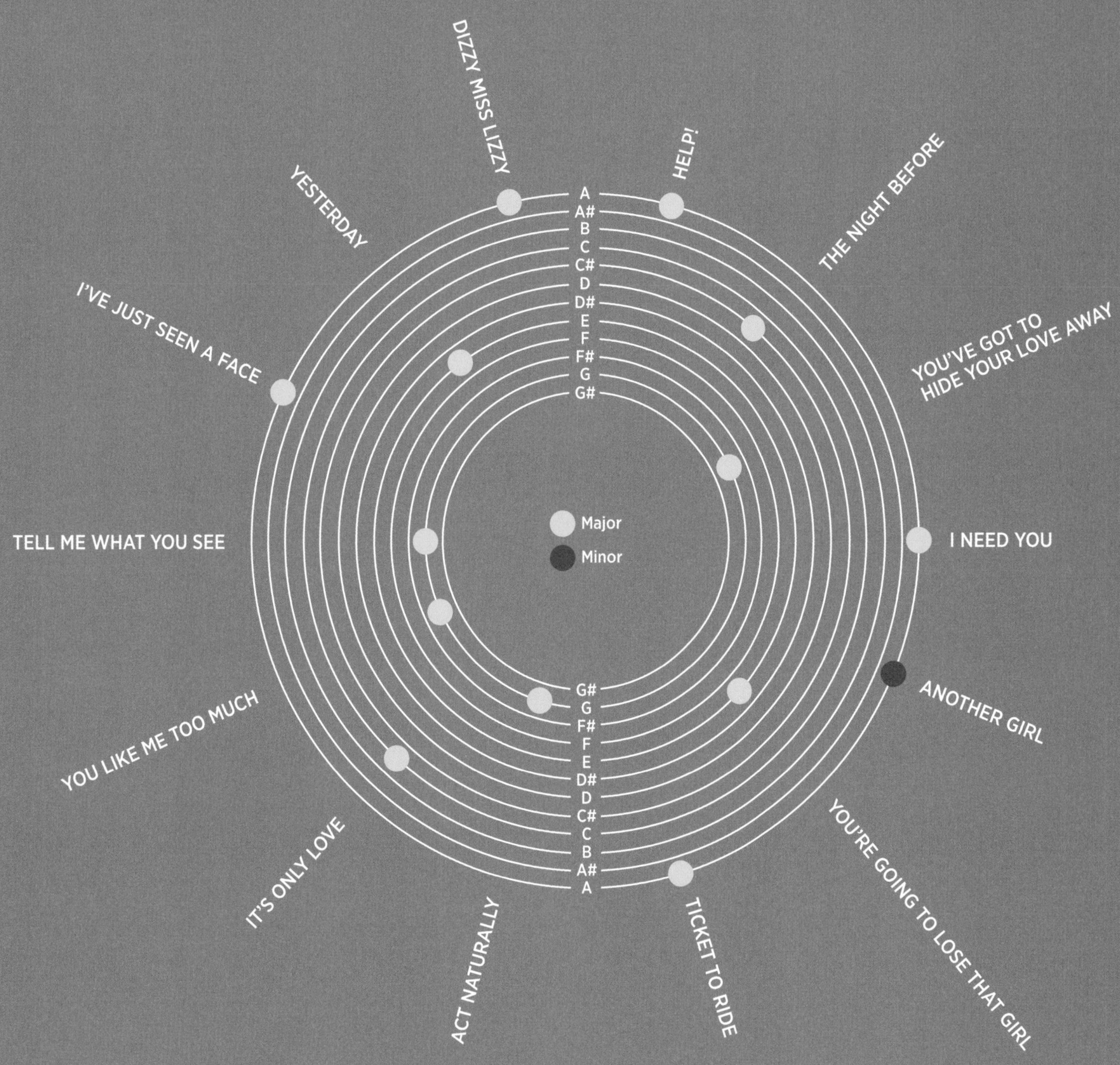
DIZZY MISS LIZZY
HELP!
YESTERDAY
THE NIGHT BEFORE
I'VE JUST SEEN A FACE
YOU'VE GOT TO HIDE YOUR LOVE AWAY
TELL ME WHAT YOU SEE
I NEED YOU
Major
Minor
ANOTHER GIRL
YOU LIKE ME TOO MUCH
IT'S ONLY LOVE
YOU'RE GOING TO LOSE THAT GIRL
ACT NATURALLY
TICKET TO RIDE
A
A#
B
C
C#
D
D#
E
F
F#
G
G#

A VISUAL REPRESENTATION OF THE VOLUME AND INTENSITY OF EACH TRACK ON THE ALBUM

SUCCESS

UK SINGLE RELEASES

McCartney wrote his most famous song 'Yesterday' for this album. It wasn't released as a single at the time because McCartney performed it on his own (this was the first Beatles song to feature just one member of the group) but it later charted in the UK on the 1976 re-release. It would go on to be recorded by more than 3,000 different artists, making it the most covered pop song in history. It was performed approximately 7 million times in the 20th Century. Non-album singles to reach number one during this period were 'We Can Work It Out'/'Day Tripper' (3/12/65) and 'Paperback Writer'/'Rain' (10/6/66).

HELP!
THE NIGHT BEFORE
YOU'VE GOT TO HIDE YOUR LOVE AWAY
I NEED YOU
ANOTHER GIRL
YOU'RE GOING TO LOSE THAT GIRL
TICKET TO RIDE
ACT NATURALLY
IT'S ONLY LOVE
YOU LIKE ME TOO MUCH
TELL ME WHAT YOU SEE
I'VE JUST SEEN A FACE
YESTERDAY
DIZZY MISS LIZZY

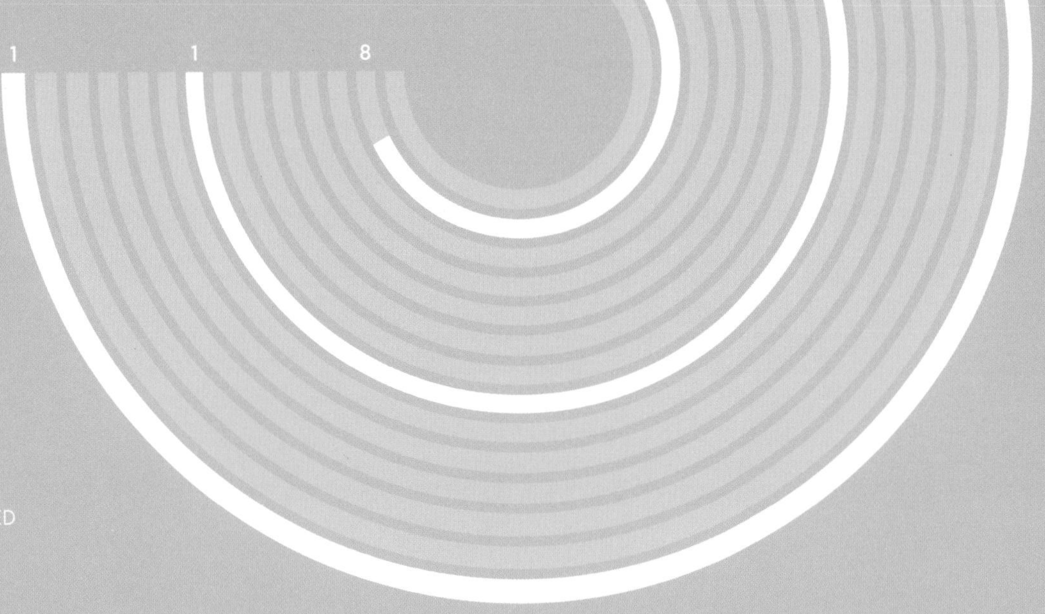

NOT RELEASED
TOP 20
TOP 10

ALBUM CHART POSITIONS

UNITED KINGDOM
Number One

GERMANY
Number One

UNITED STATES
Number One

AUSTRALIA
Number Five

INSTRUMENTS: WHAT CAN YOU HEAR?

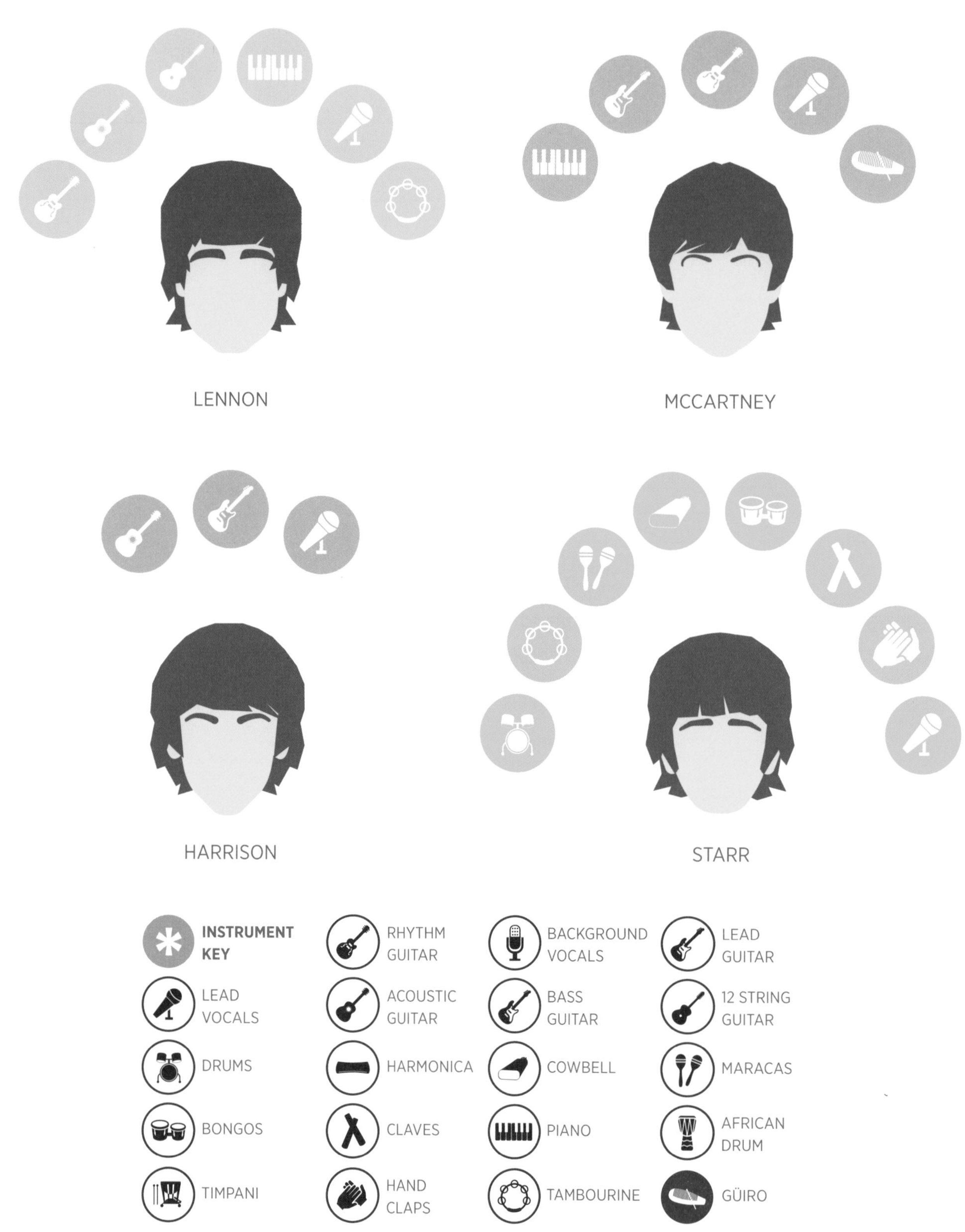

Black circle indicates instruments used for the first time in a Beatles' album

PERFORMANCES

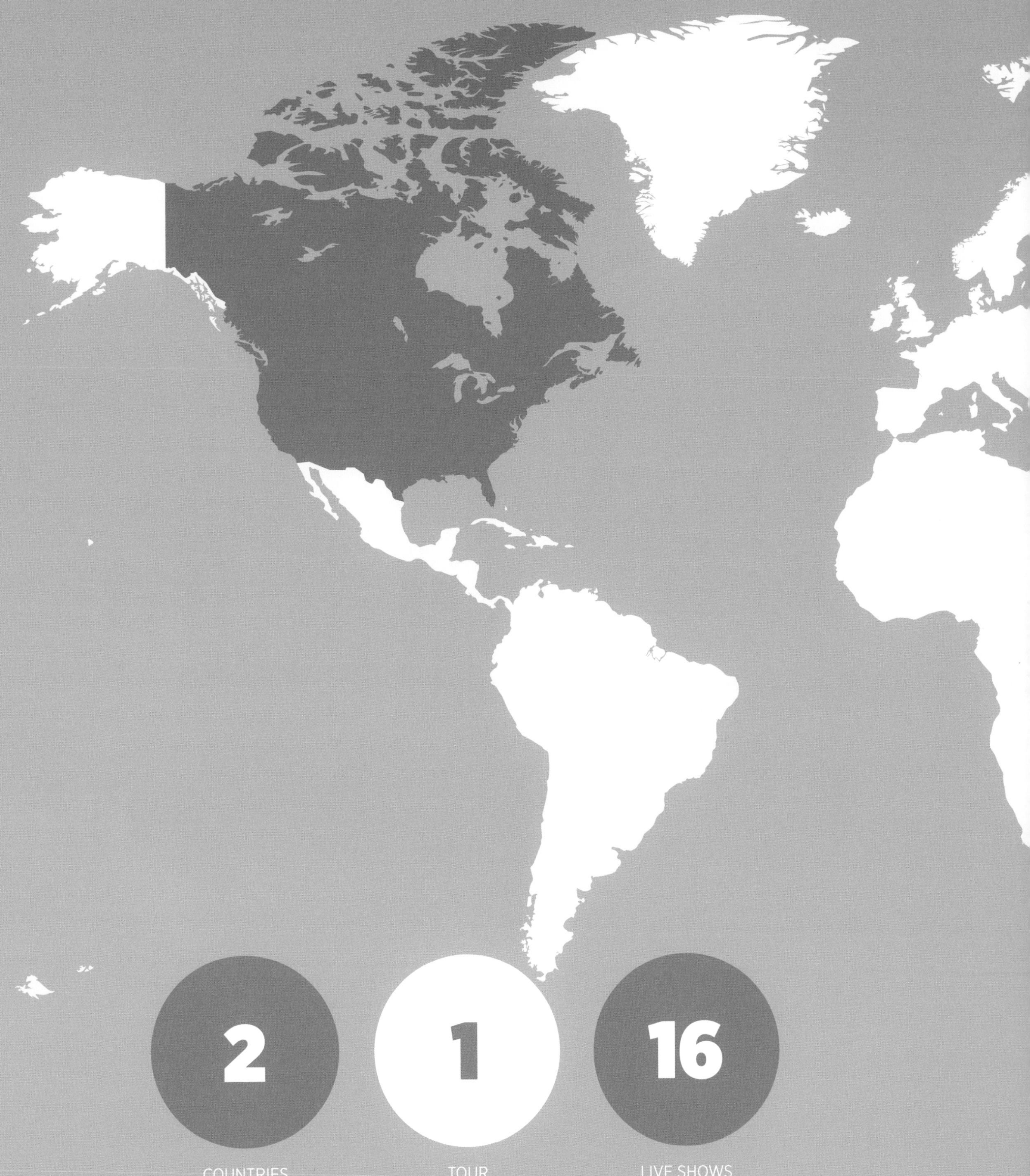

STYLE

1963
late 1963
mid 1964
late 1964

mid
1965

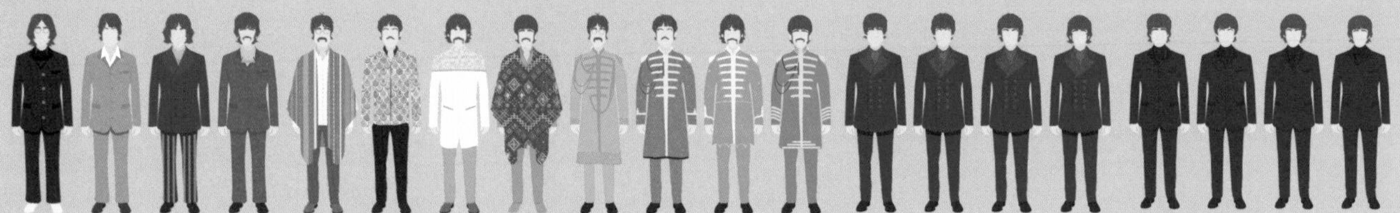
late 1968
late 1967
mid 1967
mid 1966
late 1965

early 1969
1969
1970

1970

Known as the 'Shea Stadium' suits after the famous gig where they were worn, the tan, military style jackets were paired with drainpipe trousers and Wells Fargo security officer badges from the security company that escorted the band into the venue.

US Albums

The albums released in the United States were in many cases dramatically different from those in the UK market. As a result, the experience of the band's music was an alternative one for US audiences. Here are the albums delivered to American listeners...

Introducing The Beatles (Jan 10, 1964)

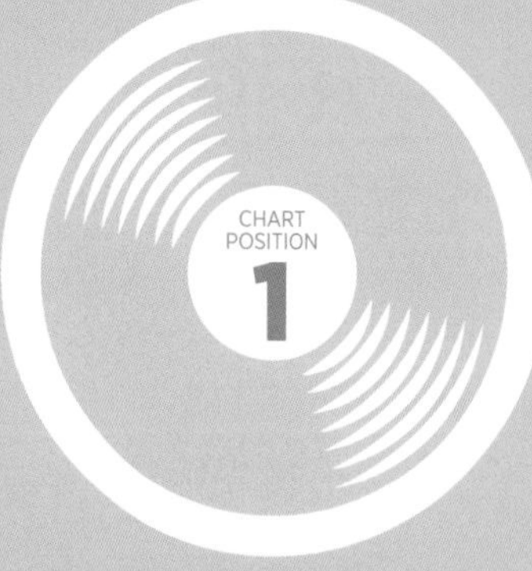

Meet the Beatles! (Jan 20, 1964)

The Beatles' Second Album! (April 10, 1964)

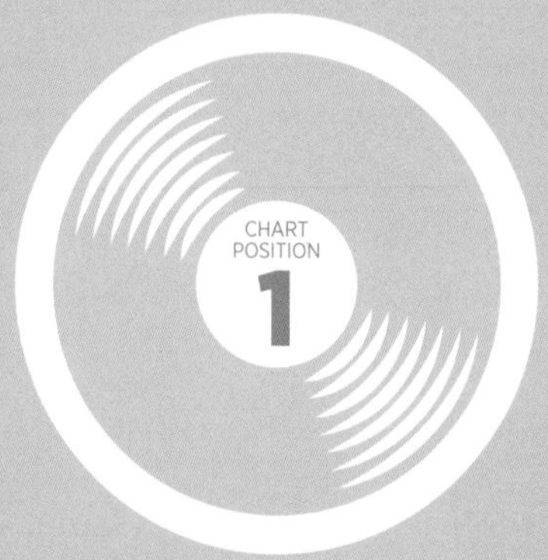

A Hard Day's Night - OST (June 26, 1964)

Something New (July 20, 1964)

The Beatles' Story (Nov 23, 1964).

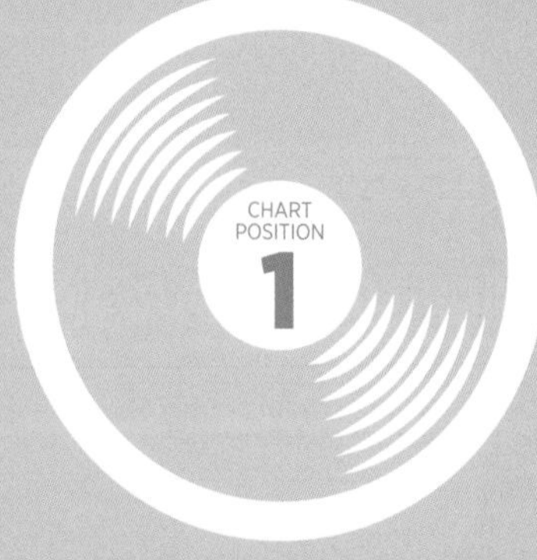

Beatles '65 (Dec 15, 1964)

The Early Beatles (Mar 22, 1965)

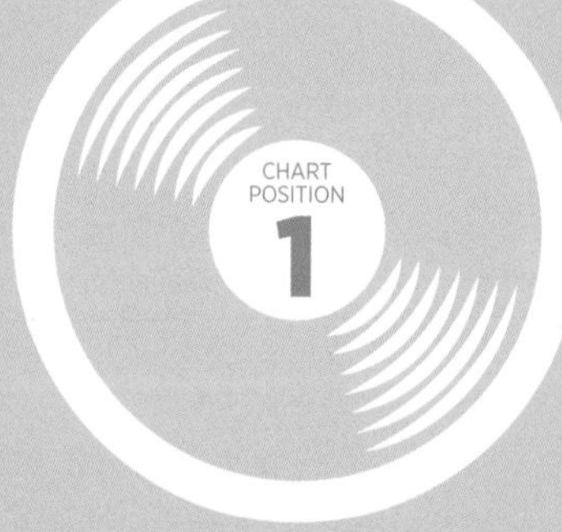

Beatles VI (June 14, 1965)

OST = Official Soundtrack

Help – OST (Aug 13, 1965)

Rubber Soul (Dec 6, 1965)

Yesterday And Today (June 20, 1966)

Revolver (Aug 8, 1966)

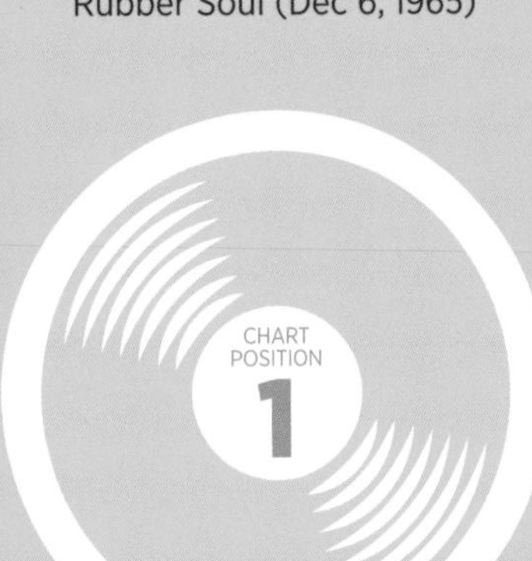

Sgt Pepper's Lonely Hearts Club Band (June 2, 1967)

Magical Mystery Tour (Nov 27, 1967)

The Beatles (Nov 25, 1968)

Yellow Submarine – OST (Jan 13, 1969)

Abbey Road (Oct 1, 1969)

Hey Jude/The Beatles Again (Feb 26, 1970)

Let It Be – OST (May 18, 1970)

ALBUM OVERVIEW

Released: 3 December 1965
Producer: George Martin
Engineer: Norman Smith

Rubber Soul signalled a change in direction for the Beatles. It marked the first time the band took full control in the studio and moved away from their early puppy love songs to exploring different subject matters, songwriting styles and instrumentation. It could be argued that *Rubber Soul* is Lennon's songwriting peak, featuring some of his most memorable creations.

There was, however, a bit of a rush to complete the album in time for Christmas, so they bought in some older songs, including 'Wait', which had been written for *Help!*, and 'Michelle', which McCartney wrote in 1959. The album title came from a comment a US musician had made about The Rolling Stones, saying they were 'plastic soul'.

DECEMBER 1965

RUBBER SOUL

TIMELINE: DECEMBER 1965-JULY 1966

December 12, 1965
End of the Beatles' last ever UK tour, Capitol Cinema Cardiff

February 3, 1966
The unmanned Soviet Luna 9 spacecraft makes the first controlled rocket assisted landing on the Moon

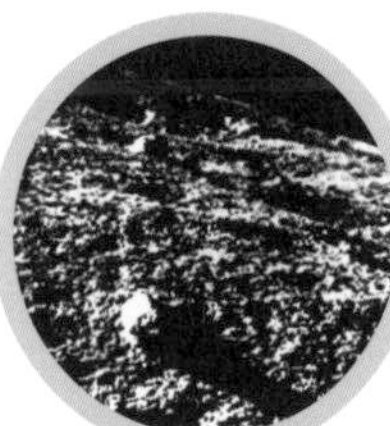

March 1, 1966
The British Government announces plans for the decimalisation of the pound sterling, to come into effect in 1971

March 4, 1966
John Lennon claims the Beatles are now 'more popular than Jesus'

April 21, 1966
The opening of the Parliament of the United Kingdom is televised for the first time

December 5, 1965
The Beatles perform in Liverpool for the last time, at the Empire Theatre

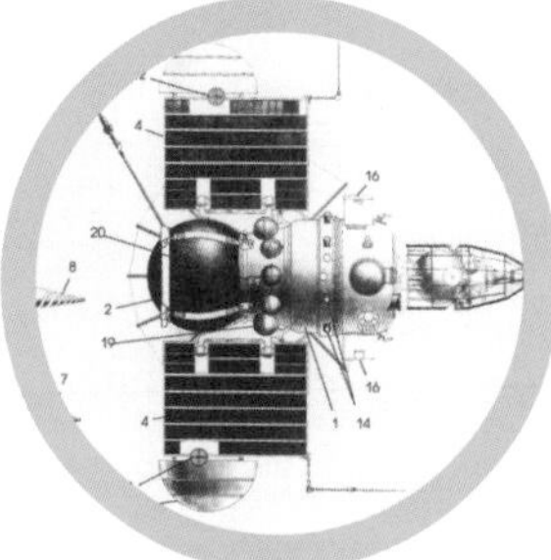

January 21, 1966
George Harrison marries Pattie Boyd

February 14, 1966
The Australian dollar is introduced at a rate of 2 dollars per pound, or 10 shillings per dollar

March 1, 1966
Soviet space probe Venera 3 crashes on Venus, becoming the first spacecraft to land on another planet's surface

April 6, 1966
The first recording session for *Revolver* takes place at Abbey Road

June 30, 1966
The Beatles play the first
of 5 shows in Tokyo, Japan

July 30, 1966
England beat West Germany
4–2 to win the 1966 FIFA World Cup
at Wembley after extra time

April 29, 1966
U.S. troops in Vietnam
total 250,000

April 30, 1966
Regular hovercraft service
begins over the English channel

July 4, 1966
The Beatles perform
in the Philippines

May 16, 1966
The legendary album
Pet Sounds by The Beach
Boys is released

April 21, 1966
An artificial heart is
installed in the chest of
Marcel DeRudder in a
Houston, Texas hospital

July 18, 1966
Gemini 10 is launched.
After docking with an Agena target
vehicle, the astronauts then set a
world altitude record of 474 miles

ALBUM COVER DESIGN

Rubber Soul was the first album by the band not to include the group's name on its cover. Instead it featured another photograph taken by Robert Freeman, this time at John Lennon's house in Weybridge. It was stretched, at the Beatles' request, making their faces longer. The original non-stretched photo might have looked something like this.

The distinctive lettering was designed by Charles Front, a London-based art director. In 2007 the lettering was auctioned by Bonhams, with a guide price of £10,000.

WE WERE JUST GETTING BETTER

TECHNICALLY AND MUSICALLY, THAT'S ALL

JOHN LENNON

1971, ON THE ALBUM 'RUBBER SOUL'

COVERS VS. ORIGINALS

SONGWRITING: WHO WROTE WHAT?

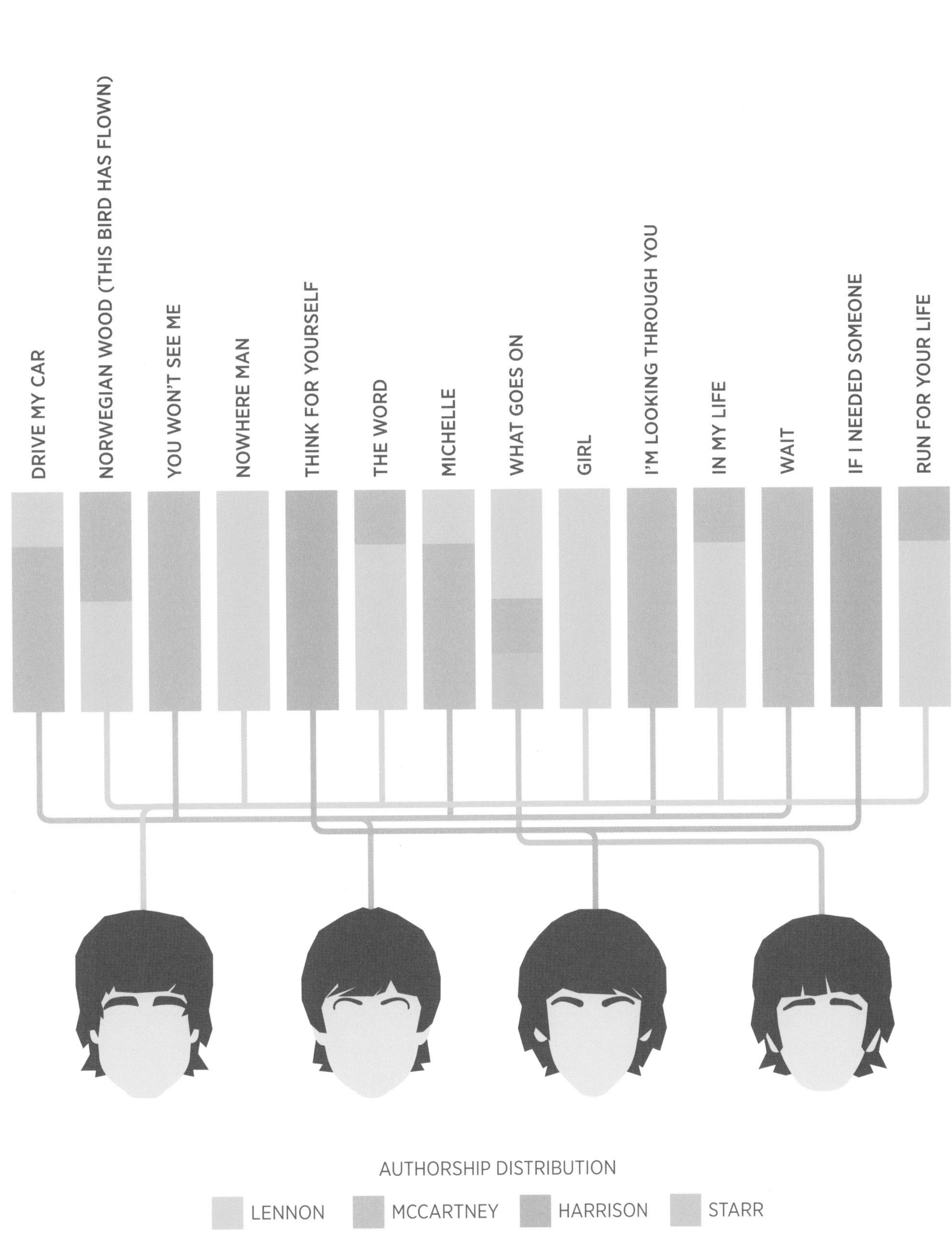

VOCALS: WHICH BEATLE TOOK THE LEAD?

Where band members shared lead vocals both are listed as singing lead vocals (as a result numbers may add up to more than the total number of tracks on the album).

SONG KEYS

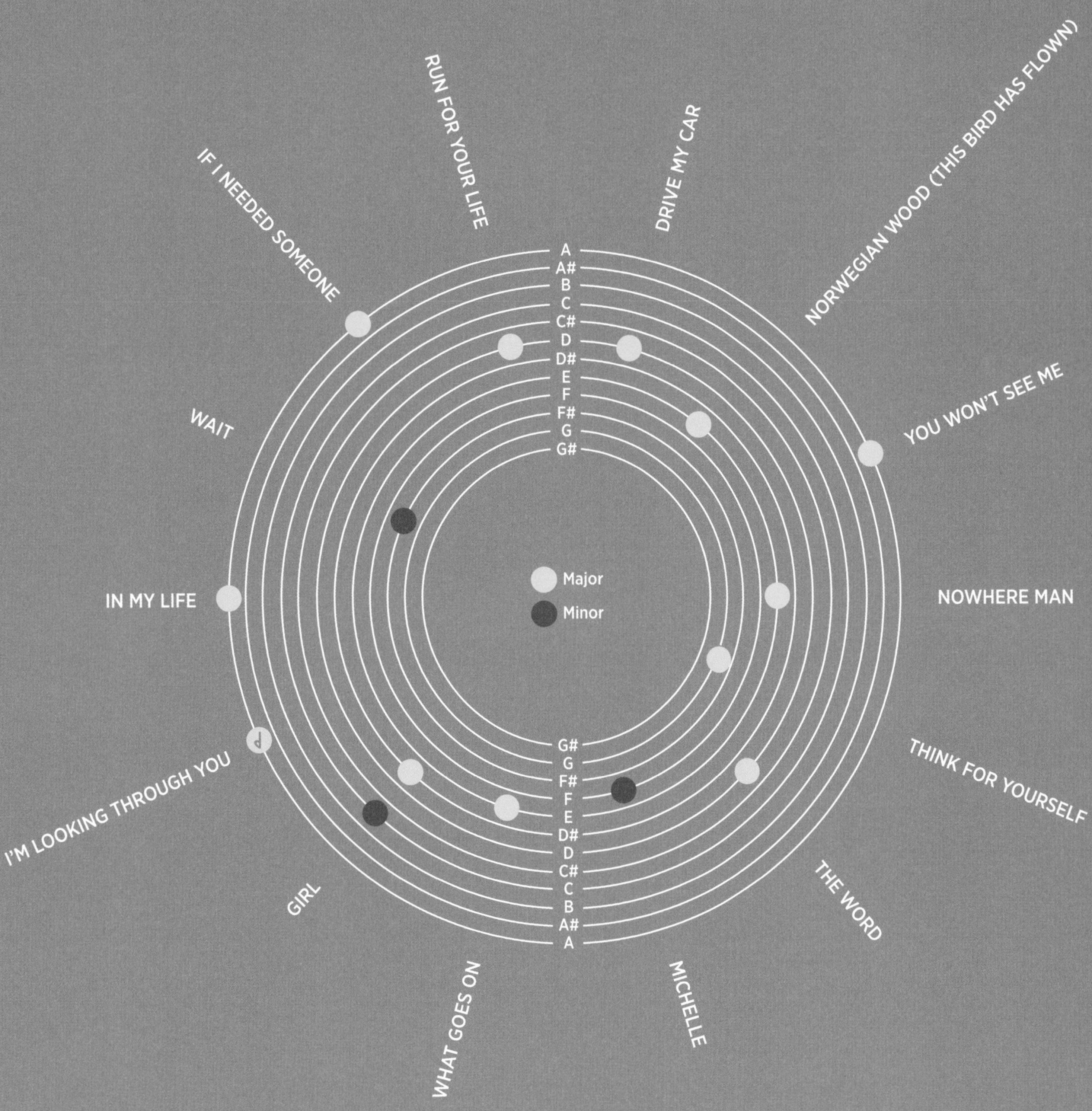

RUN FOR YOUR LIFE
DRIVE MY CAR
IF I NEEDED SOMEONE
NORWEGIAN WOOD (THIS BIRD HAS FLOWN)
WAIT
YOU WON'T SEE ME
IN MY LIFE
NOWHERE MAN
I'M LOOKING THROUGH YOU
THINK FOR YOURSELF
GIRL
THE WORD
WHAT GOES ON
MICHELLE
A
A#
B
C
C#
D
D#
E
F
F#
G
G#
Major
Minor

LENGTH: TRACKS AND ALBUM

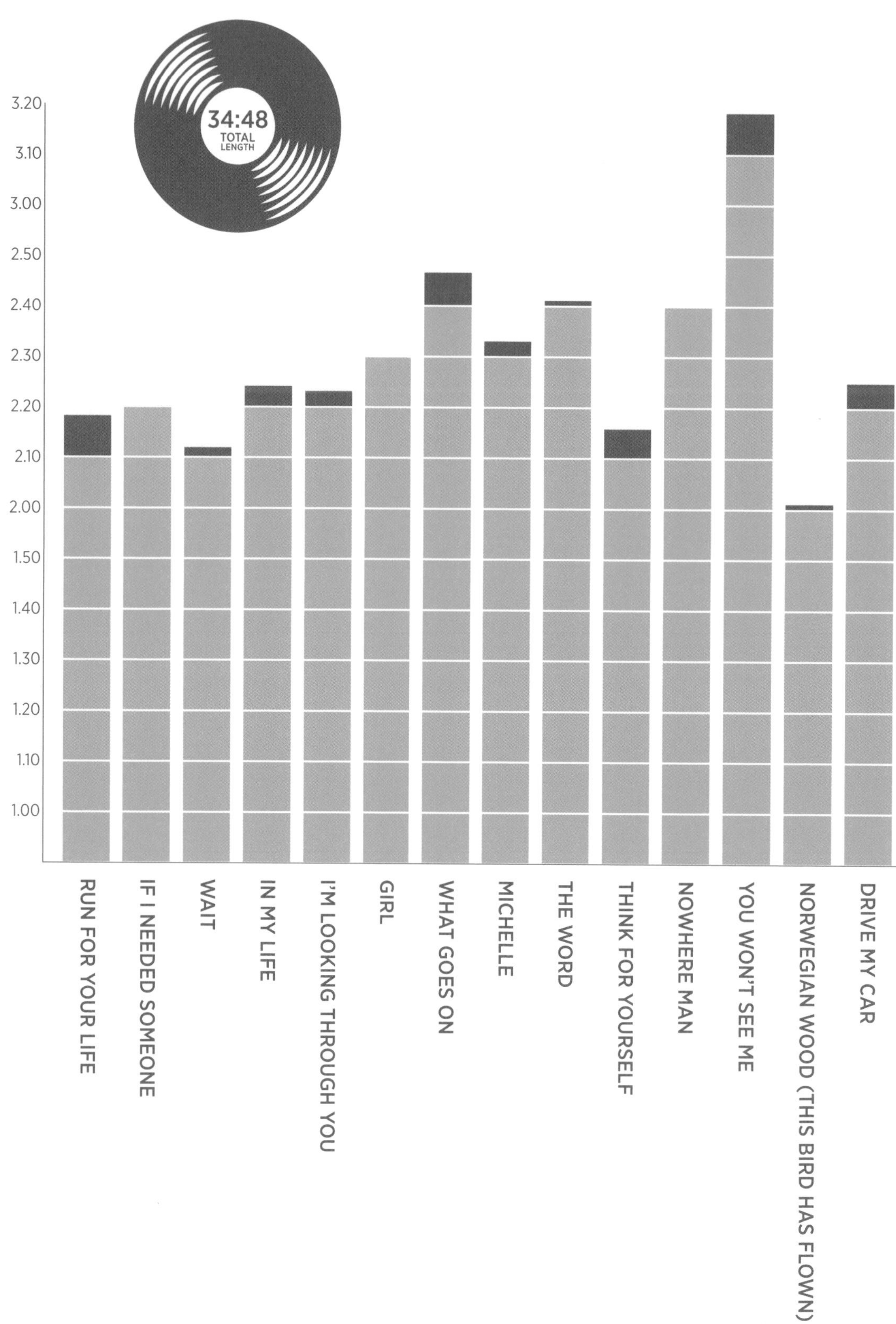

SUCCESS

UK SINGLE RELEASES

DRIVE MY CAR
NORWEGIAN WOOD (THIS BIRD HAS FLOWN)
YOU WON'T SEE ME
NOWHERE MAN
THINK FOR YOURSELF
THE WORD
MICHELLE
WHAT GOES ON
GIRL
I'M LOOKING THROUGH YOU
IN MY LIFE
WAIT
IF I NEEDED SOMEONE
RUN FOR YOUR LIFE

No songs from *Rubber Soul* were released as singles, however the band recorded 'We Can Work It Out' and 'Day Tripper' (which were released as a double A-side single on the same day as the album) in the same studio sessions. *Rubber Soul* replaced *Help!* at the top of the charts on Christmas Day and spent nine weeks at no. 1, remaining in the charts for 42 weeks. In 2012 it was ranked number five on *Rolling Stone* magazine's list of the '500 Greatest Albums of All Time'.

ALBUM CHART POSITIONS

UNITED KINGDOM
Number One

GERMANY
Number One

UNITED STATES
Number One

AUSTRALIA
Number One

INSTRUMENTS: WHAT CAN YOU HEAR?

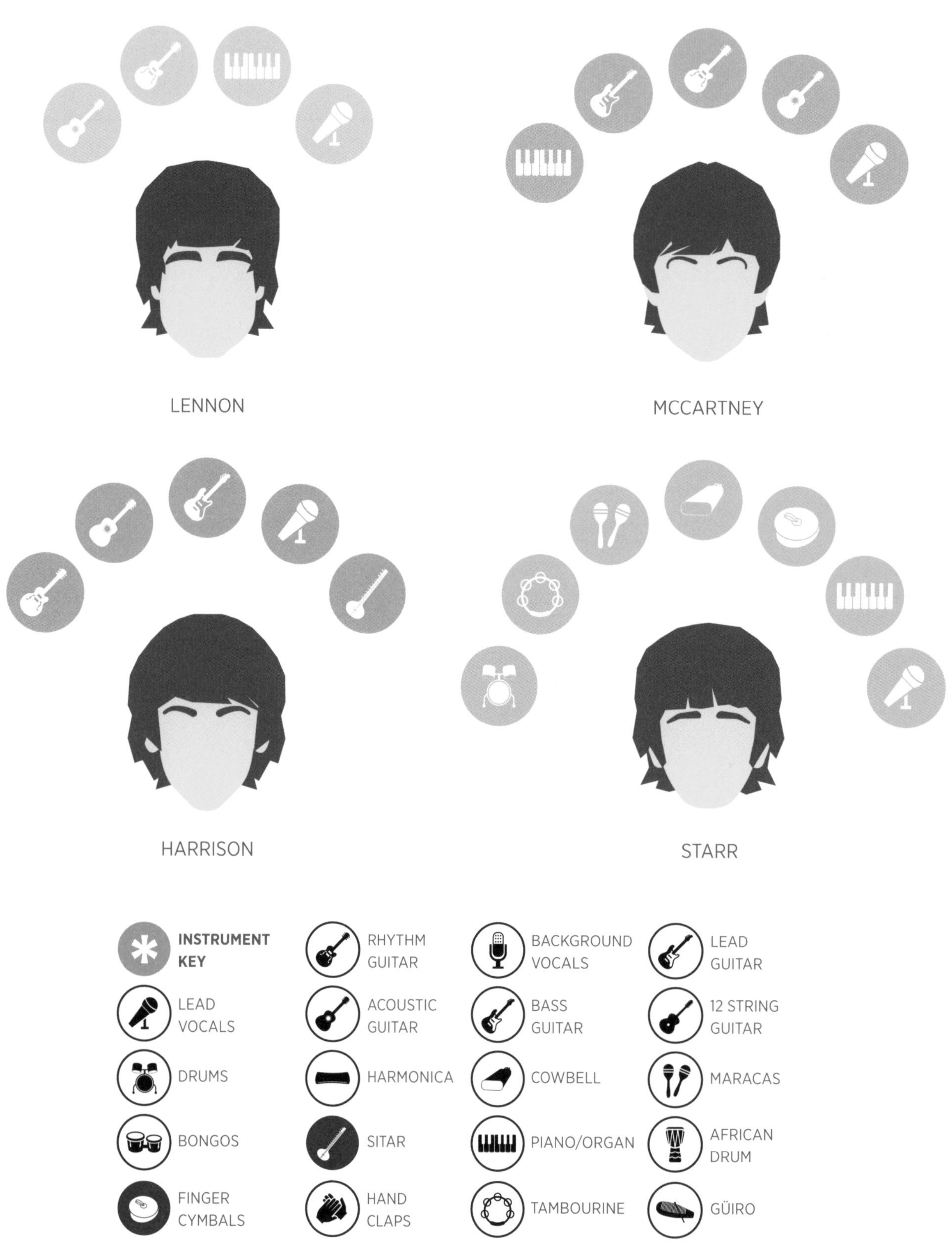

Black circle indicates instruments used for the first time in a Beatles' album

PERFORMANCES

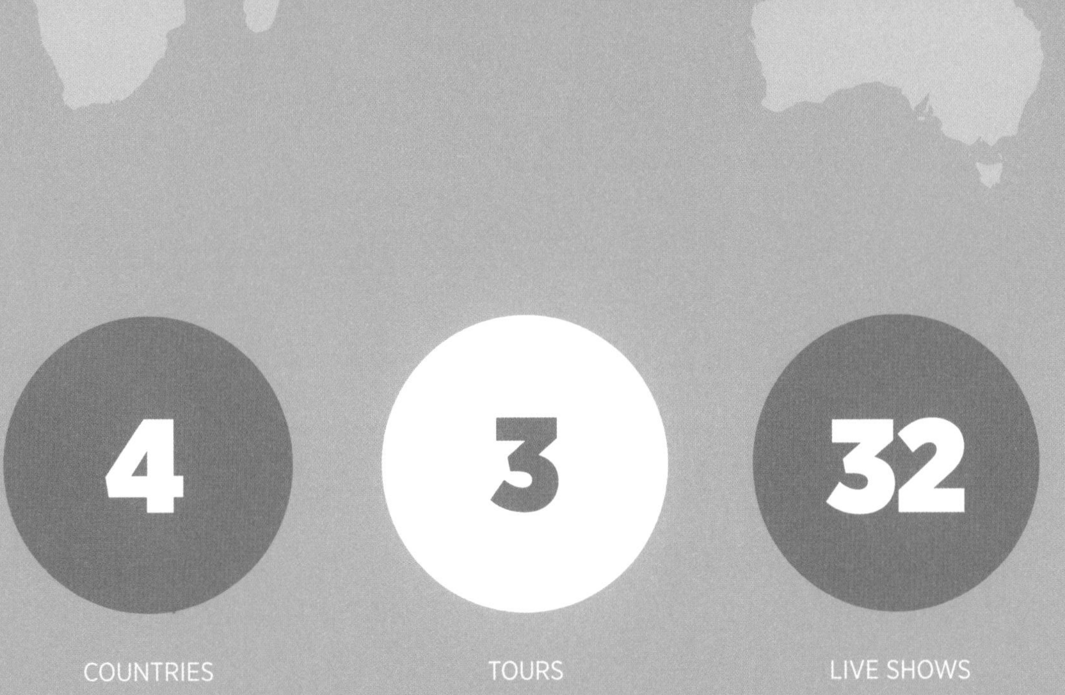

COUNTRIES

TOURS

LIVE SHOWS

STYLE

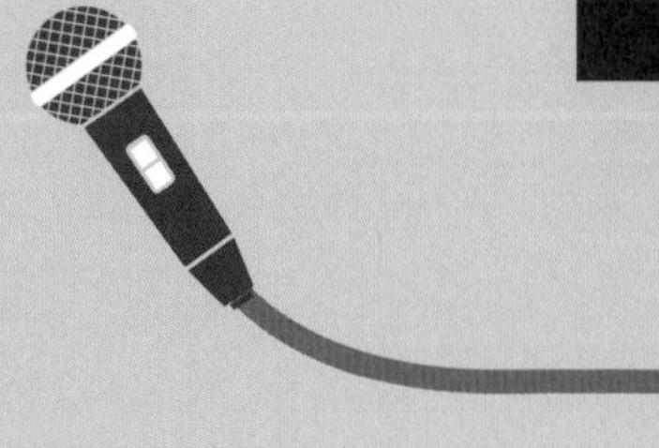

1963

late 1963

mid 1964

late 1964

mid 1965

Despite the fashions between band members beginning to change during this period, they still often wore matching suits at gigs. This time a dark blue classic fit suit paired with a black polo neck jumper for a more relaxed look.

late 1965

mid 1966

mid 1967

late 1967

late 1968

early 1969

1970

1970

1969

VOLUME AND INTENSITY

A VISUAL REPRESENTATION OF THE VOLUME AND INTENSITY OF EACH TRACK ON THE ALBUM

ALBUM OVERVIEW

Released: 5 August 1966
Producer: George Martin
Engineers: Geoff Emerick, Peter Vince

Revolver is considered by many to be the band's finest work, with all four members collaborating and at their creative peak. It marked another distinct shift in the group's music, demonstrating how they had grown-up as musicians and heralding the start of an era of experimentation, particularly when it came to studio recording techniques.

These included ADT (artificial double tracking), a method that allowed the band to; firstly, double track their vocals without having to overdub a second vocal performance (this would go on to become a well-used and established production technique); and, secondly, to speed up and slow down their recordings via an oscillator. The implementation of backwards recording on 'I'm Only Sleeping' and 'Tomorrow Never Knows' was another innovation. Tape loops were used extensively.

AUGUST

1966

REVOLVER

TIMELINE: AUGUST 1966-MAY 1967

August 5, 1966
The Caesars Palace hotel and casino opens in Las Vegas

August 29, 1966
The Beatles end their US tour with a concert at Candlestick Park in San Francisco. It is their last performance as a live touring band

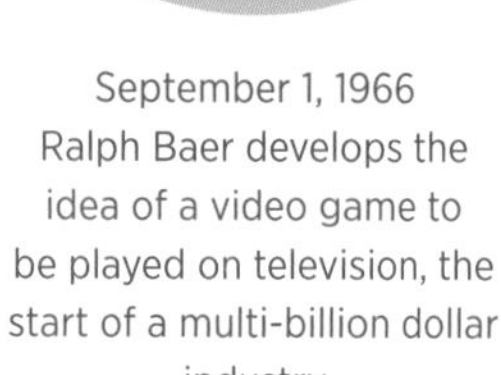

September 1, 1966
Ralph Baer develops the idea of a video game to be played on television, the start of a multi-billion dollar industry

September 8, 1966
Star Trek, the science fiction television series, debuts on NBC in the United States

October 6, 1966
LSD is made illegal in the United States

October 26, 1966
NATO moves its HQ from Paris to Brussels

November 9, 1966
John Lennon meets Yoko Ono at the Indica Gallery, London

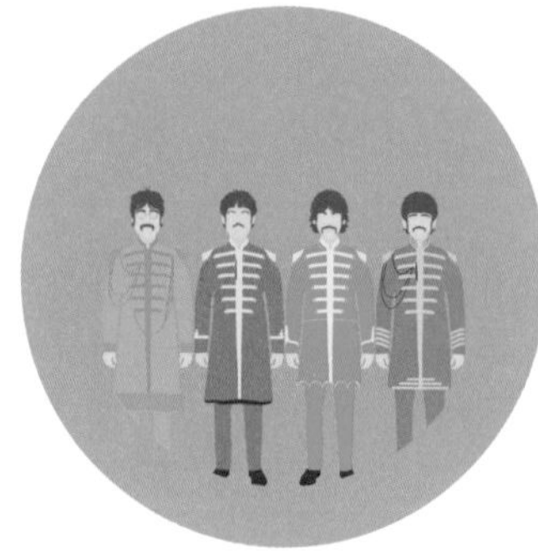

November 24, 1966
The Beatles begin recording sessions for their *Sgt. Pepper's Lonely Hearts Club Band* L.P.

January 27, 1967
The United States, Soviet Union
and United Kingdom sign the Outer Space Treaty

February 17, 1967
Strawberry Fields Forever
is released, but fails to reach
No.1 in the UK chart

April 8, 1967
Puppet on a String by Sandie Shaw wins the
Eurovision Song Contest 1967 for the United Kingdom

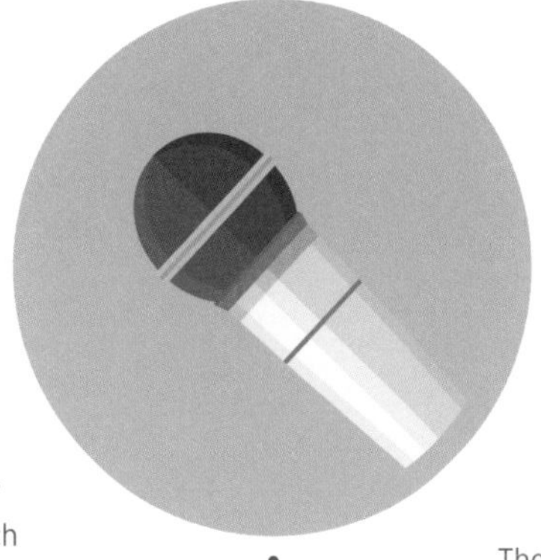

April 9, 1967
The first Boeing 737
takes its maiden flight

May 11, 1967
The United Kingdom and Ireland
apply officially for European Economic
Community membership

December 15, 1966
Walt Disney dies while
producing The Jungle Book,
the last animated feature
under his personal supervision

March 4, 1967
The first North Sea gas
is pumped ashore at Easington,
East Riding of Yorkshire

April 28, 1967
Muhammad Ali refuses military
service. He is stripped of his boxing title and
not allowed to fight for three years

REVOLVER

ALBUM COVER DESIGN

The cover artwork for *Revolver* was done by Klaus Voormann, an artist and musician the band met in Hamburg. It was mostly made up of pen drawings but it also contained collage sections which included photographs by Robert Freeman and Robert Whitaker.

Voormann was invited by the band to work on the cover and they brought him into the studio to listen to the *Revolver* recordings before he started. Voormann then worked on the covers from his studio in Parliament Hill, London, spending two weeks on the concept. He won the Grammy Award for Best Album Cover, Graphic Arts in 1967.

THEY GAVE ME AN AWFUL LOT OF
ENCOURAGEMENT

THEIR REACTION HAS BEEN VERY GOOD. IF IT HADN'T I WOULD HAVE JUST CRAWLED AWAY

— GEORGE HARRISON —

ON SHOWING SONGS TO PAUL AND JOHN

Revolver: The Alternatives

Any creative process is an iterative one, and there will always be a certain number of unused ideas that never see the light of day. Here are some of the album titles that were considered for *Revolver*...

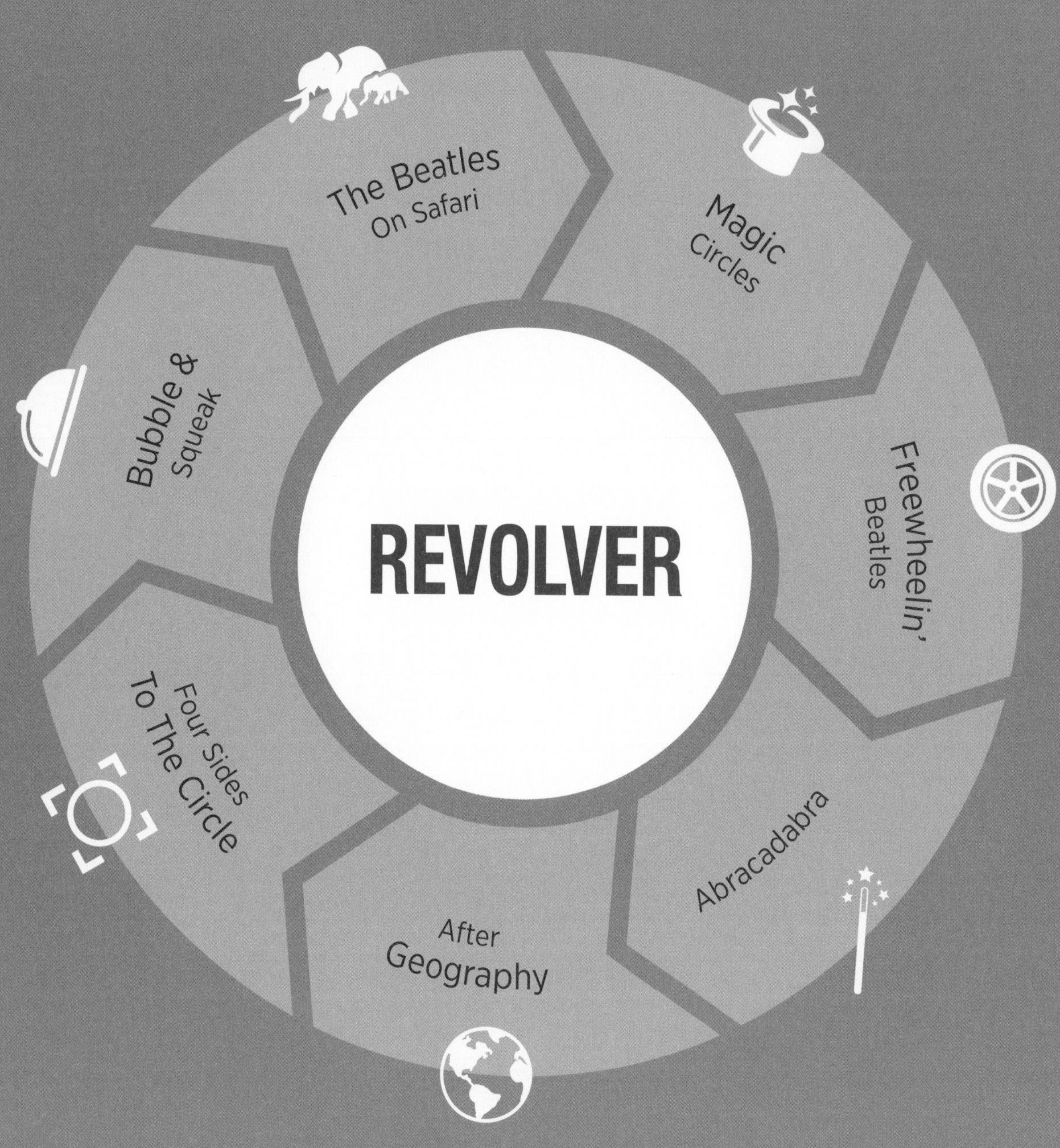

VOCALS: WHICH BEATLE TOOK THE LEAD?

Where band members shared lead vocals both are listed as singing lead vocals (as a result numbers may add up to more than the total number of tracks on the album).

Tomorrow Never Knows
Taxman
Eleanor Rigby
I'm Only Sleeping
Love You To
Here, There and Everywhere
Yellow Submarine
She Said She Said
Good Day Sunshine
And Your Bird Can Sing
For No One
Doctor Robert
I Want to Tell You
Got to Get You into My Life
0 COVERS
VS
14 ORIGINALS

SONGWRITING: WHO WROTE WHAT?

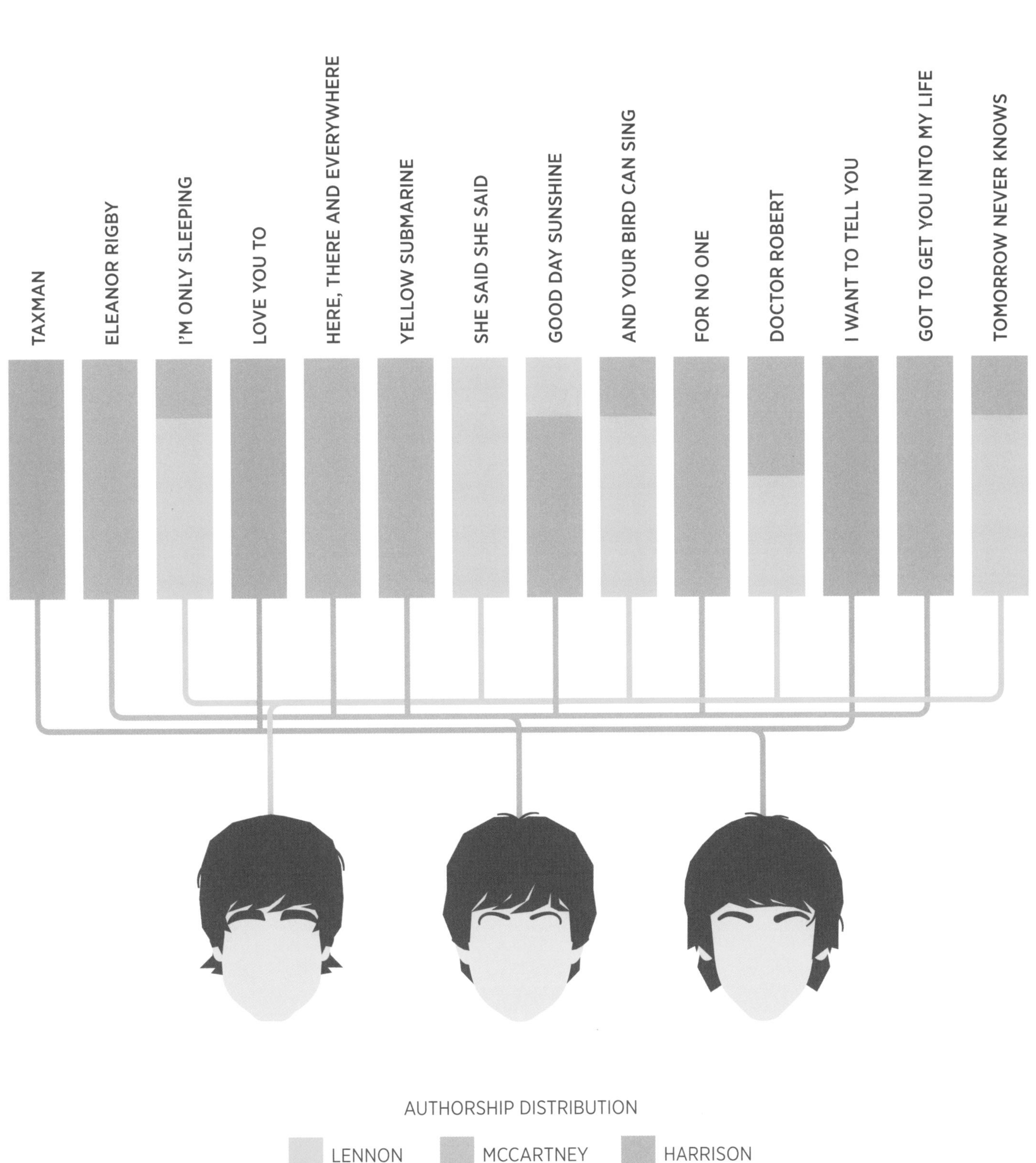

LENGTH: TRACKS AND ALBUM

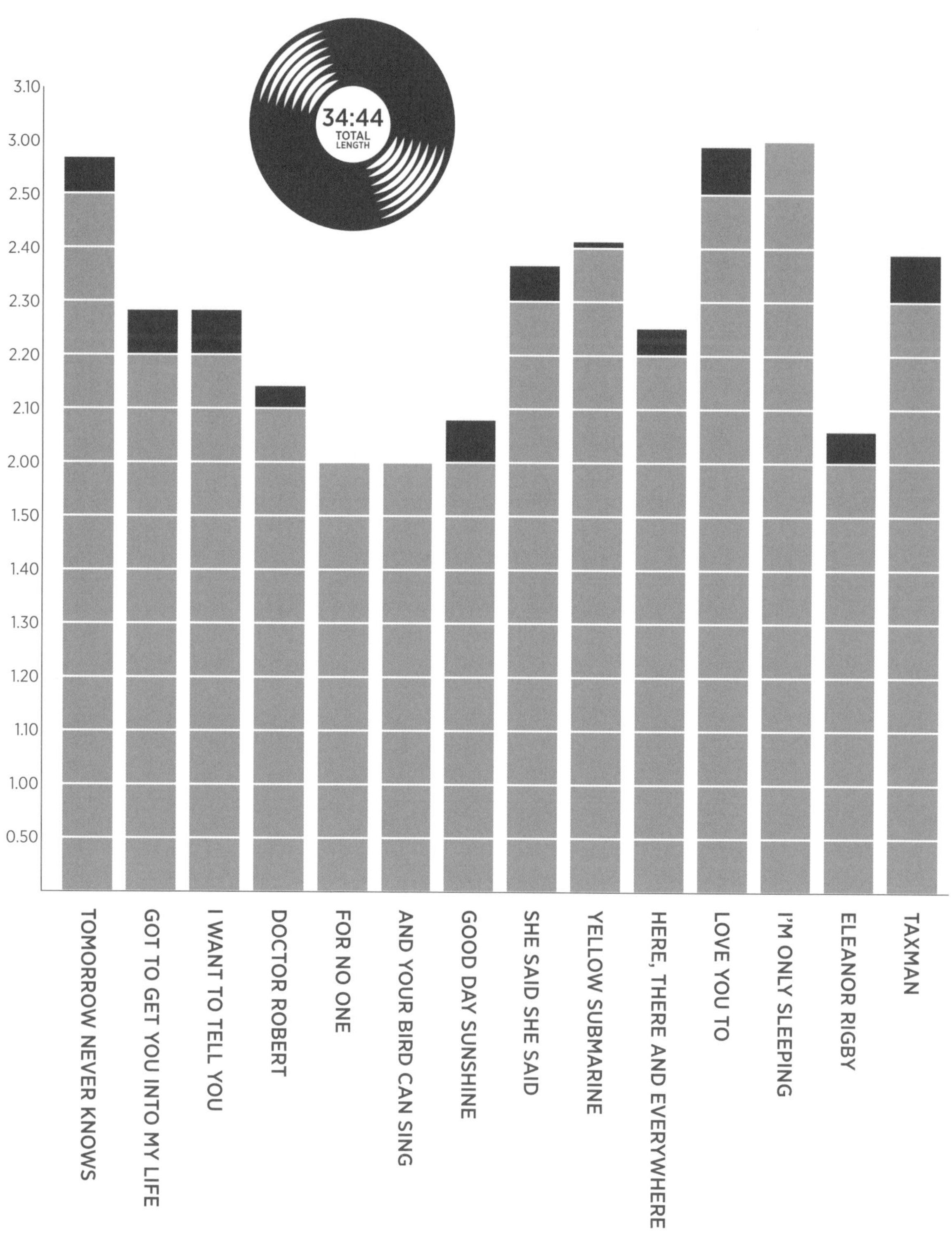

SONG KEYS

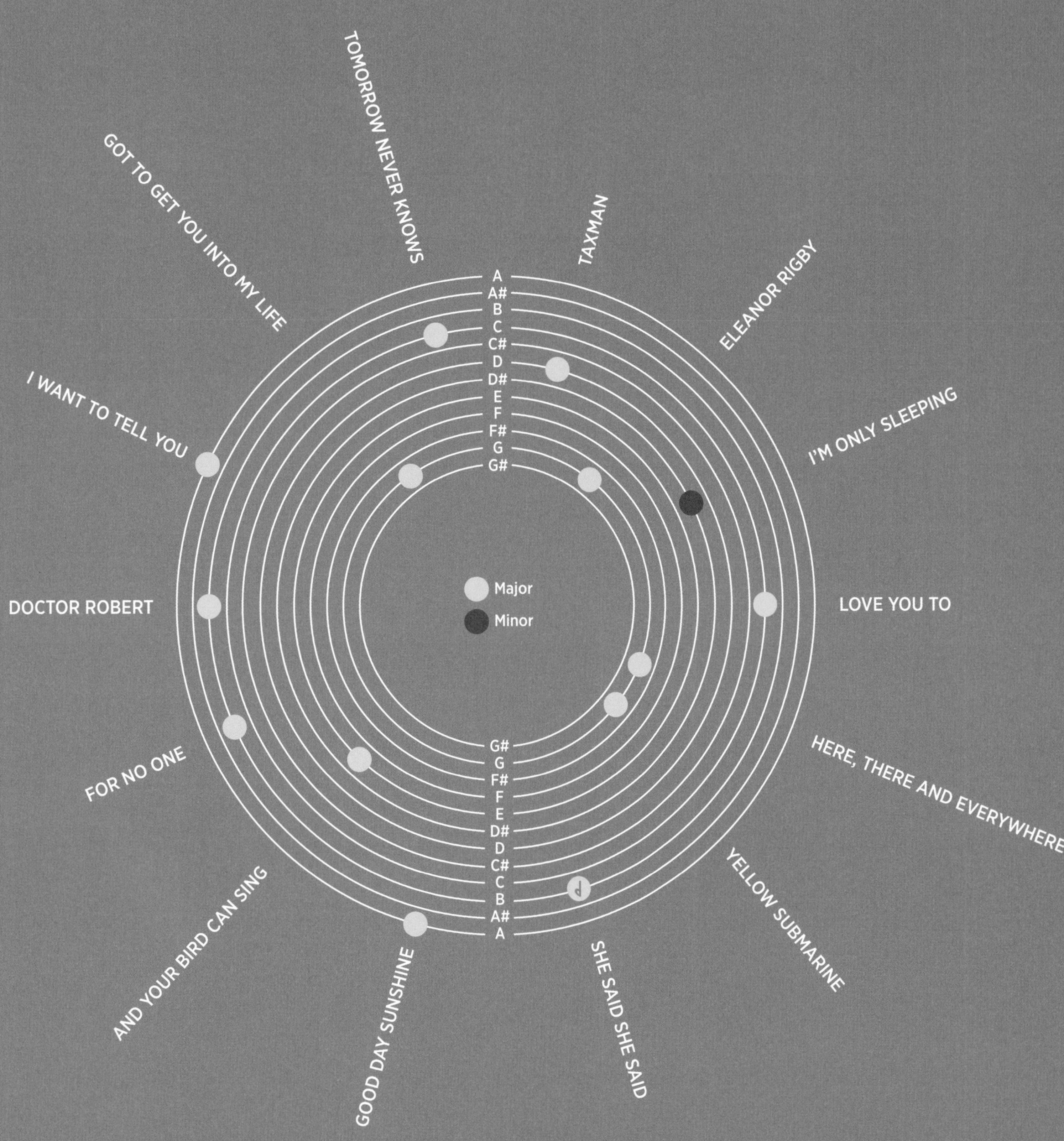

TOMORROW NEVER KNOWS
TAXMAN
GOT TO GET YOU INTO MY LIFE
ELEANOR RIGBY
I WANT TO TELL YOU
I'M ONLY SLEEPING
DOCTOR ROBERT
LOVE YOU TO
FOR NO ONE
HERE, THERE AND EVERYWHERE
AND YOUR BIRD CAN SING
YELLOW SUBMARINE
GOOD DAY SUNSHINE
SHE SAID SHE SAID
A
A#
B
C
C#
D
D#
E
F
F#
G
G#
Major
Minor

A VISUAL REPRESENTATION OF THE VOLUME AND INTENSITY OF EACH TRACK ON THE ALBUM

SUCCESS

UK SINGLE RELEASES

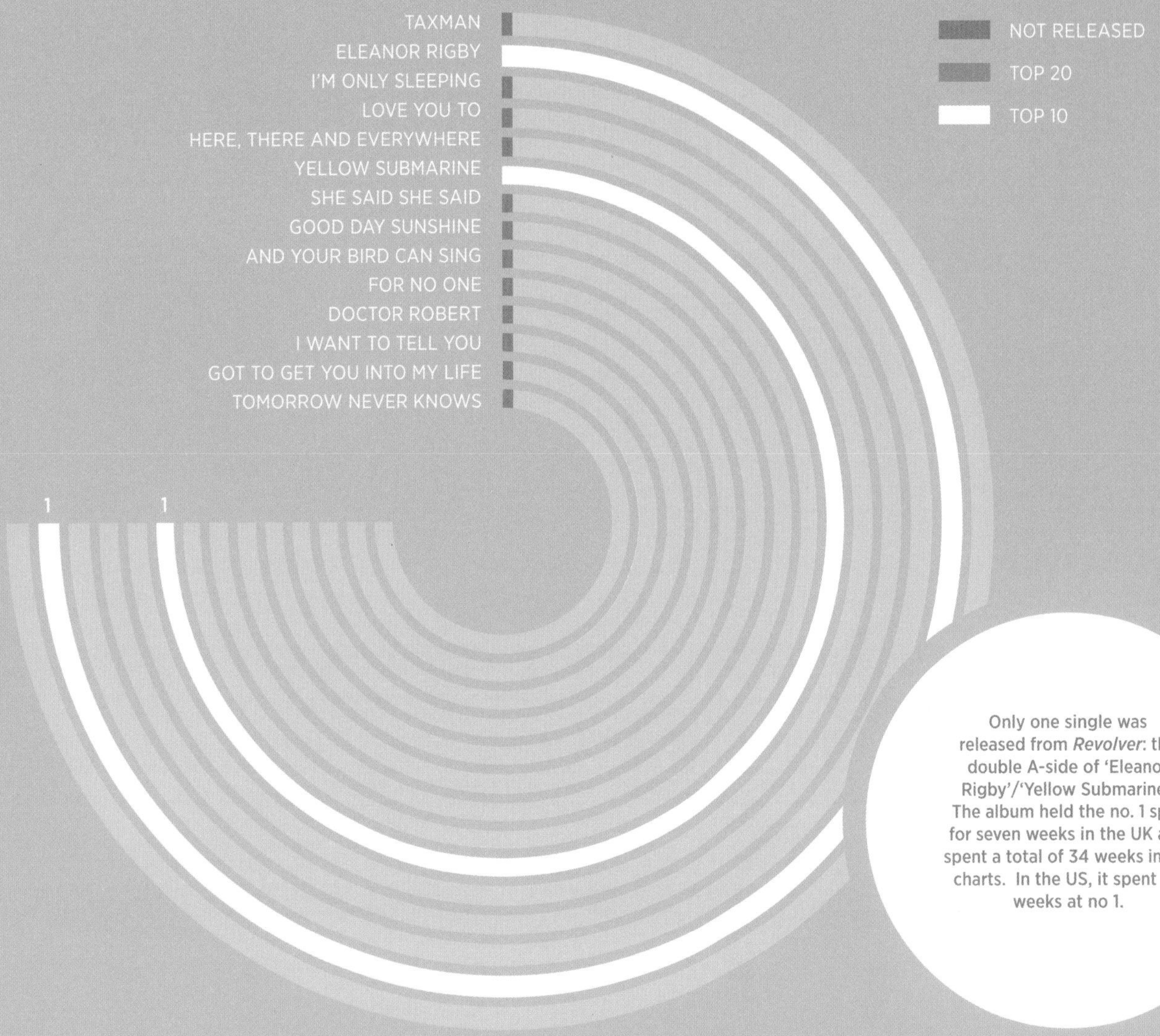

TAXMAN
ELEANOR RIGBY
I'M ONLY SLEEPING
LOVE YOU TO
HERE, THERE AND EVERYWHERE
YELLOW SUBMARINE
SHE SAID SHE SAID
GOOD DAY SUNSHINE
AND YOUR BIRD CAN SING
FOR NO ONE
DOCTOR ROBERT
I WANT TO TELL YOU
GOT TO GET YOU INTO MY LIFE
TOMORROW NEVER KNOWS

NOT RELEASED
TOP 20
TOP 10

1
1

Only one single was released from *Revolver*: the double A-side of 'Eleanor Rigby'/'Yellow Submarine'. The album held the no. 1 spot for seven weeks in the UK and spent a total of 34 weeks in the charts. In the US, it spent six weeks at no 1.

ALBUM CHART POSITIONS

UNITED KINGDOM
Number One

GERMANY
Number One

UNITED STATES
Number One

AUSTRALIA
Number One

NORWAY
Number One

SWEDEN
Number One

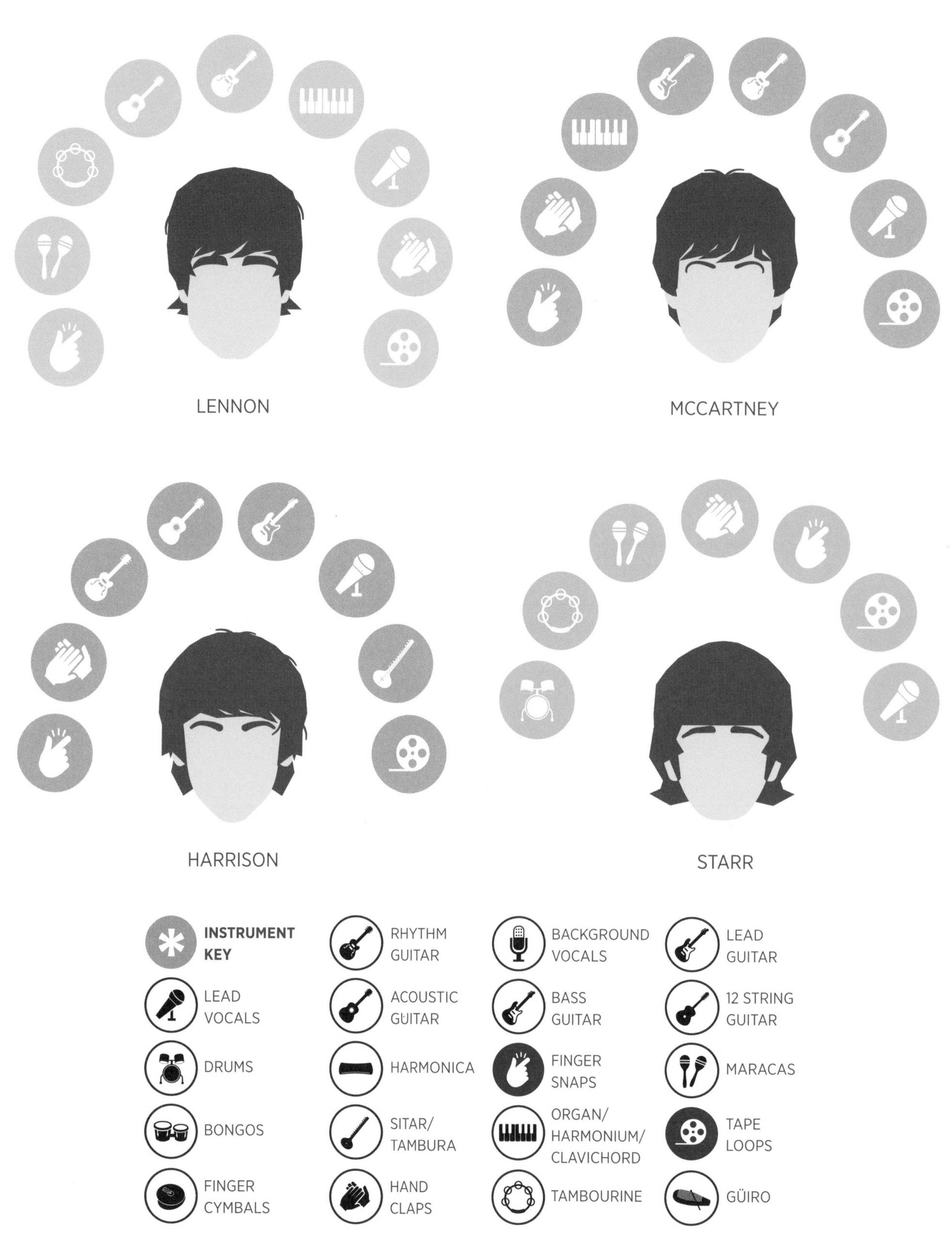

Black circle indicates instruments used for the first time in a Beatles' album

2

COUNTRIES

1

TOUR

19

LIVE SHOWS

1963
late 1963
mid 1964

late 1964
mid 1965
late 1965

mid
1966

mid 1967
late 1967

late 1968
early 1969
1969
1970

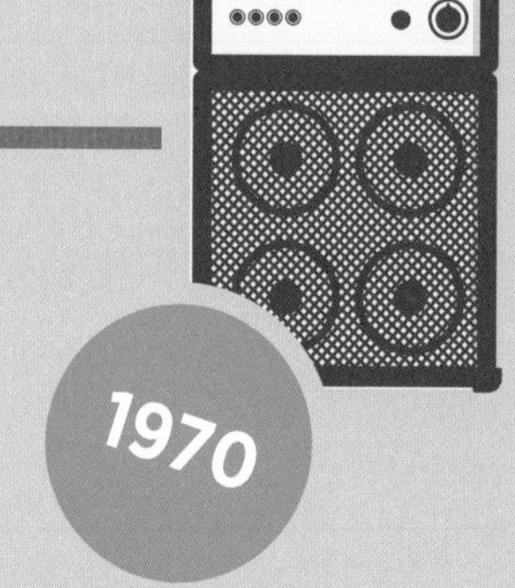
1970

Throughout 1966, the Beatles took to the stage wearing one of two iconic designs: a dark double-breasted suit with a green trim known as the 'Budokan', and a cream-coloured number with oxblood pinstripes. The former was clearly the preferred choice, as the band wore it twice as much as the pinstripe model. It is also the suit to feature in their final concert at Candlestick Park in San Francisco.

ALBUM OVERVIEW

Released: 1 June 1967
Producer: George Martin
Engineers: Geoff Emerick, Adrian Ibbetson, Malcolm Addey, Ken Townsend, Peter Vince

The band's eighth UK album played a huge part in defining the mid-sixties period and, in particular, the '67 'Summer of Love'. Many consider this album, which took over 400 hours to record during a 129-day period, to be a significant step in the progression of modern music. It certainly pushed the boundaries of what was possible in studio recording, producing sounds that were completely unique for the time. Numerous session musicians and orchestras were utilised, combining several different styles of music.

Before the release of the album, many music journalists suspected the Beatles were finished. They were no longer touring and had retreated from the public. Music papers had explicitly questioned where the band were and speculated that their creativity had run dry. Paul has said that before writing the album they had become bored of being the Beatles and thought of themselves as artists rather than just performers. *Sgt. Pepper's* was a way for the band to develop alter egos and project a different image to the world.

The album won four Grammy Awards in 1968 and, in 2003, was ranked number one by *Rolling Stone* magazine in their '500 Greatest Albums of All Time'.

JUNE 1967

SGT. PEPPER'S LONELY HEARTS CLUB BAND

TIMELINE: JUNE-NOVEMBER 1967

June 25, 1967
400 million viewers watch *Our World*, the first live, international, satellite television production. It features the live debut of The Beatles' song 'All You Need Is Love'

July 1, 1967
Canada celebrates its first one hundred years of Confederation

July 4, 1967
The British Parliament decriminalises homosexuality

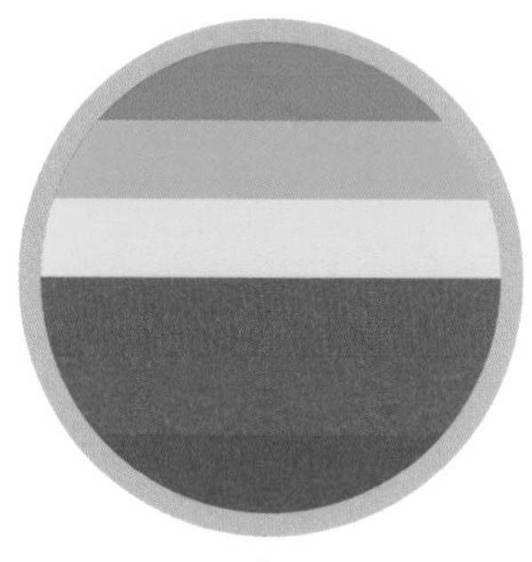

July 10, 1967
New Zealand decimalises its currency from pound to dollar

June 19, 1967
Paul admits taking LSD in an interview, sending the press wild

June 27, 1967
The first automatic cash machine (voucher-based) is installed, in the office of the Barclays Bank in Enfield, England

July 1, 1967
The first UK colour television broadcasts begin on BBC2. The first one is from the Wimbledon tennis championships

July 7, 1967
All You Need Is Love is released in the UK

October 3, 1967
An X-15 research aircraft with test pilot William J. Knight establishes an unofficial world fixed-wing speed record of Mach 6.7

August 13, 1967
The first line-up of Fleetwood Mac makes their live debut at the Windsor Jazz and Blues Festival

August 27, 1967
Beatles manager Brian Epstein is found dead in his locked bedroom

November 28, 1967
The first pulsar named PSR B1919+21 was discovered by Jocelyn Bell Burnell and Antony Hewish

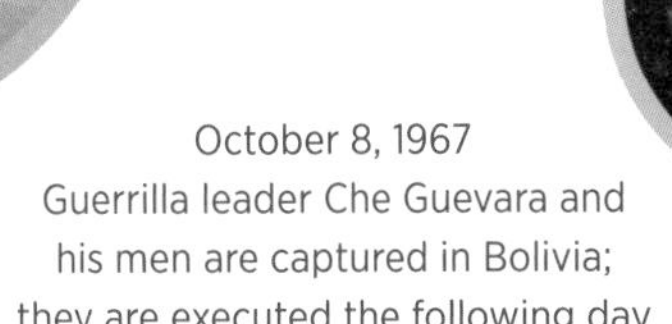

October 8, 1967
Guerrilla leader Che Guevara and his men are captured in Bolivia; they are executed the following day

August 5, 1967
Pink Floyd release their debut album *The Piper at the Gates of Dawn*

September 3, 1967
At 5:00 a.m. local time, all road traffic in Sweden switches from a left-hand traffic pattern to right-hand traffic

November 8, 1967
The BBC's first local radio station (BBC Radio Leicester) is launched

ALBUM COVER DESIGN

Originally, the Beatles wanted to use an illustration by The Fool, a design group that painted the mural on the side of the Apple shop in London, for the cover. They were, however, talked out of it by Robert Fraser, their art director. He suggested husband and wife Peter Blake and Jann Haworth instead.

The band, along with Fraser and Blake, made lists of who they would like to invite to an imaginary *Sgt. Pepper's* concert. Various people were chosen from these lists and featured in the background of the cover (including Carl Jung, Bob Dylan, Stuart Sutcliffe, Aldous Huxley, Edgar Allan Poe, Marilyn Monroe, Albert Einstein, Karl Marx, Laurel and Hardy, Oscar Wilde, Lewis Carroll and Marlene Dietrich). We've visualised the incredible outfits the band wore here.

SGT. PEPPER'S IS ONE OF THE MOST IMPORTANT STEPS OF OUR CAREER IT HAD TO BE JUST RIGHT

JOHN LENNON

1967, ON 'SGT. PEPPER'S'

A VISUAL REPRESENTATION OF THE VOLUME AND INTENSITY OF EACH TRACK ON THE ALBUM

VOCALS: WHICH BEATLE TOOK THE LEAD?

Sgt. Pepper is the first pop album to be mastered without the momentary gaps between songs as a point of demarcation. Instead, it used two crossfades that blended songs together, giving the impression of a continuous live performance. The album saw Paul emerge as the leading creative force, writing most of the songs on the album and deciding on much of the arrangement.

Where band members shared lead vocals both are listed as singing lead vocals (as a result numbers may add up to more than the total number of tracks on the album).

Sgt. Pepper's Lonely Hearts Club Band
With a Little Help from My Friends
Lucy in the Sky with Diamonds
Getting Better
Fixing a Hole
She's Leaving Home
Being for the Benefit of Mr Kite!
Within You Without You
When I'm Sixty-Four
Lovely Rita
Good Morning Good Morning
Sgt. Pepper's Lonely Hearts Club Band (Reprise)
A Day in the Life
0 COVERS
VS
13 ORIGINALS

SONGWRITING: WHO WROTE WHAT?

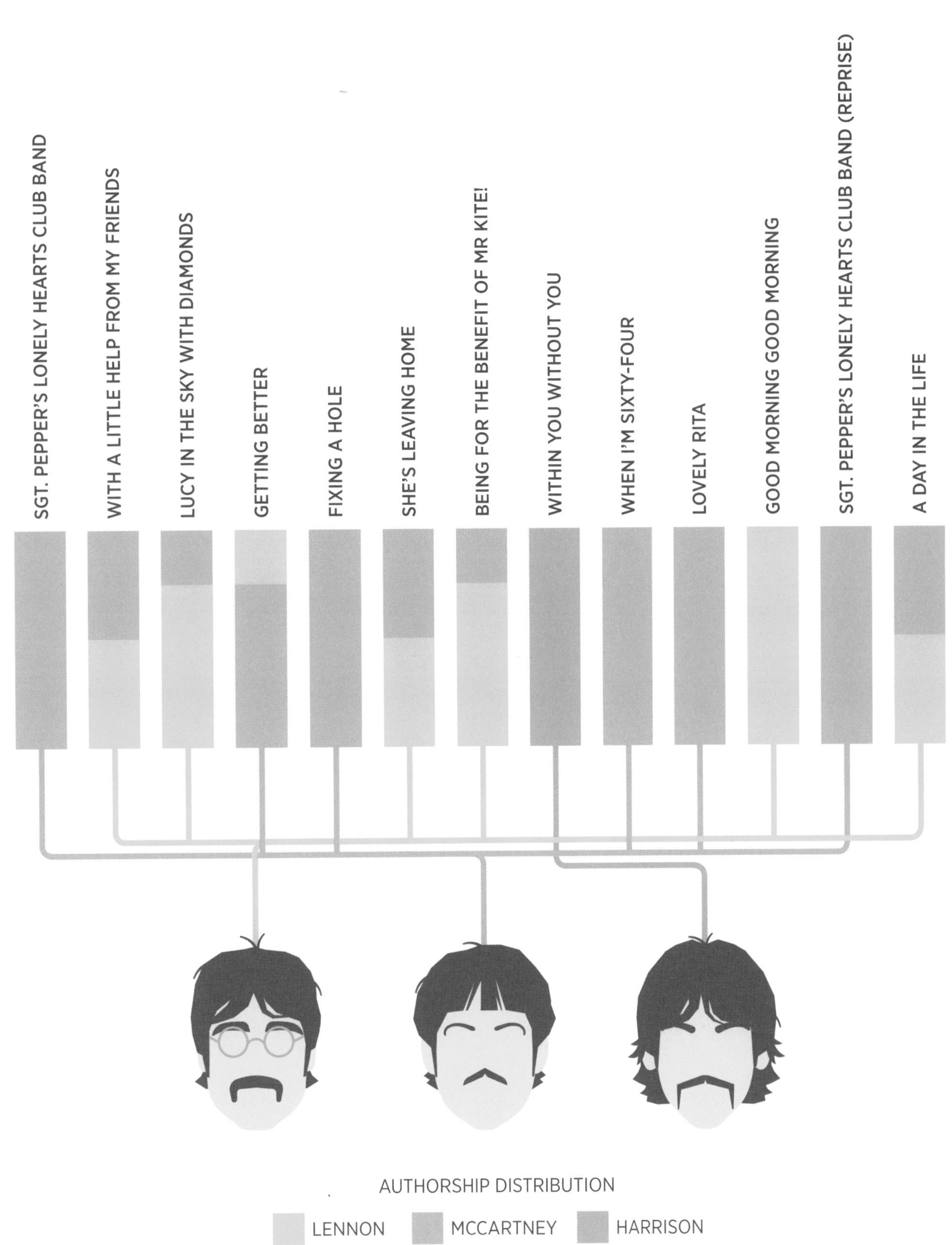

LENGTHS: TRACK AND ALBUM

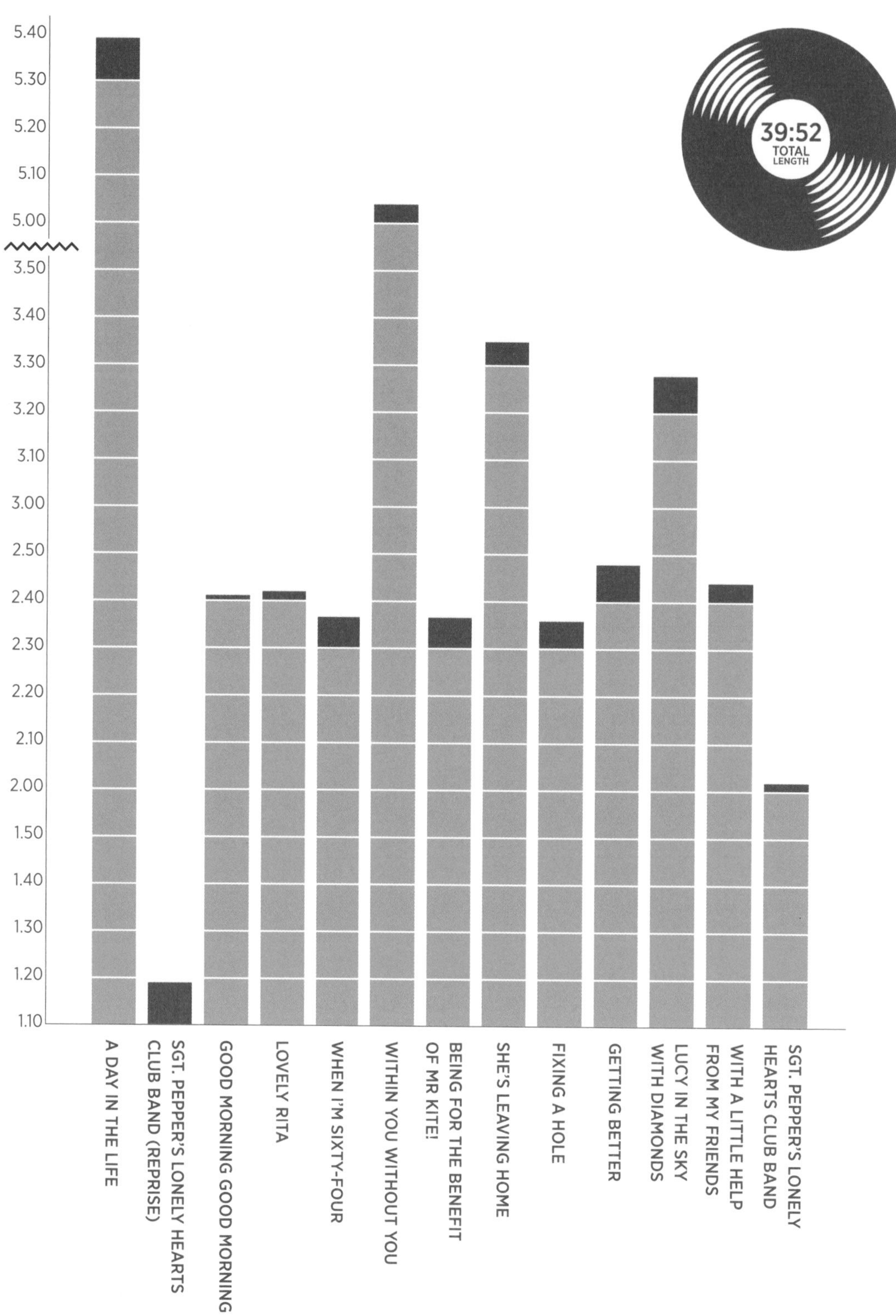

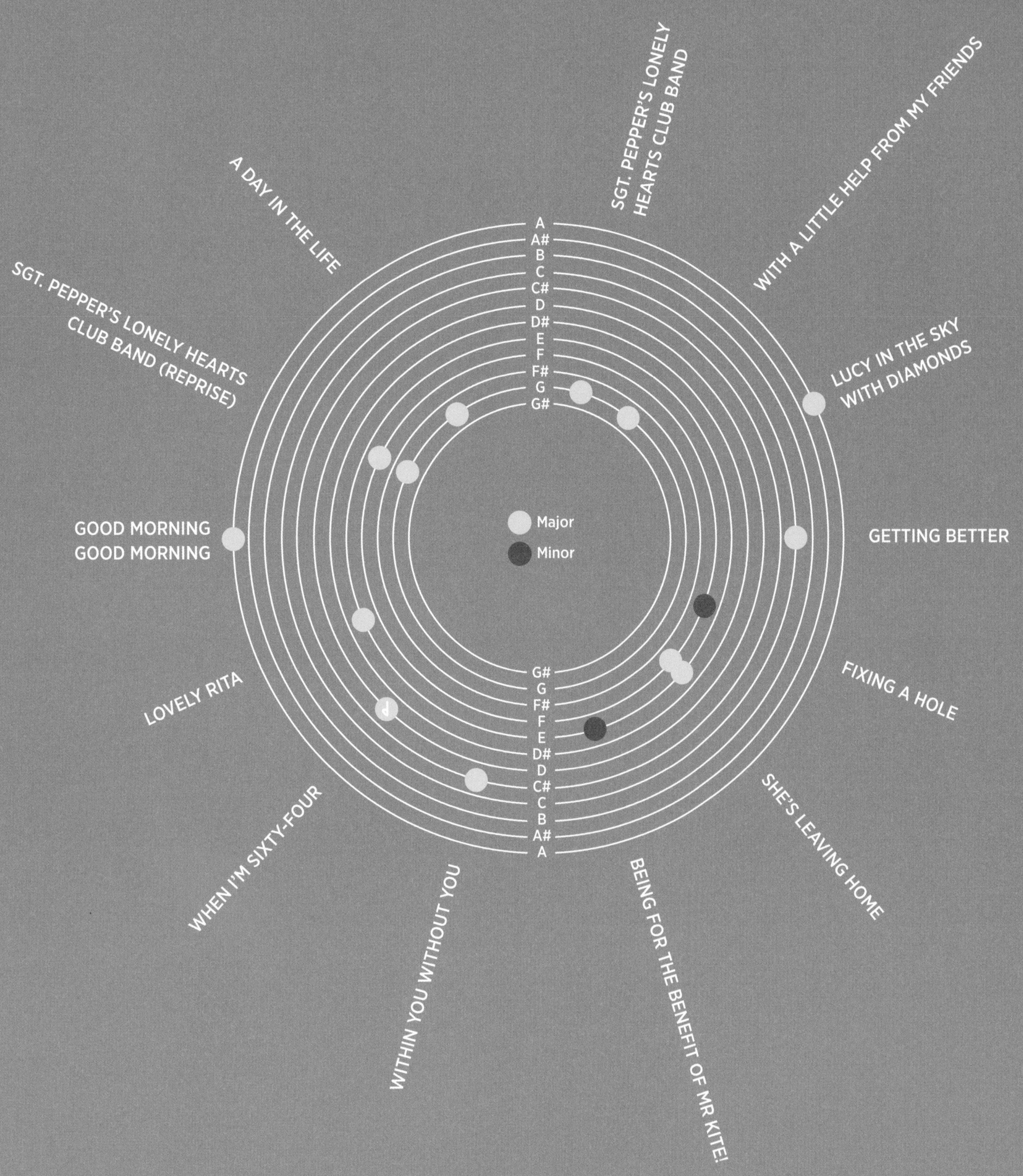
SGT. PEPPER'S LONELY HEARTS CLUB BAND
WITH A LITTLE HELP FROM MY FRIENDS
LUCY IN THE SKY WITH DIAMONDS
GETTING BETTER
FIXING A HOLE
SHE'S LEAVING HOME
BEING FOR THE BENEFIT OF MR KITE!
WITHIN YOU WITHOUT YOU
WHEN I'M SIXTY-FOUR
LOVELY RITA
GOOD MORNING GOOD MORNING
SGT. PEPPER'S LONELY HEARTS CLUB BAND (REPRISE)
A DAY IN THE LIFE
A
A#
B
C
C#
D
D#
E
F
F#
G
G#
Major
Minor

INSTRUMENTS: WHAT CAN YOU HEAR?

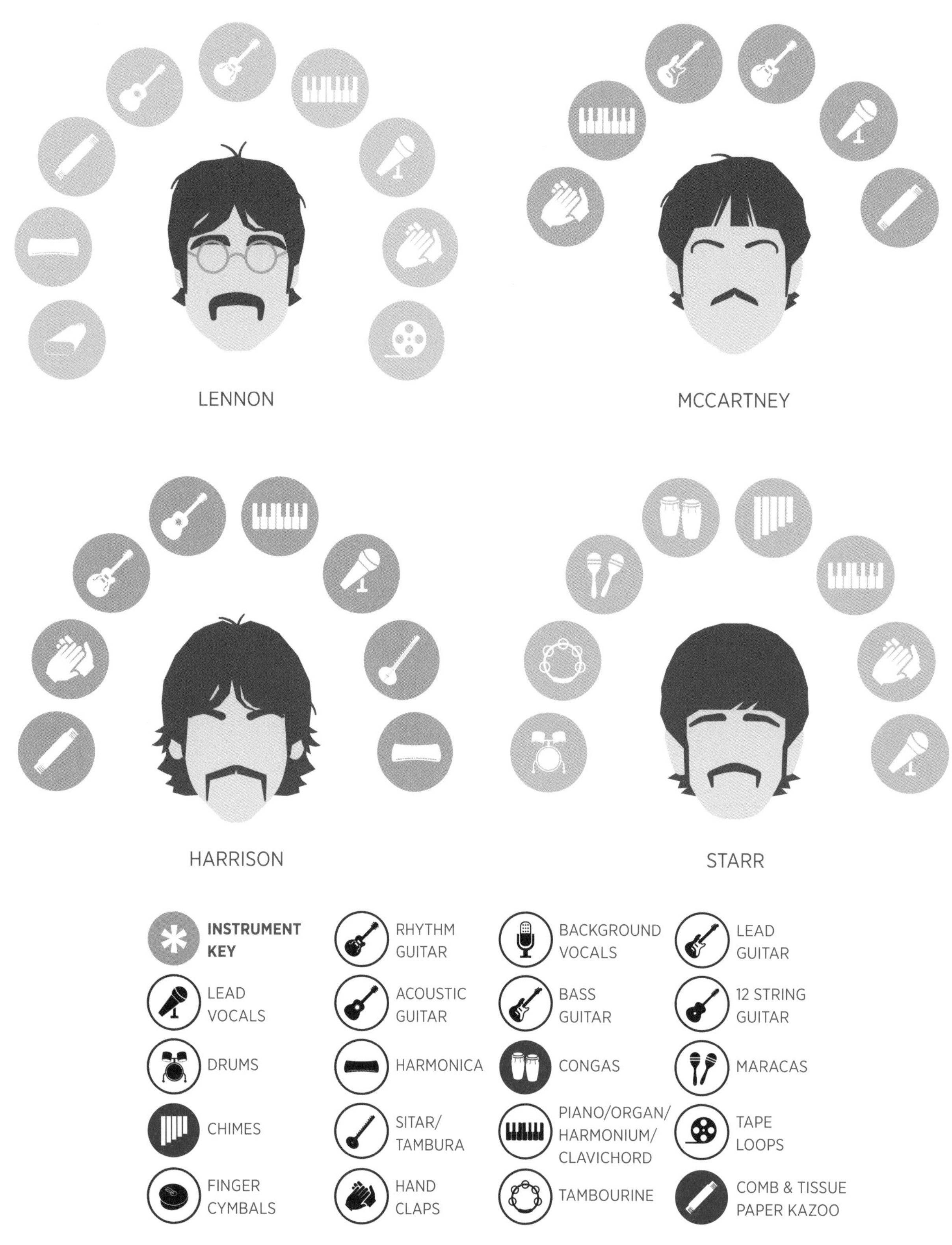

Black circle indicates instruments used for the first time in a Beatles' album

SUCCESS

UK SINGLE RELEASES

SGT. PEPPER'S LONELY HEARTS CLUB BAND
WITH A LITTLE HELP FROM MY FRIENDS
LUCY IN THE SKY WITH DIAMONDS
GETTING BETTER
FIXING A HOLE
SHE'S LEAVING HOME
BEING FOR THE BENEFIT OF MR KITE!
WITHIN YOU WITHOUT YOU
WHEN I'M SIXTY FOUR
LOVELY RITA
GOOD MORNING GOOD MORNING
SGT. PEPPER'S (REPRISE)
A DAY IN THE LIFE

No singles were taken from the album (initially given a working title of 'One Down, Six To Go' in reference to their recording contract with EMI). But 'Sgt. Pepper's Lonely Hearts Club Band' and 'With A Little Help From My Friends' charted in 1978 on the re-release (with A Day In The Life' as the B-side). The album topped the UK charts for a total of 27 weeks, 23 of them consecutive, and remained in the charts for 148 weeks. Worldwide, it sold 30 million copies and spent 15 weeks at no. 1 in the US charts.

ALBUM CHART POSITIONS

UNITED KINGDOM	GERMANY	UNITED STATES	AUSTRALIA	NORWAY	SWEDEN	CANADA
Number One	Number One	Number One	Number One	Number One	Number One	Number One

1963
late 1963
mid 1964

late 1964
mid 1965
late 1965
mid 1966

mid
1967

late 1967
late 1968

early 1969
1969
1970

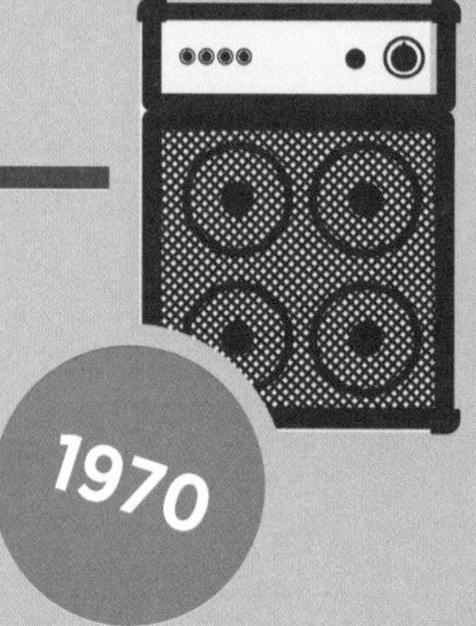
1970

The iconic psychedelic outfits worn for the cover of *Sgt. Pepper's* are one of the most recognisable Beatles images of all time. The group are dressed as members of the Lonely Hearts Club Band and the faux military uniforms were designed to poke fun at the vogue in Britain for military fashions.

BEATLES ISLAND

In the summer of 1967, the Beatles agreed to buy a set of Greek islands in the Aegean sea, totalling approximately 100 acres. Encouraged in particular by John Lennon, the band wanted to purchase what could have been known as 'Beatles Island' as a base for them to live and work, alongside friends and family.

The main island was surrounded by four smaller islands, where the band were to have separate villas, with the main island serving as a base for all Beatles-related operations.

Ultimately, the purchase didn't go through because by the time the band managed to get permission to move the required £90,000 from Britain to Greece, they had cooled on the idea and moved on to other plans. Luckily however, in selling the dollars back to the government the band made over £10,000 profit.

ALBUM OVERVIEW

Released: 8 December 1967
Producers: George Martin, Dave Harries
Engineers: Geoff Emerick, Dave Harries, Malcolm Addey, Keith Grant, Eddie Kramer, John Timperley, Peter Vince, Ken Scott

This album came about in the wake of Brian Epstein's death (27 August 1967), leaving the band suddenly without the direction and guidance of their manager. *Magical Mystery Tour* was Paul McCartney's idea. He wanted to produce a TV special about a group of ordinary people taking a mystery coach trip. The album is the soundtrack to the programme broadcast by the BBC in December 1967. Four of the six songs from the EP were recorded before filming began on 11 September 1967. Despite the film being slated by critics and public audiences, the soundtrack was well received and a commercial success. It was the first album to be issued in both mono and stereo.

The US version of the album contained five other songs released by the Beatles in 1967, contrary to the wishes of the band. In 1976 the full album version was released in the UK, and in 1987 this became the standard version worldwide when the band's back catalogue was re-released on CD.

DECEMBER

1967

MAGICAL MYSTERY TOUR

TIMELINE: DECEMBER 1967-OCTOBER 1968

December 26, 1967
The Beatles' film Magical Mystery Tour receives its world premiere on BBC Television in the UK

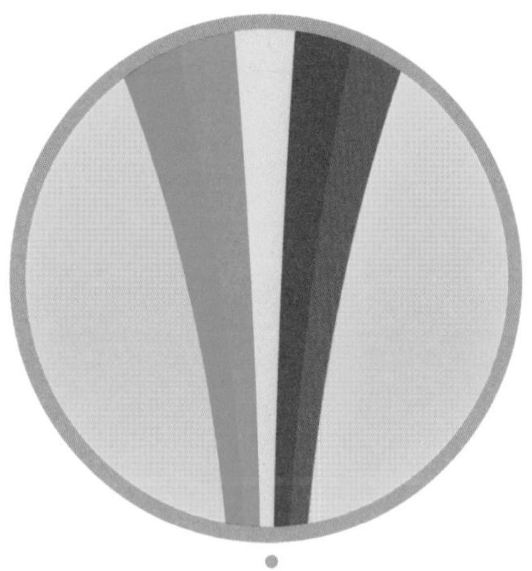

February 11, 1968
Madison Square Garden in New York City opens at its current location

April 2, 1968
The film 2001: A Space Odyssey premieres in Washington, D.C.

April 22, 1968
Ringo Starr temporarily leaves the band before being persuaded to return a couple of weeks later

December 31, 1967
Evel Knievel attempts to jump 141 feet over the Caesars Palace Fountains on the Las Vegas Strip

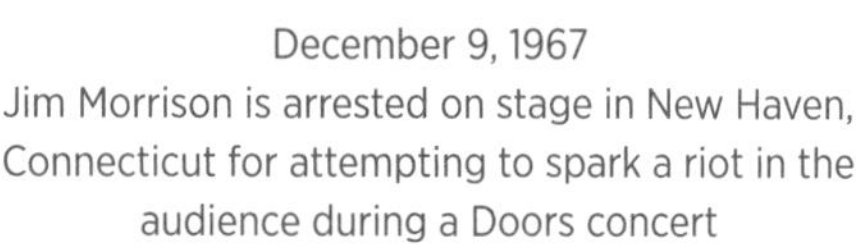

December 9, 1967
Jim Morrison is arrested on stage in New Haven, Connecticut for attempting to spark a riot in the audience during a Doors concert

February, 1968
The Beatles journey to India with their partners for a meditation course

April 4, 1968
Martin Luther King, Jr. is shot dead at the Lorraine Motel in Memphis, Tennessee. Riots erupt in major American cities, lasting for several days afterwards

July 20, 1968
The first International Special Olympics Summer Games are held at Soldier Field in Chicago, Illinois

May 29, 1968
Manchester United win the European Cup Final, becoming the first English team to do so

October 15, 1968
Led Zeppelin perform their first live gig at Surrey University in England

June 5, 1968
U.S. presidential candidate Robert F. Kennedy is shot at the Ambassador Hotel in Los Angeles

September 30, 1968
Boeing officially rolls out its new 747 for the media and the public

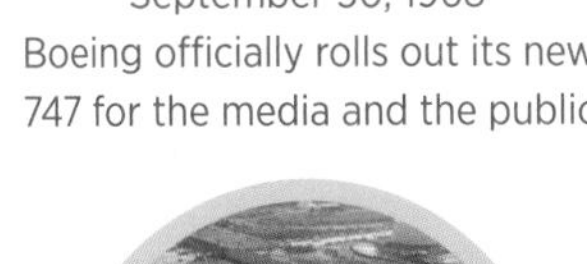

May 14, 1968
The Beatles announce the creation of Apple Records in a New York press conference

July 18, 1968
The semiconductor company Intel is founded

October 11, 1968
NASA launches Apollo 7, the first manned Apollo mission. Goals include the first live television broadcast from orbit and testing the lunar module docking manoeuvre

ALBUM COVER DESIGN

This cover was an explosion of colour. The photograph on the front features the four band members in the animal costumes they wore for the *Magical Mystery Tour* film. John Lennon wore a walrus costume, Paul McCartney a hippopotamus costume, George Harrison a rabbit costume and Ringo Starr a chicken costume.

The double EP had a gatefold cover, with a 24-page booklet containing photographs from the filming of *Magical Mystery Tour,* as well as a cartoon strip telling the story of the film. The EP also contained a four-page lyrics section in the centre of the booklet.

MAGICAL MYSTERY TOUR IS ONE OF MY FAVOURITE ALBUMS BECAUSE IT WAS SO WEIRD

JOHN LENNON

1974, ON 'MAGICAL MYSTERY TOUR'

SONGWRITING: WHO WROTE WHAT?

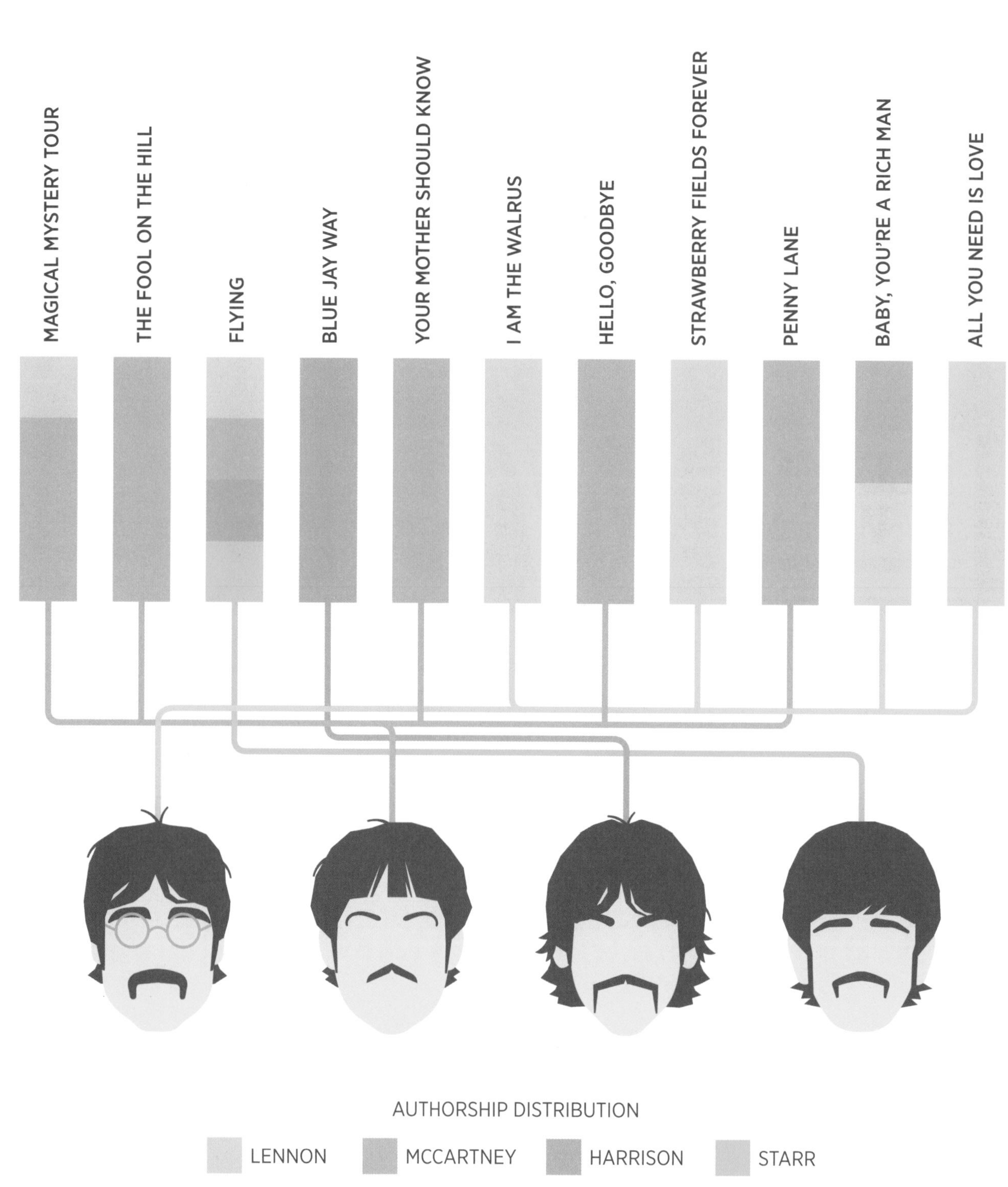

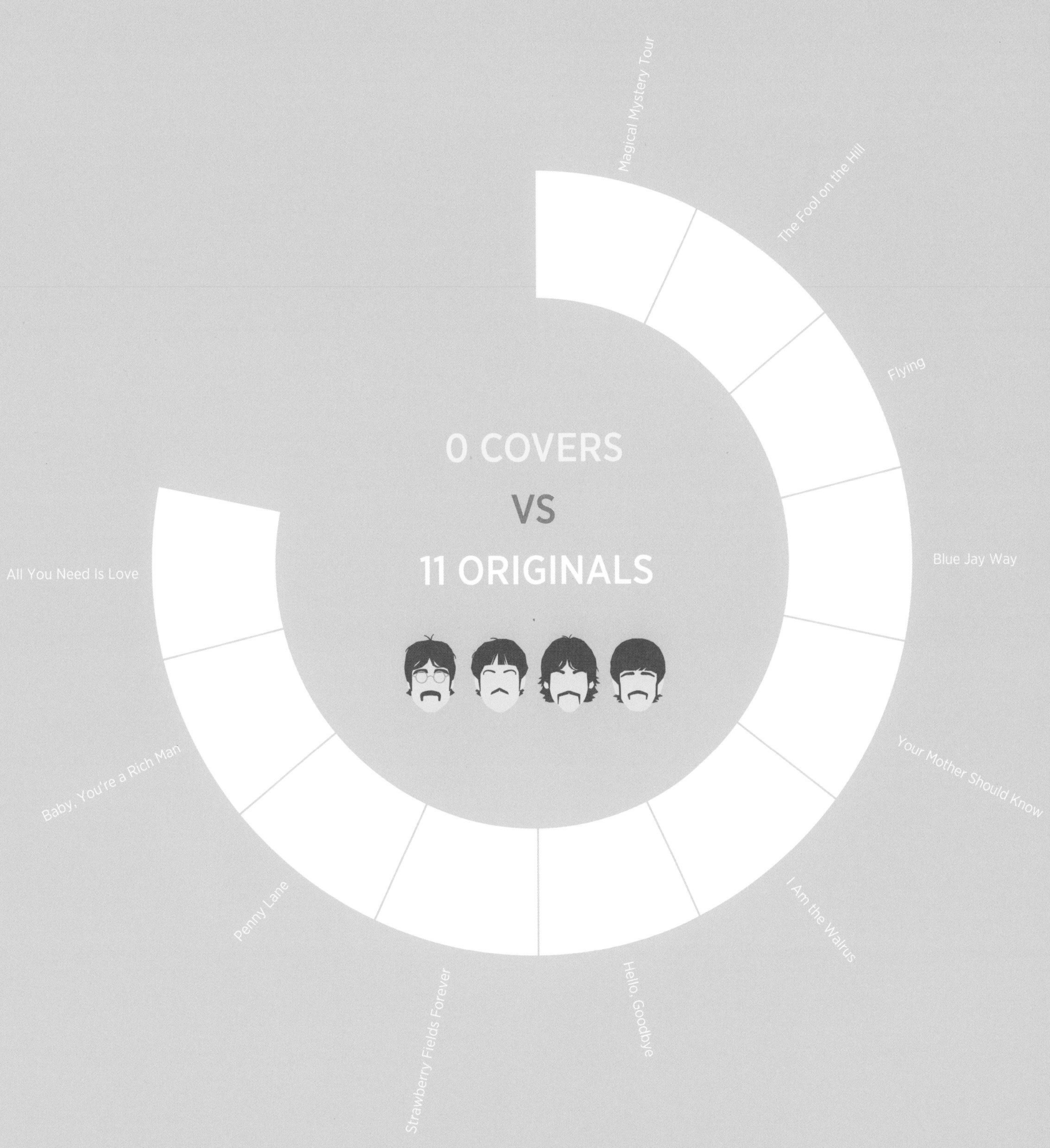
Magical Mystery Tour
The Fool on the Hill
Flying
Blue Jay Way
Your Mother Should Know
I Am the Walrus
Hello, Goodbye
Strawberry Fields Forever
Penny Lane
Baby, You're a Rich Man
All You Need Is Love
0 COVERS
VS
11 ORIGINALS

VOCALS: WHICH BEATLE TOOK THE LEAD?

Where band members shared lead vocals both are listed as singing lead vocals (as a result numbers may add up to more than the total number of tracks on the album).

SONG KEYS

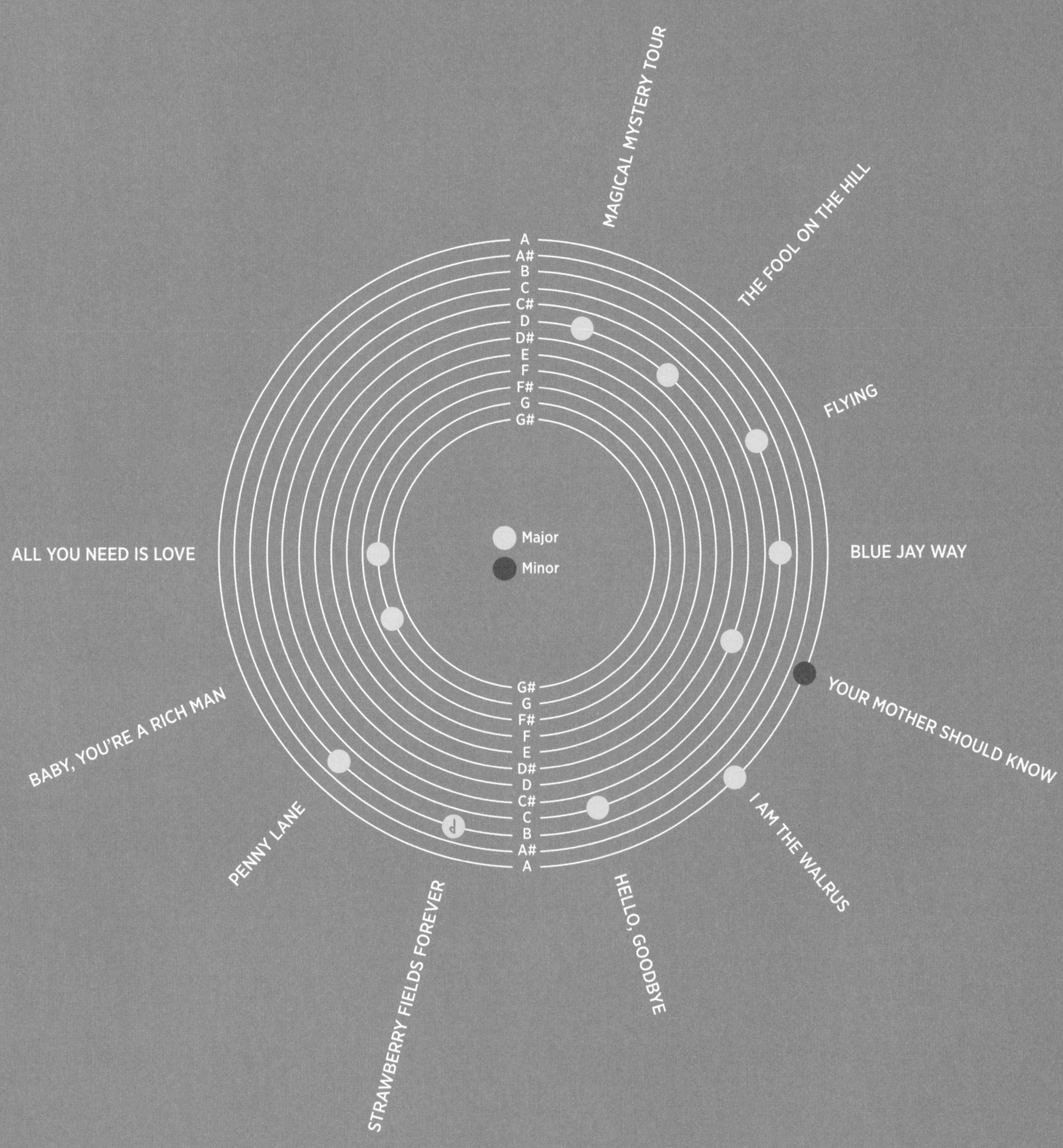

MAGICAL MYSTERY TOUR
THE FOOL ON THE HILL
FLYING
BLUE JAY WAY
YOUR MOTHER SHOULD KNOW
I AM THE WALRUS
HELLO, GOODBYE
STRAWBERRY FIELDS FOREVER
PENNY LANE
BABY, YOU'RE A RICH MAN
ALL YOU NEED IS LOVE
A
A#
B
C
C#
D
D#
E
F
F#
G
G#
Major
Minor

INSTRUMENTS: WHAT CAN YOU HEAR?

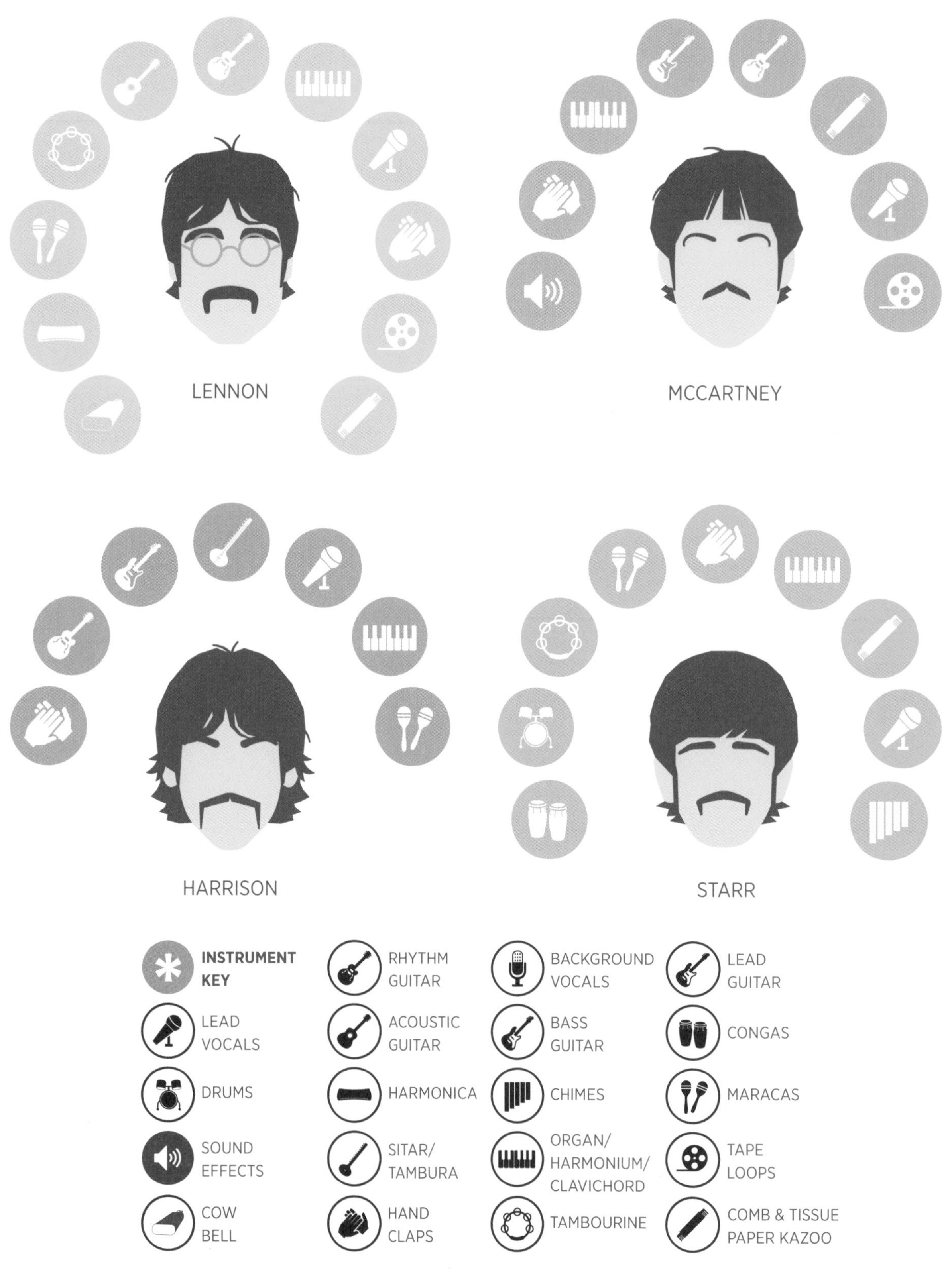

Black circle indicates instruments used for the first time in a Beatles' album

UK SINGLE RELEASES

MAGICAL MYSTERY TOUR
THE FOOL ON THE HILL
FLYING
BLUE JAY WAY
YOUR MOTHER SHOULD KNOW
I AM THE WALRUS
HELLO, GOODBYE
STRAWBERRY FIELDS FOREVER
PENNY LANE
BABY, YOU'RE A RICH MAN
ALL YOU NEED IS LOVE

1 1 2 2 1 1

NOT RELEASED
TOP 20
TOP 10

In total, *Magical Mystery Tour* spent twelve weeks at no 2. The US version of the album was imported into the UK and peaked at no. 31 in the charts in Jan 1968, despite the fact that it wasn't officially available in the UK. Across the pond, *Magical Mystery Tour* enjoyed the largest initial sales figure of any album in history, selling $8 million worth in only three weeks.

ALBUM CHART POSITIONS

UNITED KINGDOM
Number Two

UNITED STATES
Number One

FRANCE
Number Two

GERMANY
Number Eight

Filmography

As well as musical performances, the Beatles turned their hand to acting several times. Four films were made featuring the Fab Four in various guises:

A Hard Day's Night (1964)

Written by Alun Owen during the height of Beatlemania, *A Hard Day's Night* gives viewers a glimpse into several days in the lives of the band. It's often credited as being one of the most influential music films of all time, inspiring countless pop videos, spy films and even *The Monkees* TV show.

Budget

£189,000

Length

87 mins

Rating

Locations

London
Somerset
Devon
Sussex

Magical Mystery Tour (1967)

Magical Mystery Tour originally aired on Boxing Day 1967 on BBC1. It is the story of a group of people on a coach trip embarking on a mystery tour around Britain. The initial showing of the film was poorly received by critics and audiences, although it is now warmly regarded by many fans.

Budget

£30,000

Length

55 mins

Rating

Locations

Cornwall
Kent
Surrey
Nice

Help! (1965)

The second feature film, *Help!* is a comedy adventure that sees the Beatles come up against an evil cult, that is trying to obtain a sacrificial ring worn by Ringo. *Help!* was given positive reviews at the time of release and is often regarded as a huge influence on the development of music videos.

Budget

$1,500,000

Length

92 mins

Rating

Locations

Salzburg
Bahamas
Liverpool
Wiltshire
London
Buckinghamshire

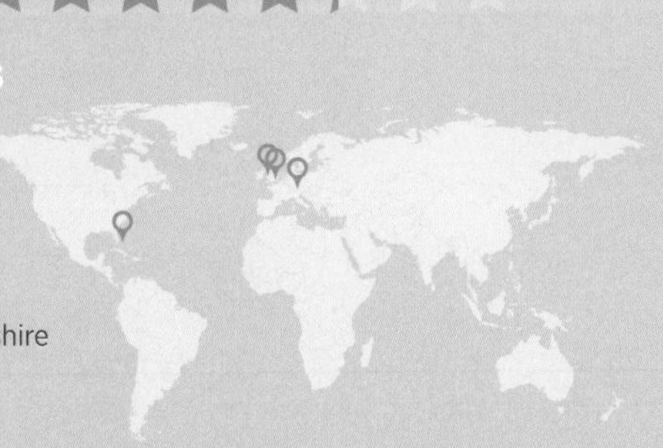

Yellow Submarine (1968)

The final Beatles film was an animated musical comedy, inspired by the music of the band. Although the Beatles composed and performed the songs, they only participated in the closing scene of the film and the on-screen characters were voiced by actors. *Yellow Submarine* was extremely well received and is credited with positioning animation as a serious art form.

Budget

£250,000

Length

90 mins

Rating

Locations

London
(TVC Animation
Studios)

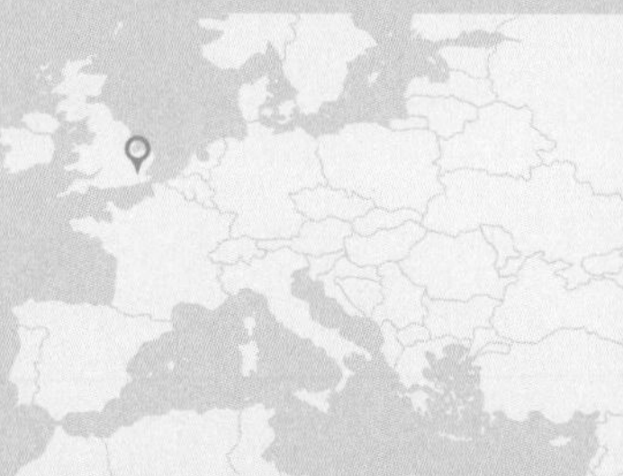

A VISUAL REPRESENTATION OF THE VOLUME AND INTENSITY OF EACH TRACK ON THE ALBUM

1963
late 1963
mid 1964

late 1964
mid 1965
late 1965
mid 1966

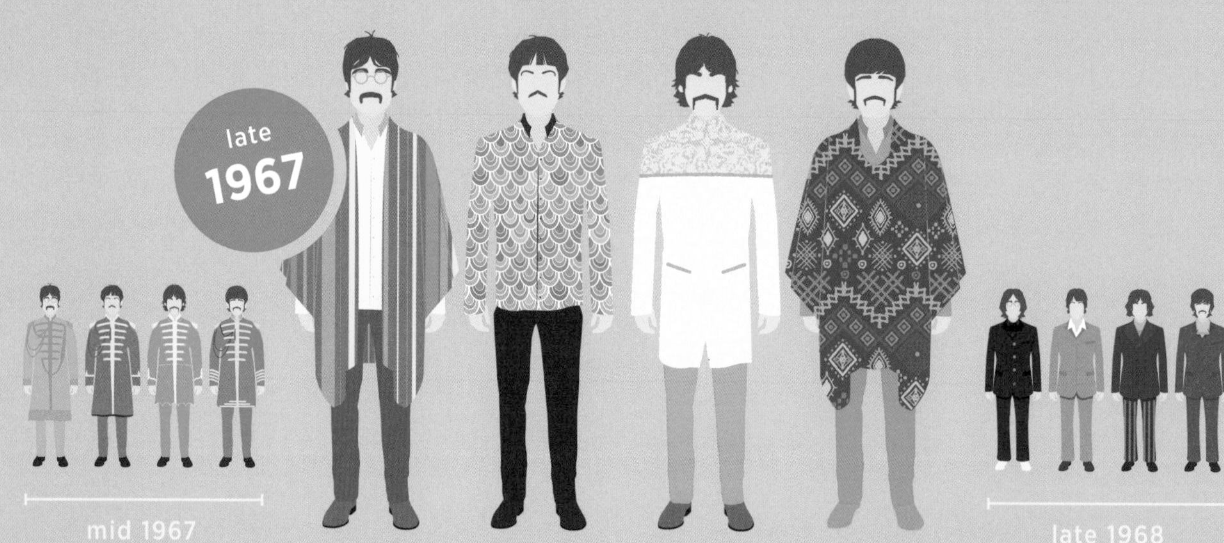
late 1967
mid 1967
late 1968

early 1969
1969
1970

1970

The outfits worn throughout *Magical Mystery Tour* show the continuation of the psychedelic theme running through this period of the Beatles' careers. A wide range of colours and patterns give an eclectic look, with a real mix of styles.

ALBUM OVERVIEW

Released: 22 November 1968
Producers: George Martin, Chris Thomas,
John Lennon, Paul McCartney
Engineers: Geoff Emerick, Peter Bown, Ken Scott,
Barry Sheffield, Ken Townsend

The album is called *The Beatles* but is commonly known as 'The White Album' to fans. It was the band's first double-length release, consisting of 30 songs, many of which were written in India. George Martin wanted to cut some of the weaker ones and release a stronger single-disc album instead, but the Beatles insisted. During the writing and recording, the band were setting up Apple Corps, and dealing with press speculation, substance abuse, relationship issues and problems with the authorities.

They were now working more separately and sessions often drifted without any direction. By the third month of recording, tensions began to rise in the studio. There were frequent conflicts and disagreements, and the authority of George Martin began to lessen. In August, Ringo Starr walked out. It was only when he returned two weeks later that the band finally began working together again, and the album started to fully take shape.

NOVEMBER

1968

THE BEATLES (WHITE ALBUM)

TIMELINE: NOVEMBER-DECEMBER 1968

November 20, 1968
The Farmington Mine disaster in Farmington, West Virginia, kills seventy-eight men

December 9, 1968
Douglas Engelbart publicly demonstrates his pioneering hypertext system, NLS, in San Francisco

December 10, 1968
Japan's biggest heist, the never-solved "300 million yen robbery", occurs in Tokyo

November 8, 1968
John and Cynthia Lennon divorce

November 22, 1968
"Plato's Stepchildren", 12th episode of Star Trek 3rd season is aired, featuring the first-ever interracial kiss on U.S. national television between Lieutenant Uhura and Captain James T. Kirk

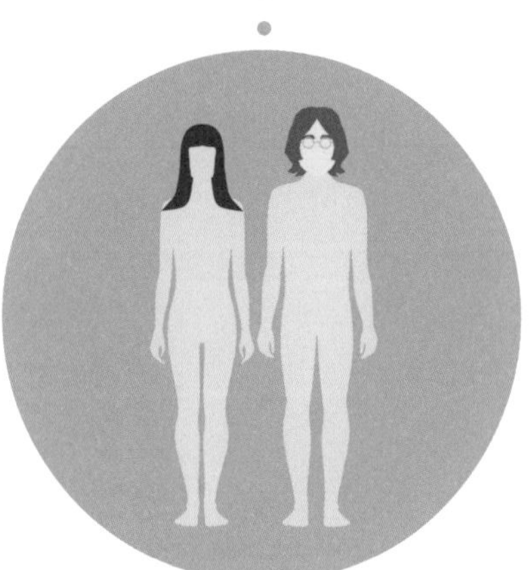

December 18, 1968
John Lennon and Yoko Ono release Two Virgins

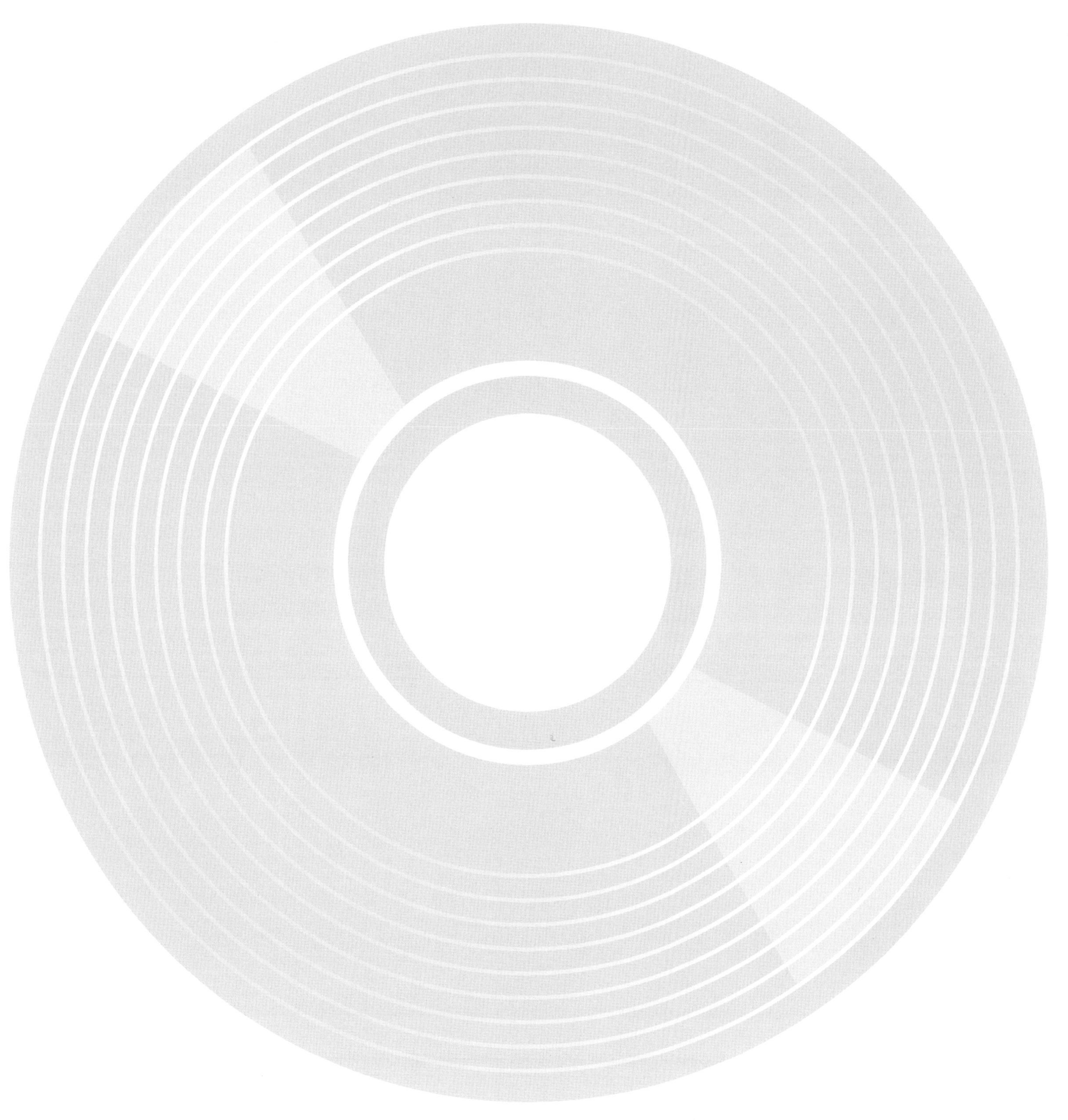

ALBUM COVER DESIGN

The band enlisted pop artist Richard Hamilton to design the cover. He suggested a minimalist approach and numbered sleeves, which early copies of the album had. The band originally intended it to have a see-through sleeve but were told it couldn't be done and settled on a plain white one with 'The Beatles' lightly embossed on one side. Here we've visualised how the album might have looked if the Beatles' had got their way.

NUMBER
ROUND
RIGHT
9
I'D
JULIA
GUN
TELL
SON
CRY
GUITAR
GOES
I'VE
DIE
MM
NIGHT
KNOW
LOVE
GONNA
EASY
ROCKY
ROAD
HEY
MAKE
COME
NOW
OLD
AH
SMILE
GIRL
DON'T
AH
BOY
WELL
PIE
SEE
SING
YEAH
BUNGALOW
DEAR
LET
TU
LA
GO
OOH
I'M
BACK
BILL
DA
LIFE
GOOD
YES
HONEY
LIKE
FLY
GET
KILL
TAKE
JOY
OH

LOOK WHAT MEDITATION'S DONE FOR

RINGO

AFTER ALL THIS TIME HE'S WRITTEN

HIS FIRST SONG

JOHN LENNON

ON SONGWRITING FOR 'THE WHITE ALBUM'

INSTRUMENTS: WHAT CAN YOU HEAR?

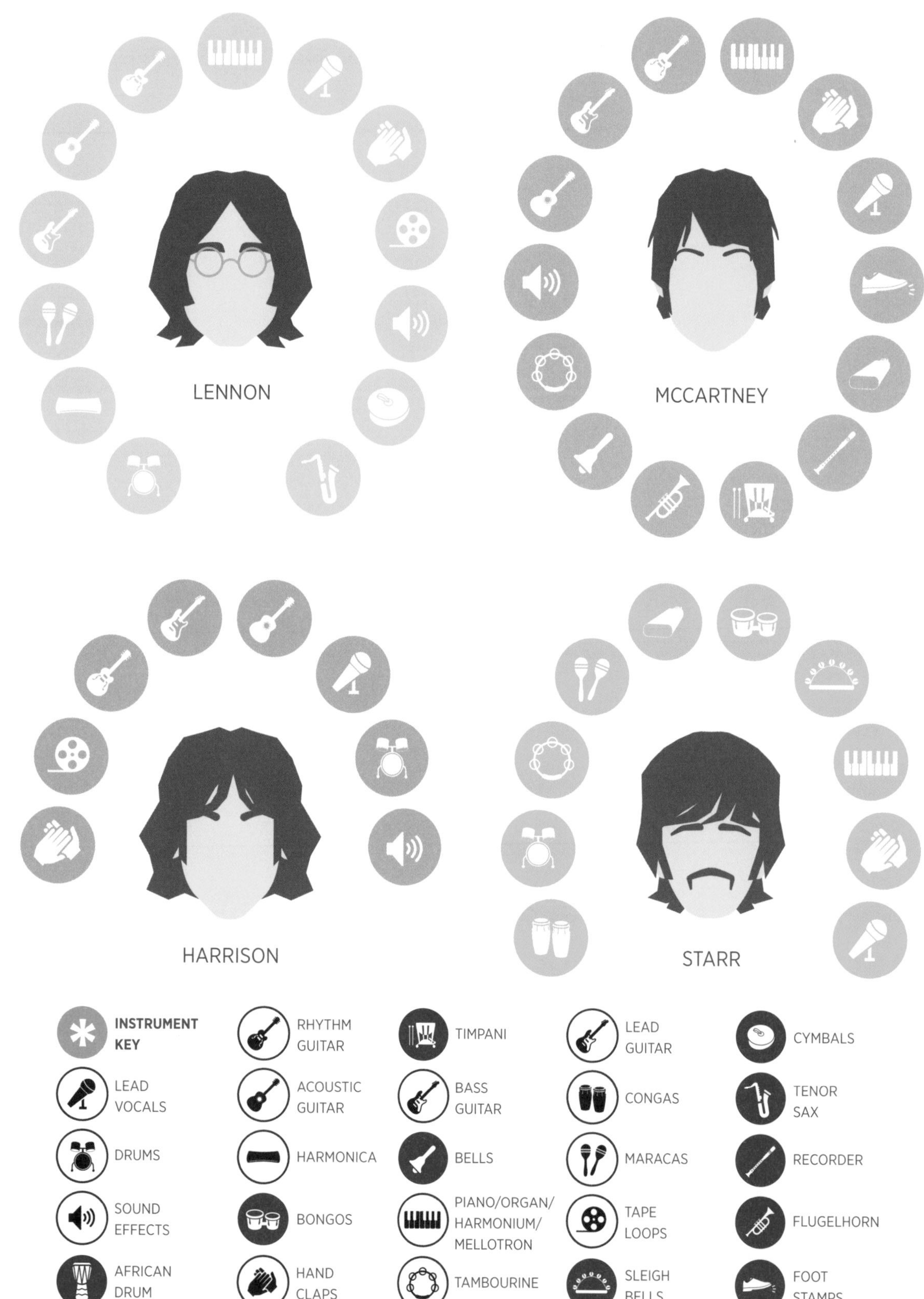

Black circle indicates instruments used for the first time in a Beatles' album

VOCALS: WHICH BEATLE TOOK THE LEAD?

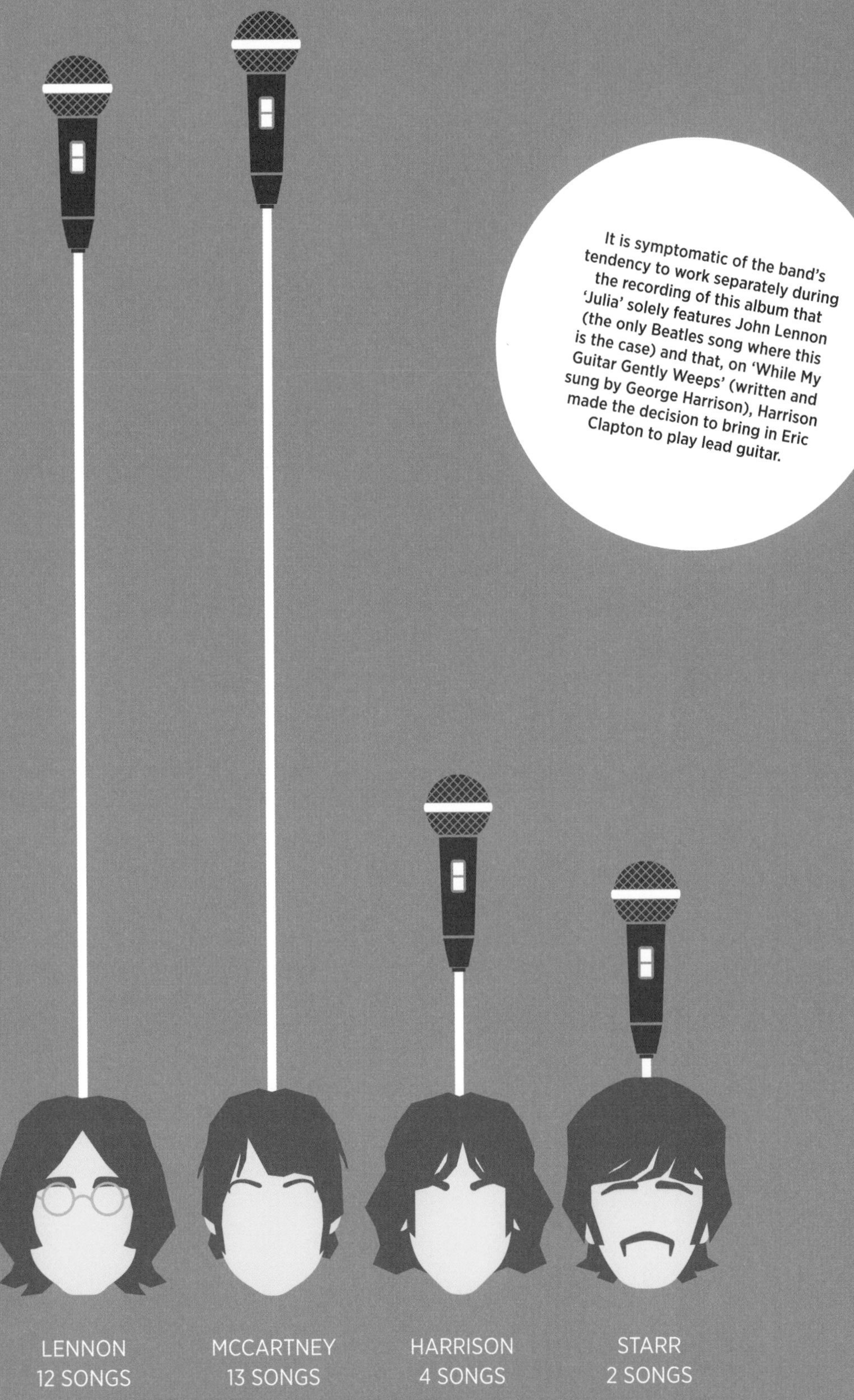

It is symptomatic of the band's tendency to work separately during the recording of this album that 'Julia' solely features John Lennon (the only Beatles song where this is the case) and that, on 'While My Guitar Gently Weeps' (written and sung by George Harrison), Harrison made the decision to bring in Eric Clapton to play lead guitar.

Where band members shared lead vocals both are listed as singing lead vocals (as a result numbers may add up to more than the total number of tracks on the album).

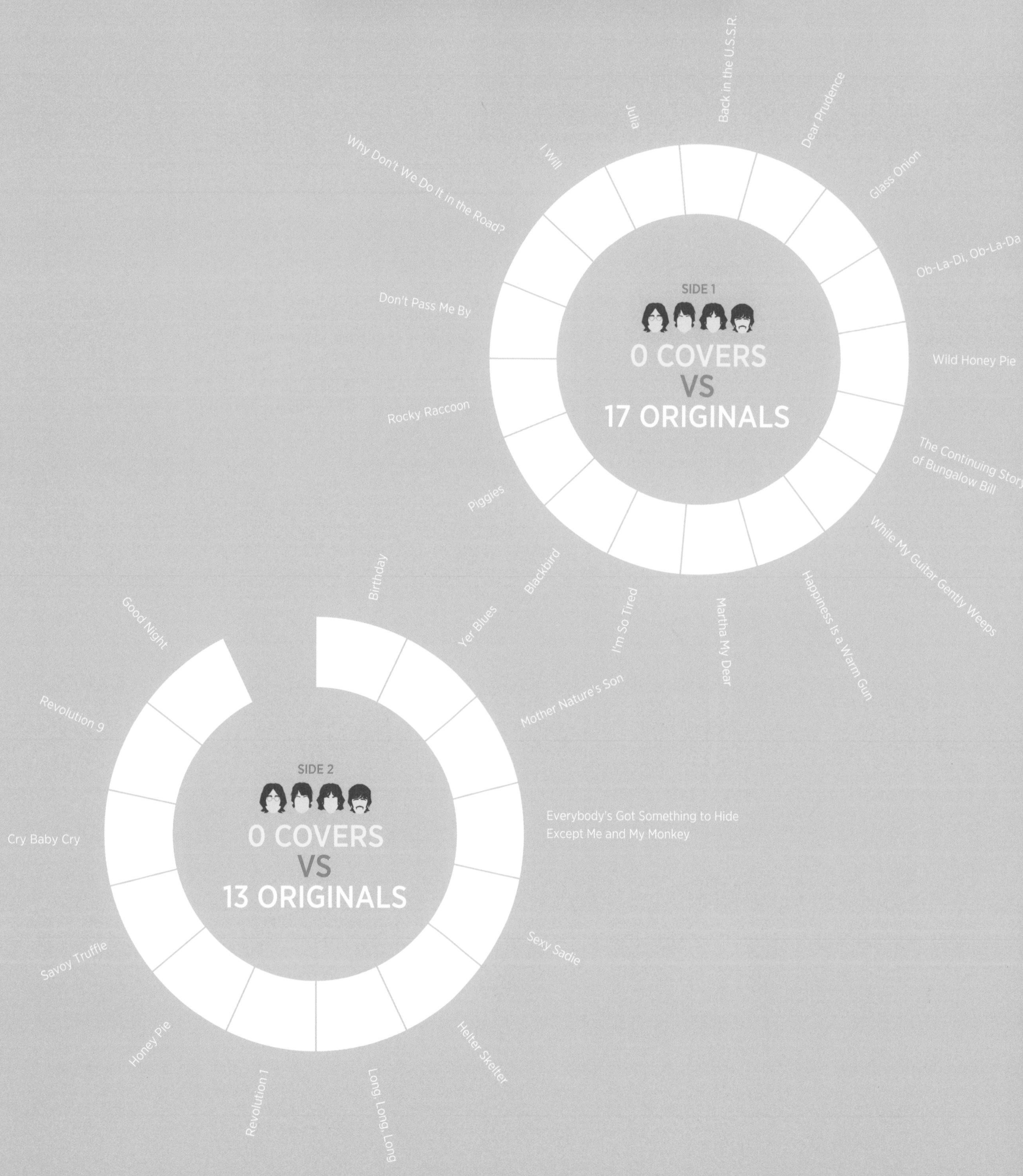
SIDE 1
0 COVERS
VS
17 ORIGINALS
Back in the U.S.S.R.
Dear Prudence
Glass Onion
Ob-La-Di, Ob-La-Da
Wild Honey Pie
The Continuing Story of Bungalow Bill
While My Guitar Gently Weeps
Happiness Is a Warm Gun
Martha My Dear
I'm So Tired
Blackbird
Piggies
Rocky Raccoon
Don't Pass Me By
Why Don't We Do It in the Road?
I Will
Julia
SIDE 2
0 COVERS
VS
13 ORIGINALS
Birthday
Yer Blues
Mother Nature's Son
Everybody's Got Something to Hide Except Me and My Monkey
Sexy Sadie
Helter Skelter
Long, Long, Long
Revolution 1
Honey Pie
Savoy Truffle
Cry Baby Cry
Revolution 9
Good Night

SONGWRITING: WHO WROTE WHAT?

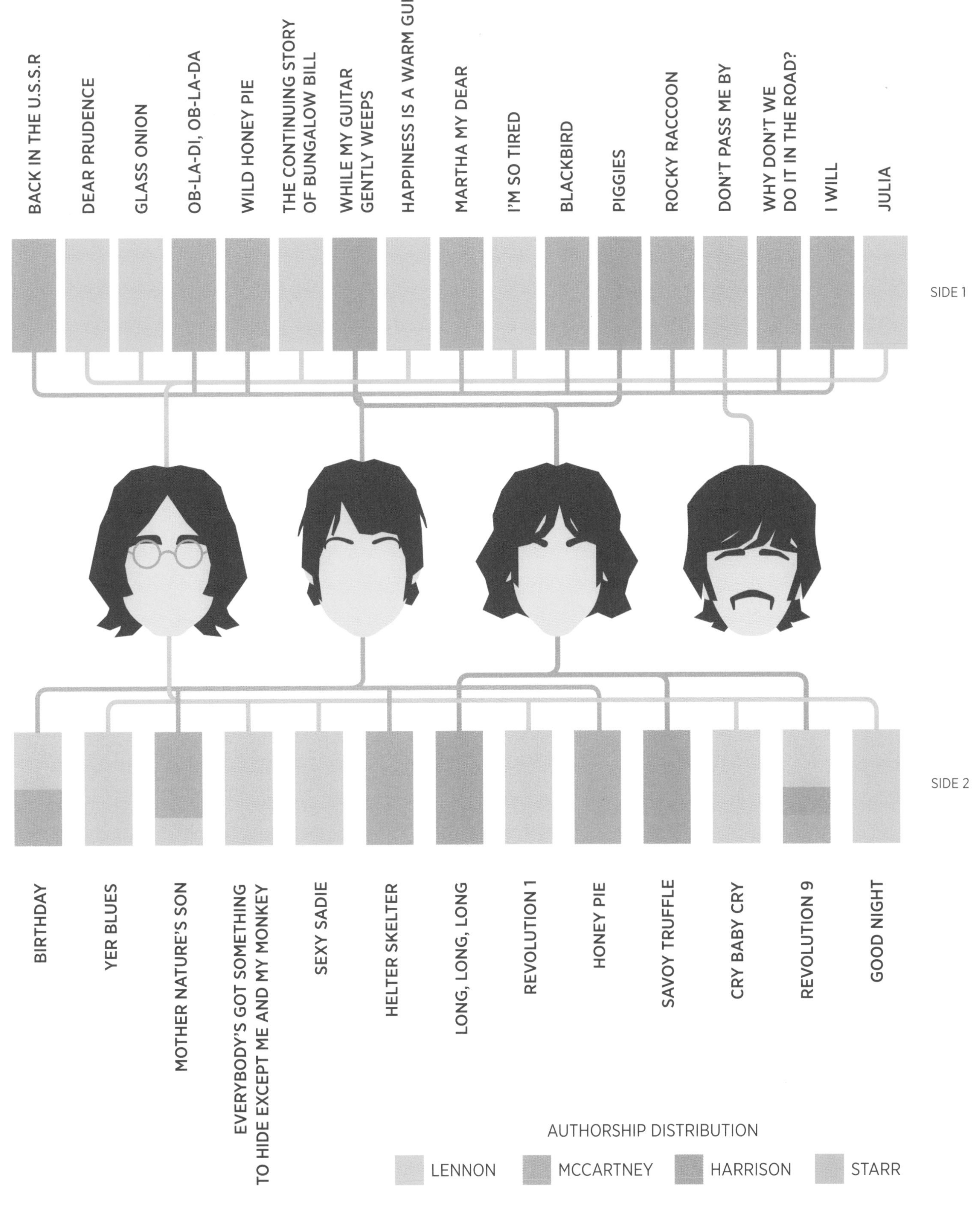

LENGTHS: TRACK AND ALBUM (SIDE 1)

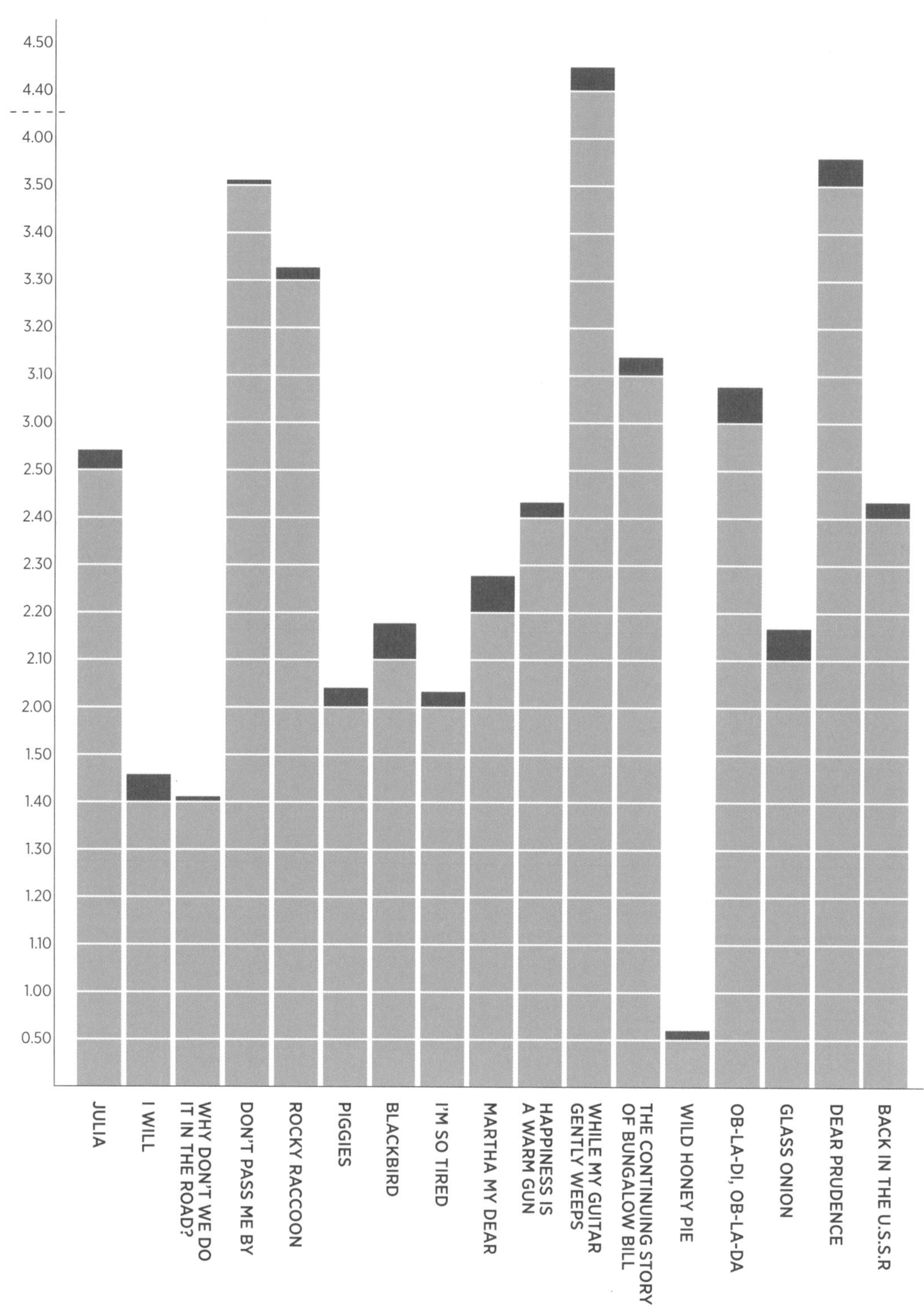

SONG KEYS (SIDE 1)

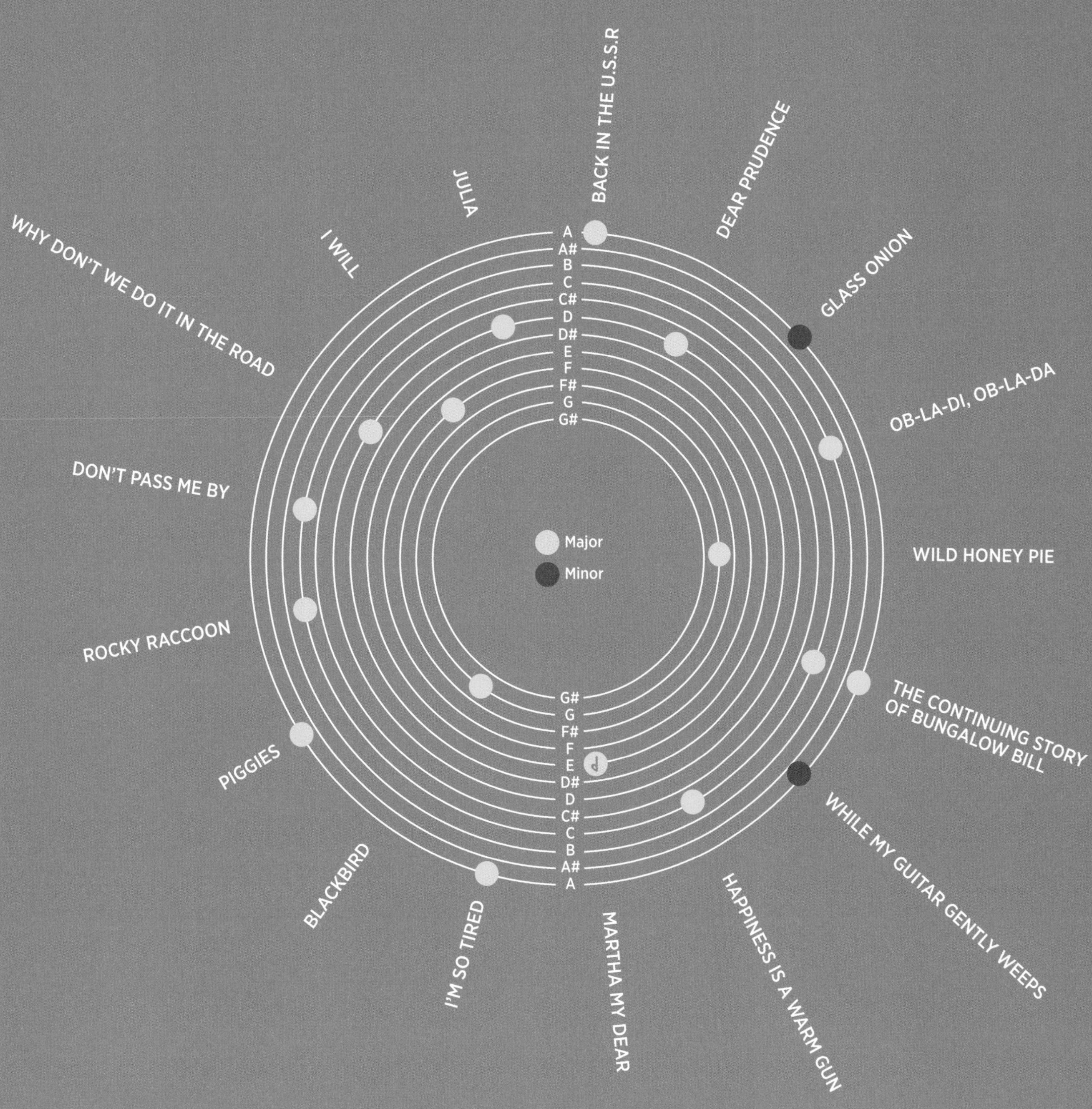

LENGTHS: TRACK AND ALBUM (SIDE 2)

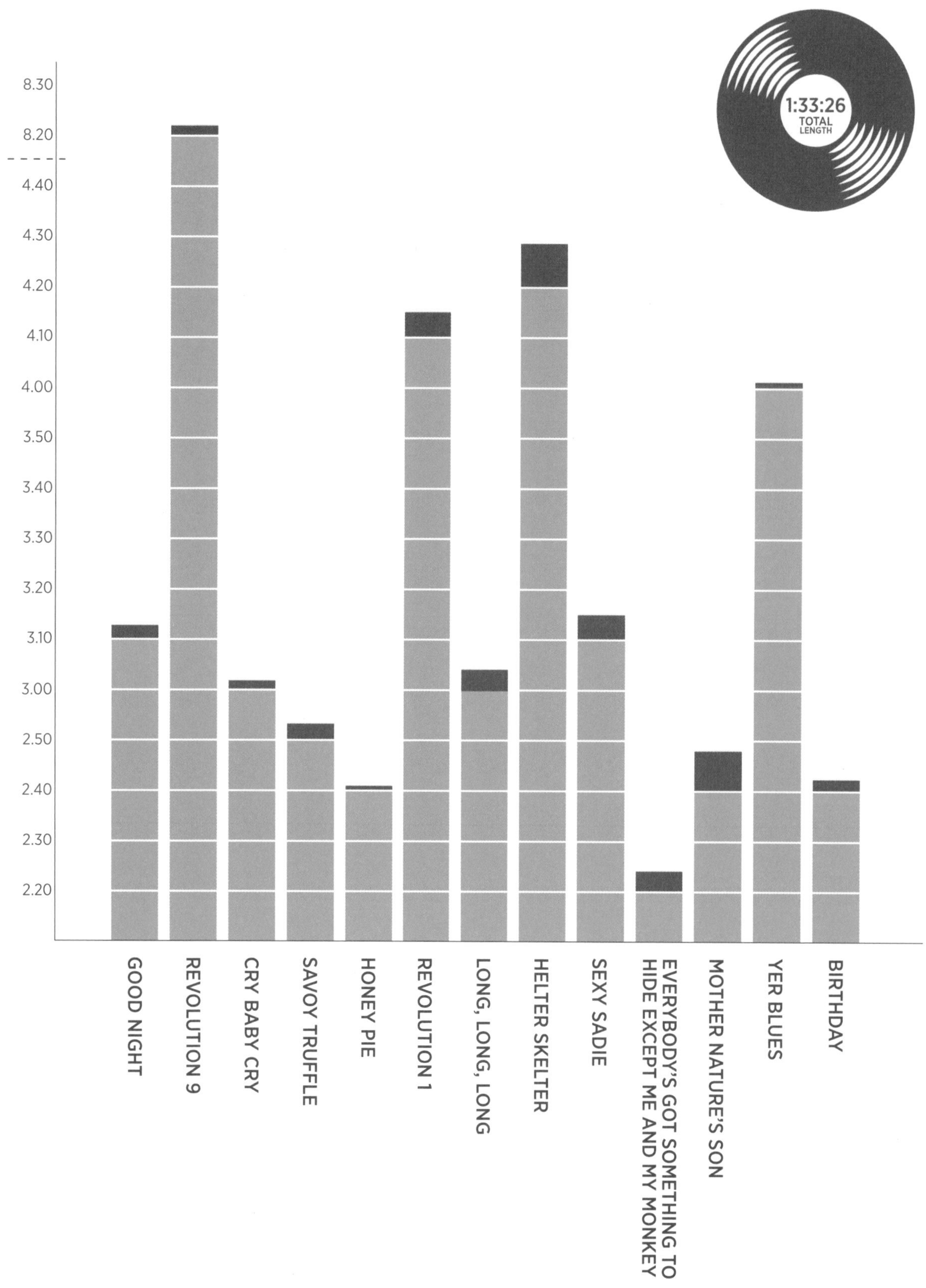

SONG KEYS (SIDE 2)

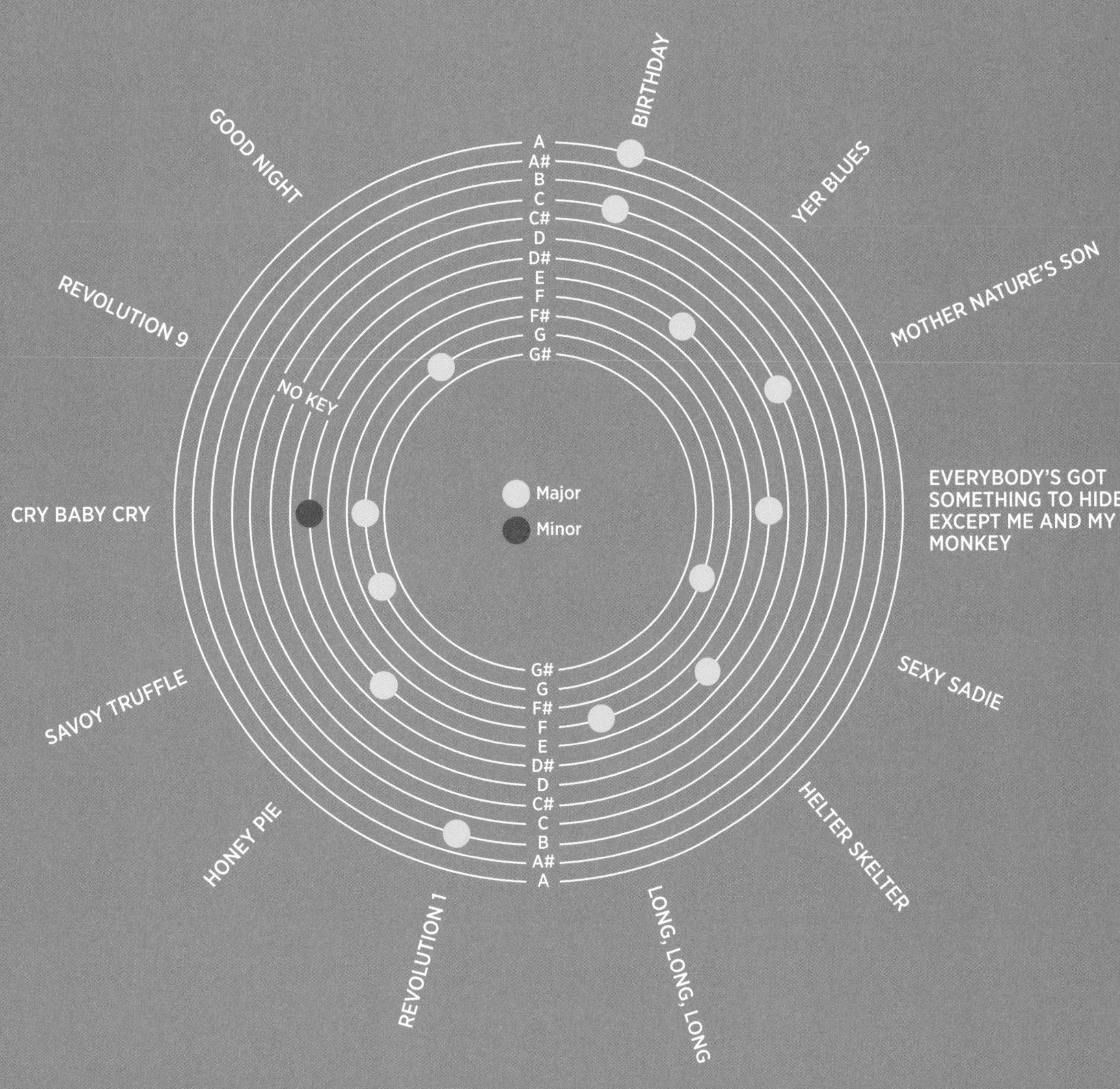

A VISUAL REPRESENTATION OF THE VOLUME
AND INTENSITY OF EACH TRACK ON SIDE 1 OF THE ALBUM

SUCCESS

UK SINGLE RELEASES (SIDE 1)

BACK IN THE U.S.S.R
DEAR PRUDENCE
GLASS ONION
OB-LA-DI, OB-LA-DA
WILD HONEY PIE
THE CONTINUING STORY OF BUNGALOW BILL
WHILE MY GUITAR GENTLY WEEPS
HAPPINESS IS A WARM GUN
MARTHA MY DEAR
I'M SO TIRED
BLACKBIRD
PIGGIES
ROCKY RACCOON
DON'T PASS ME BY
WHY DON'T WE DO IT IN THE ROAD
I WILL
JULIA

19*

NOT RELEASED
TOP 20
TOP 10

*Charted in the UK on the 1976 rerelease.

After the creative failure of the *Magical Mystery Tour* television film, and the release of the accompanying EP and Lady Madonna single, there was widespread speculation from music writers that the band had finished. But *The White Album* debuted at number one in the UK chart, spending a total of seven weeks there and 24 weeks in the charts in total. In the US, the album spent nine weeks at number one, and 155 weeks on the Billboard 200. No singles were taken from *The White Album*, although 'Hey Jude'/'Revolution' was recorded during the same sessions and released as a standalone single. 'Back in the USSR' charted in the UK on the 1976 rerelease.

ALBUM CHART POSITIONS

UNITED KINGDOM
Number One

GERMANY
Number One

CANADA
Number One

SPAIN
Number Two

FRANCE
Number One

AUSTRALIA
Number One

UNITED STATES
Number One

NORWAY
Number Two

SWEDEN
Number One

STYLE

1963
late 1963
mid 1964

late 1964
mid 1965
late 1965
mid 1966

late
1968
mid 1967
late 1967

early 1969
1969
1970

1970

On Sunday 28 July 1968, whilst in the midst of recording the White Album, the Beatles invited renowned war photographer Don McCullin to produce a new set of publicity images for them including a cover photo for *Life* magazine. McCullin jumped at the chance and, accompanied by five others with cameras, set off on a day-long jaunt around London, more famously known as the 'Mad Day Out'. These are the outfits they wore in the front cover photograph.

ALBUM OVERVIEW

Released: 17 January 1969
Producer: George Martin
Engineers: Geoff Emerick, Dave Siddle, Eddie Kramer

Yellow Submarine came about due to a contractual obligation for the band to supply new songs for the soundtrack to the *Yellow Submarine* animated film. It is reported that the band showed minimal enthusiasm for the project and didn't view it as a significant release. It only contains six songs by the Beatles. The remainder are re-recordings of the orchestral soundtrack to the film by George Martin.

The album is often criticised by music journalists, who feel it falls short of the band's usual high standards.

JANUARY

1969

YELLOW SUBMARINE

TIMELINE: JANUARY-AUGUST 1969

January 20, 1969
Richard Nixon succeeds Lyndon B. Johnson as the 37th President of the United States of America

February 3, 1969
Allen Klein becomes the Beatles' manager

March 20, 1969
John Lennon and Yoko Ono are married at Gibraltar and proceed to their honeymoon "Bed-In" for peace in Amsterdam

May 15, 1969
An American teenager known as 'Robert R.' dies in St. Louis, Missouri in what becomes the first case of HIV/AIDS in North America

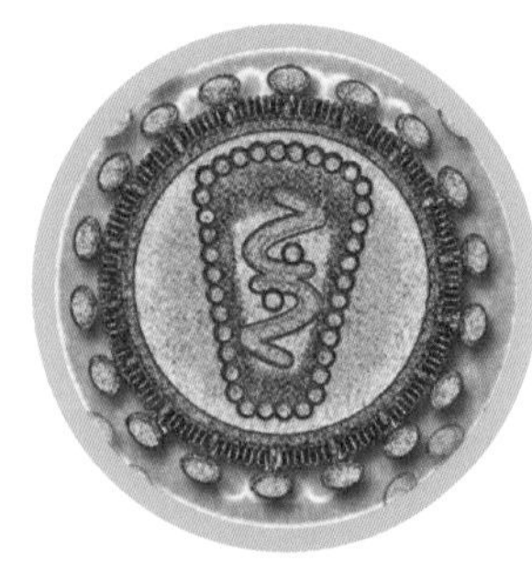

January 2, 1969
Rupert Murdoch purchases the largest selling British Sunday newspaper, *The News of the World*

January 30, 1969
The Beatles give their last public performance, filming several tracks on the roof of Apple Records, London

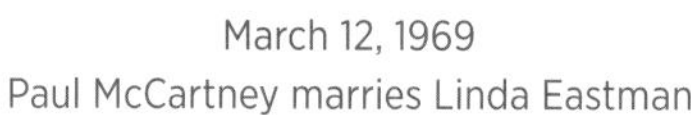

March 12, 1969
Paul McCartney marries Linda Eastman

April 22, 1969
Robin Knox-Johnston becomes the first person to sail around the world solo without stopping

July 1, 1969
Charles, Prince of Wales, is invested with his title at Caernarfon

July 14, 1969
The United States officially withdraws $500, $1,000, $5,000 and $10,000 bills from circulation

July 31, 1969
The halfpenny ceases to be legal tender in the UK

August 8, 1969
The iconic Abbey Road photo is taken by photographer Ian Macmillan

August 15-18, 1969
The Beatles gather at John's estate, Tittenhurst Park for their final photo shoot

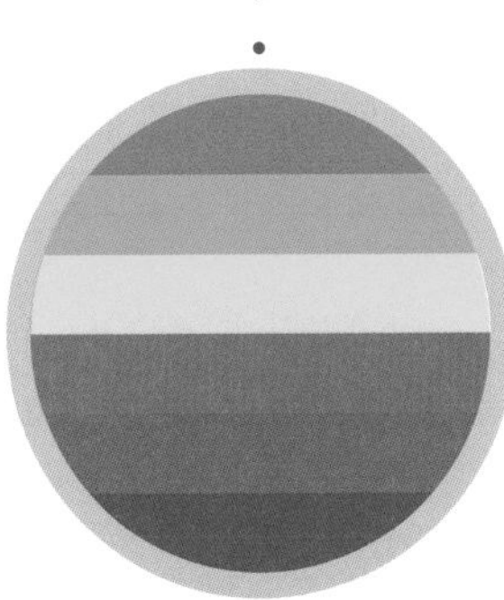

June 28, 1969
The Stonewall riots in New York City mark the start of the modern gay rights movement in the U.S

July 20, 1969
Apollo 11 lands on the Moon.
An estimated 500 million people worldwide watch in awe as Neil Armstrong takes his historic first steps on the lunar surface

August 9, 1969
Charles Manson's cult kill five people at Hollywood director Roman Polanski's house, including his wife actress Sharon Tate, in what becomes know as the 'Tate Murders'

ALBUM COVER DESIGN

If the lyrics had ever come true this might have been all we'd seen of the Beatles! In reality, the cover artwork features a drawing by Heinz Edelman of the Beatles safely on land. The back of the cover contains a review of the White Album by Tony Palmer, written for the *Observer*.

THAT SCORE PROVED ENORMOUSLY SUCCESSFUL AND EARNED ME A LOAD OF FAN MAIL

— GEORGE MARTIN —

ON THE SCORE FOR 'YELLOW SUBMARINE'

A VISUAL REPRESENTATION OF THE VOLUME
AND INTENSITY OF EACH TRACK ON THE ALBUM

VOCALS: WHICH BEATLE TOOK THE LEAD?

Where band members shared lead vocals both are listed as singing lead vocals (as a result numbers may add up to more than the total number of tracks on the album).

Yellow Submarine
Only a Northern Song
All Together Now
Hey Bulldog
It's All Too Much
All You Need Is Love
Pepperland
Sea of Time
Sea of Holes
Sea of Monsters
March of the Meanies
Pepperland Laid Waste
Yellow Submarine in Pepperland
0 COVERS
VS
13 ORIGINALS

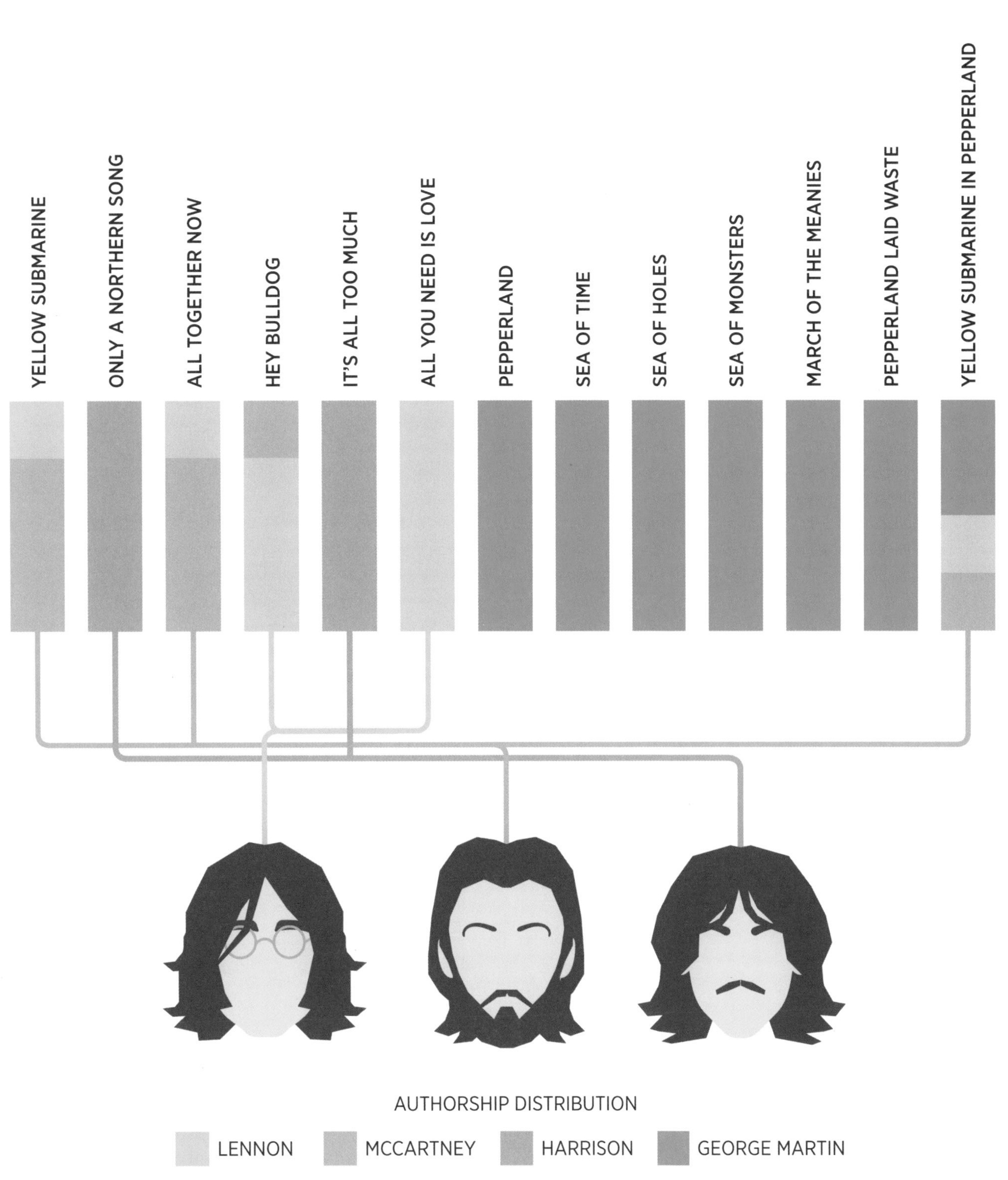
YELLOW SUBMARINE
ONLY A NORTHERN SONG
ALL TOGETHER NOW
HEY BULLDOG
IT'S ALL TOO MUCH
ALL YOU NEED IS LOVE
PEPPERLAND
SEA OF TIME
SEA OF HOLES
SEA OF MONSTERS
MARCH OF THE MEANIES
PEPPERLAND LAID WASTE
YELLOW SUBMARINE IN PEPPERLAND
AUTHORSHIP DISTRIBUTION
LENNON
MCCARTNEY
HARRISON
GEORGE MARTIN

INSTRUMENTS: WHAT CAN YOU HEAR?

Black circle indicates instruments used for the first time in a Beatles' album

SONG KEYS

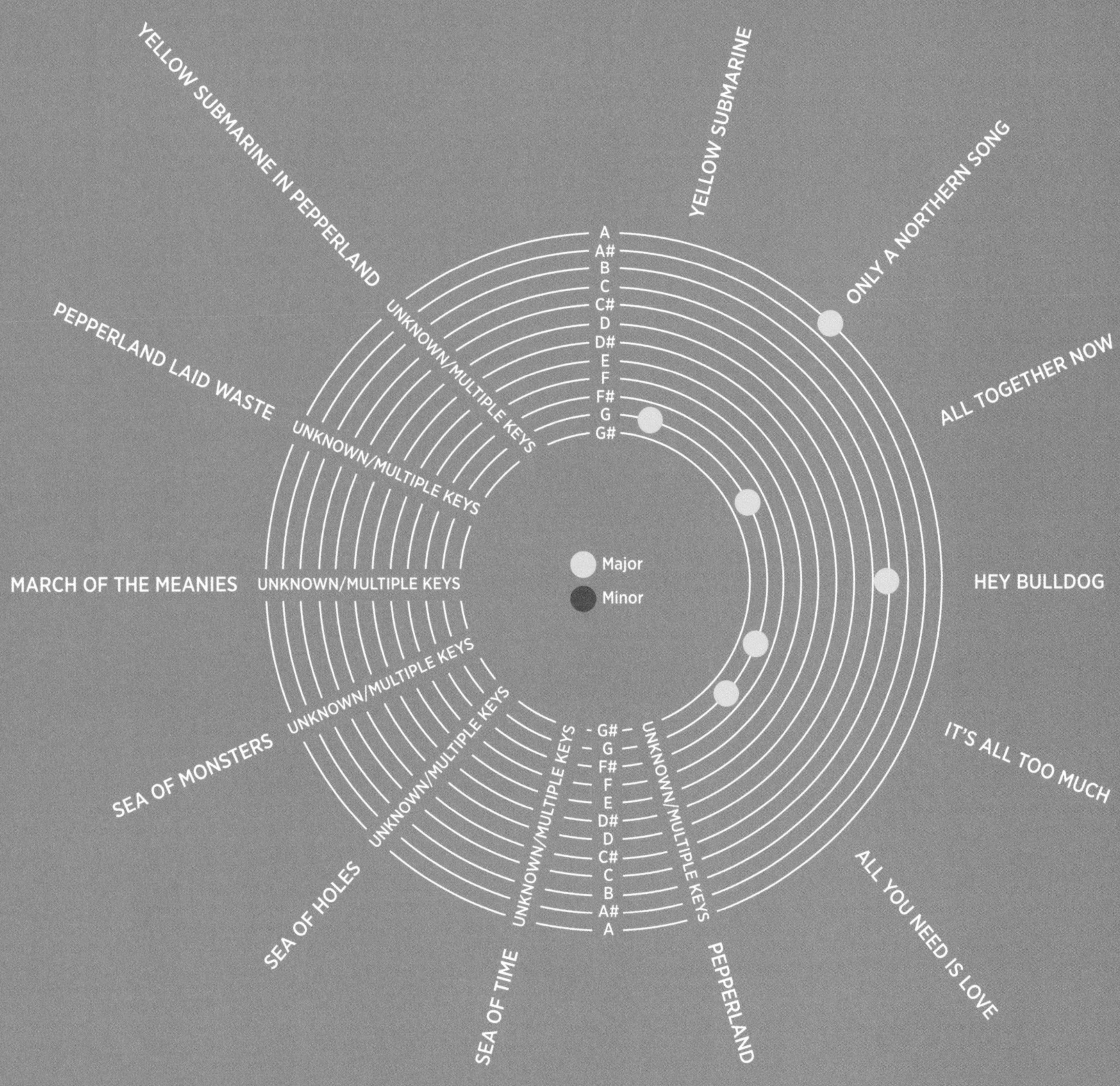

N.B The orchestral film score that comprises the second half of this album, performed by the 41-piece George Martin Orchestra, has never been released

UK SINGLE RELEASES

YELLOW SUBMARINE
ONLY A NORTHERN SONG
ALL TOGETHER NOW
HEY BULLDOG
IT'S ALL TOO MUCH
ALL YOU NEED IS LOVE
PEPPERLAND
SEA OF TIME
SEA OF HOLES
SEA OF MONSTERS
MARCH OF THE MEANIES
PEPPERLAND LAID WASTE
YELLOW SUBMARINE IN PEPPERLAND

1 1

NOT RELEASED
TOP 20
TOP 10

Yellow Submarine failed to top the charts in either the US or the UK, though the single 'Yellow Submarine' which was included in *Revolver* and charted in 1966 was included on this album as well. Martin's orchestral score is generally well-reviewed. 'All You Need Is Love' was originally released on 7 July 1967 as a non-album single.

ALBUM CHART POSITIONS

UNITED KINGDOM
Number Three

GERMANY
Number Five

UNITED STATES
Number Two

AUSTRALIA
Number Four

NORWAY
Number One

CANADA
Number One

The Rooftop Concert

After numerous plans for their final gig had fallen through (including the Sahara Desert and the QE2), John proposed that they play on top of their Apple Corps headquarters at 3 Savile Row, London. Plans were made, and on 30 January 1969, the Beatles played a show that would go down in rock history.

Along with keyboardist Billy Preston, the band played nine takes of five songs in a 42-minute set, before the Metropolitan Police service asked them to reduce the volume. This last ever live performance was filmed and footage from the performance was used in the 1970 documentary *Let It Be*.

STYLE

1963 | late 1963 | mid 1964

late 1964 | mid 1965 | late 1965 | mid 1966

mid 1967 | late 1967 | late 1968

1969 | 1970

These are the outfits the Beatles wore for the infamous 'Rooftop Concert'. Lennon wore Yoko Ono's fur coat and Starr wore his wife's red raincoat.

ALBUM OVERVIEW

Released: 26 September 1969
Producers: George Martin, Chris Thomas, Glyn Johns
Engineers: Geoff Emerick, Phil McDonald, Jeff Jarratt, Glyn Johns, Barry Sheffield, Tony Clark

Although *Abbey Road* was the penultimate album released by the band, it was the last album they ever recorded. As a result, many see it as the band's true final album and it is also thought that the band members knew it would be their swansong. The album was finished less than a month before Lennon told the group he was going to leave. Despite the tensions, Lennon remarked that once the band were together in the studio they were as strong as ever.

Lennon missed some of the recording sessions due to being injured in a car crash in Scotland. Yoko Ono also suffered injuries during the crash, and was pregnant at the time. As Lennon wanted to keep an eye on her during her recuperation, he arranged for a double bed to be delivered to the studio so she could be there while the band recorded.

Abbey Road remained untitled until the recording sessions were well underway. The working title was 'Everest', named after the cigarettes smoked by Geoff Emerick. After the band decided they didn't want to fly out to Mount Everest for a photo shoot, Paul suggested they name the album after the studio they were in. It made the building and street famous the world over and, in the early 70s, EMI changed the name from EMI Studios to Abbey Road Studios to reflect this.

SEPTEMBER 1969 ABBEY ROAD

TIMELINE: SEPTEMBER 1969-APRIL 1970

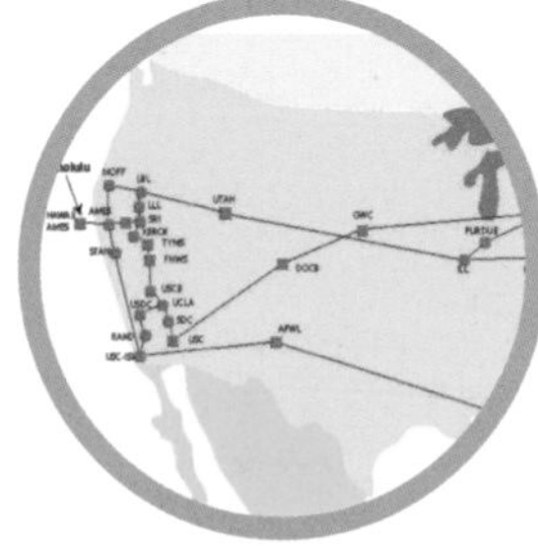

October 19, 1969
The first message is sent over ARPANET, the forerunner of the internet

November 10, 1969
Sesame Street is broadcast for the first time, on the National Educational Television (NET) network

November 19, 1969
Soccer great Pelé scores his 1,000th goal

December 2, 1969
The Boeing 747 jumbo jet makes its first passenger flight

January 1, 1970
Unix time begins at 00:00:00 UTC

February 21, 1970
Paul McCartney begins recording a solo album at Morgan Studios

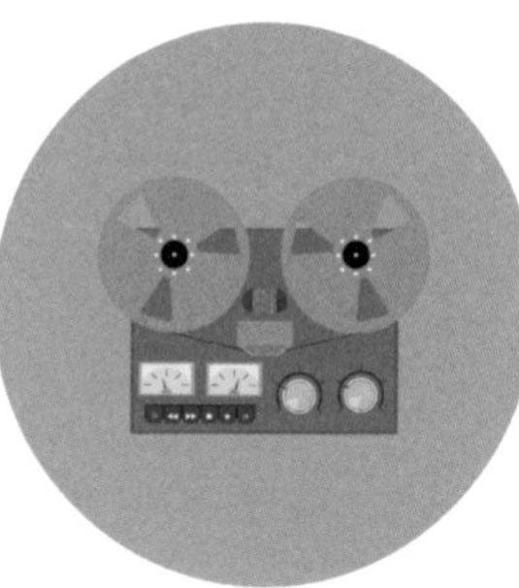

March 31, 1970
NASA's Explorer 1, the first American satellite and Explorer program spacecraft, re-enters Earth's atmosphere after 12 years in orbit

April 10, 1970
In a press release written in mock interview style, that is included in promotional copies of his first solo album, Paul McCartney announces that he has left The Beatles

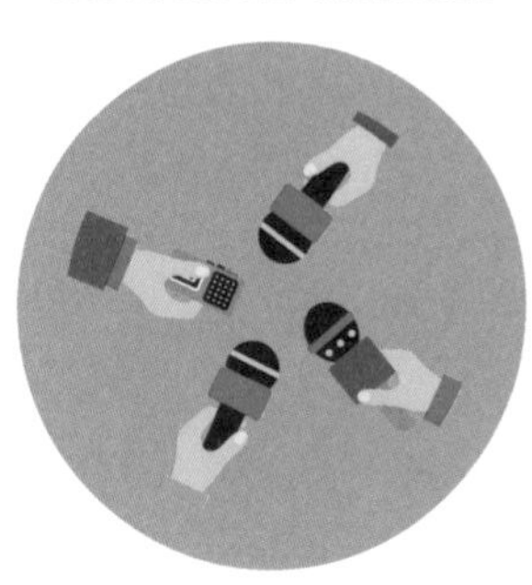

THE SECOND SIDE OF ABBEY ROAD IS MY FAVOURITE I LOVE IT

RINGO STARR

1976, ON 'ABBEY ROAD'

ALBUM COVER DESIGN

On 8 August 1969 photographer Iain Macmillan (a friend of John Lennon and Yoko Ono) set up a stepladder in the middle of Abbey Road. A policeman stopped traffic. With a Hasselblad camera, he took six photographs of the Beatles walking away from EMI Studios, a symbol of what was to come.

In shots 1, 2, 3, 4 and 6 the band were walking out of step. The fifth shot was perfect and was chosen by Paul McCartney for the album cover. The VW Beetle in the background was sold at auction in 1986 for £2,530 and is currently in the Autostadt museum in Germany

DARLING
DAY
COMES
BANG
BAD
I'LL
PAPER
HEAVY
I'D
LEAVE
OH
SLOWLY
CRY
ROUND
OCTOPUSS
GIRL
NEARLY
KNEE
DRIVING
PRETTY
WANT
CAME
BELIEVE
KNEW
HOMEWARD
SHOOT
ROLLER
HIGH
AMORE
BABE
COME
SLEEPS
GO
YES
WORLD
BLUE
SUN
I'M
FEELING
LOT
SKY
SOMEDAY
MINE
ONE
TOGETHER
SEE
LITTLE
LOVE
SHE'S
ALWAYS
MI
MAGIC
BAG
LIKE
MAD
NEVER
GONNA
CAME
BELIEVE
FREE
PAM
TRUE
HEH
LONG
YEARS
GIVE
YEAH
DON'T
CARRY
SURE
NOW
RIGHT
KNOW
GARDEN
DIDN'T
AH
WEIGHT
TELLS
THOUGH
GOT
DAY
TAKE

VOCALS: WHICH BEATLE TOOK THE LEAD?

Where band members shared lead vocals both are listed as singing lead vocals (as a result numbers may add up to more than the total number of tracks on the album).

Come Together
Something
Maxwell's Silver Hammer
Oh! Darling
Octopus's Garden
I Want You (She's So Heavy)
Here Comes the Sun
Because
You Never Give Me Your Money
Sun King
Mean Mr Mustard
Polythene Pam
She Came in Through the Bathroom Window
Golden Slumbers
Carry That Weight
The End
Her Majesty
0 COVERS
VS
17 ORIGINALS

SONGWRITING: WHO WROTE WHAT?

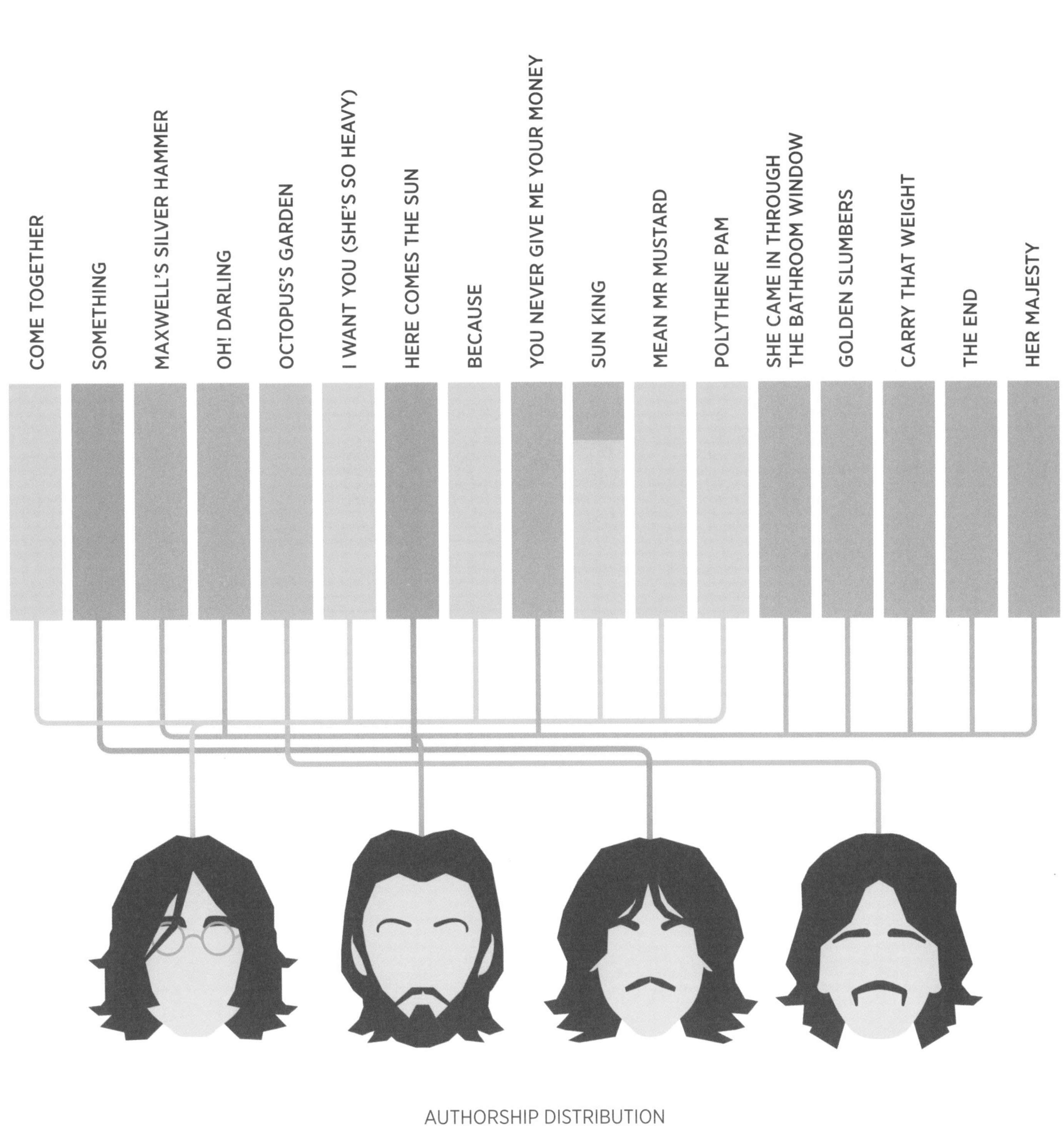

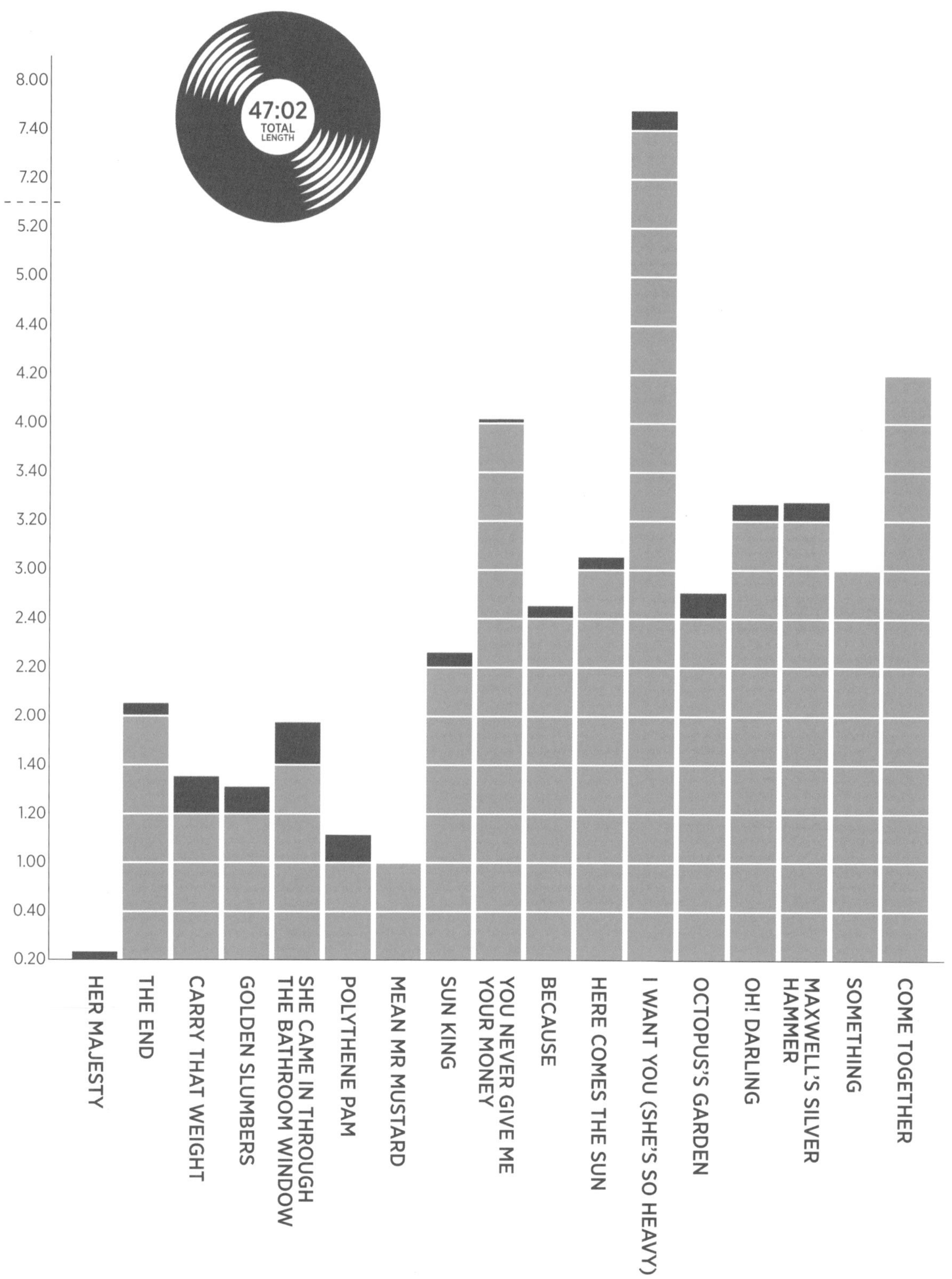
47:02
TOTAL LENGTH
8.00
7.40
7.20
5.20
5.00
4.40
4.20
4.00
3.40
3.20
3.00
2.40
2.20
2.00
1.40
1.20
1.00
0.40
0.20
HER MAJESTY
THE END
CARRY THAT WEIGHT
GOLDEN SLUMBERS
SHE CAME IN THROUGH THE BATHROOM WINDOW
POLYTHENE PAM
MEAN MR MUSTARD
SUN KING
YOU NEVER GIVE ME YOUR MONEY
BECAUSE
HERE COMES THE SUN
I WANT YOU (SHE'S SO HEAVY)
OCTOPUS'S GARDEN
OH! DARLING
MAXWELL'S SILVER HAMMER
SOMETHING
COME TOGETHER

SONG KEYS

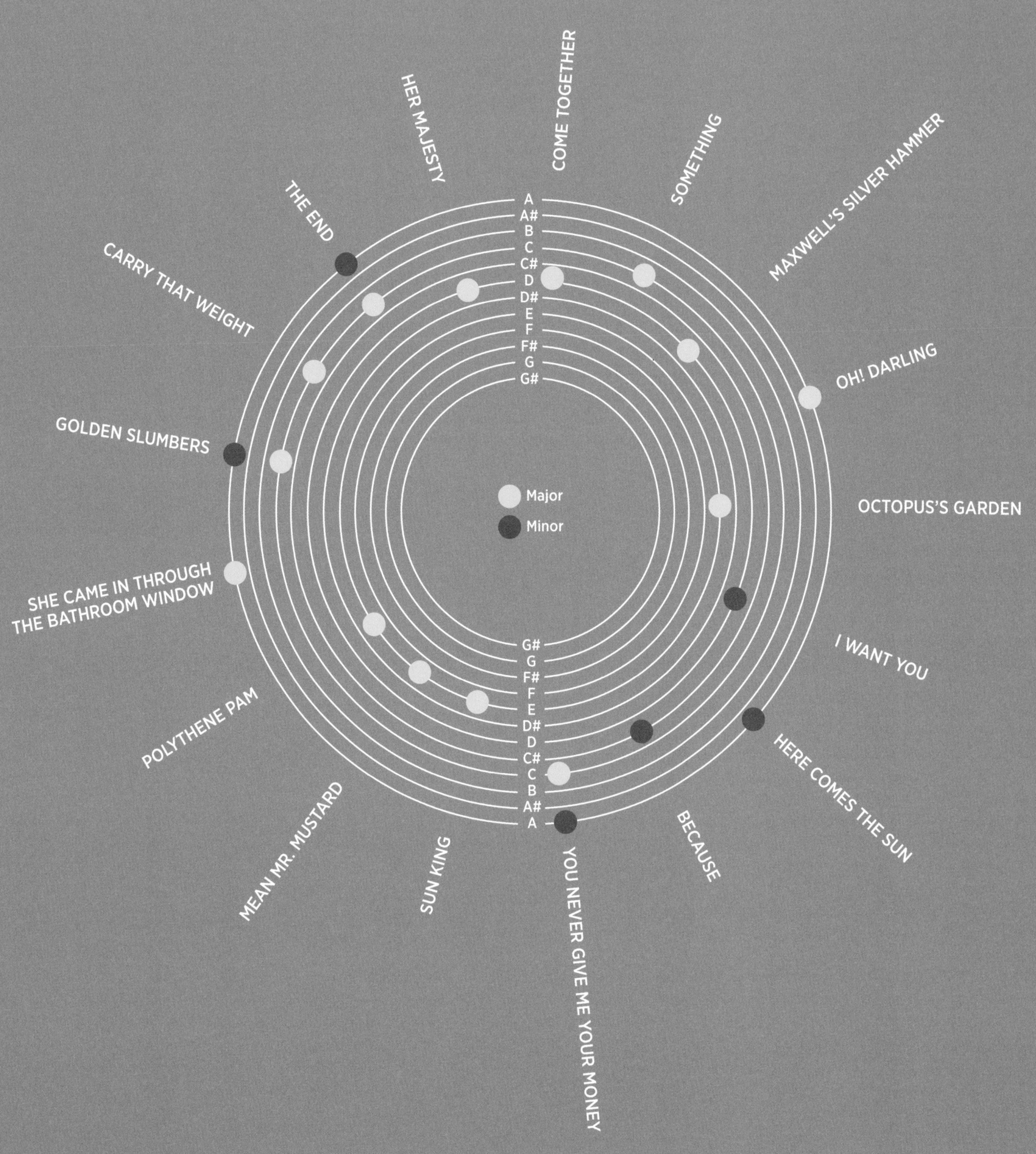

COME TOGETHER
SOMETHING
MAXWELL'S SILVER HAMMER
OH! DARLING
OCTOPUS'S GARDEN
I WANT YOU
HERE COMES THE SUN
BECAUSE
YOU NEVER GIVE ME YOUR MONEY
SUN KING
MEAN MR. MUSTARD
POLYTHENE PAM
SHE CAME IN THROUGH THE BATHROOM WINDOW
GOLDEN SLUMBERS
CARRY THAT WEIGHT
THE END
HER MAJESTY
A
A#
B
C
C#
D
D#
E
F
F#
G
G#
Major
Minor

BEATLES GUITARS

INSTRUMENTS: WHAT CAN YOU HEAR?

Black circle indicates instruments used for the first time in a Beatles' album

UK SINGLE RELEASES

Abbey Road was the first Beatles album to sell more than 10 million copies worldwide. It is the UK's best selling album of 1969 and the fourth highest selling album of the 1960s, entering the charts at no. 1 and staying there for eleven consecutive weeks. In the US, *Abbey Road* spent eleven (non-consecutive) weeks at no. 1 and was in the top 200 for 83 weeks in total.

Non-album singles that reached no. 1 at this time include 'Get Back'/'Don't Let Me Down' with Billy Preston (11/4/69) and 'The Ballad of John and Yoko'/'Old Brown Shoe' (30/5/69).

ALBUM CHART POSITIONS

UNITED KINGDOM
Number One

GERMANY
Number One

CANADA
Number One

NETHERLANDS
Number One

SPAIN
Number One

JAPAN
Number Three

AUSTRALIA
Number One

UNITED STATES
Number One

NORWAY
Number One

SWEDEN
Number One

A VISUAL REPRESENTATION OF THE VOLUME AND INTENSITY OF EACH TRACK ON THE ALBUM

1963
late 1963
mid 1964

late 1964
mid 1965
late 1965
mid 1966

mid 1967
late 1967
late 1968
early 1969

1969
1970
1970

These are the outfits the band wore for the iconic Abbey Road photoshoot. It sees the band in semi-formal style, but with interesting tweaks such as Paul barefoot and George in his now trademark denim outfit.

Turn me on, dead man ☠

One of the most enduring Beatles conspiracy theories centres around the supposed death of Paul McCartney, and subsequent replacement by the winner of a lookalike competition. A phone call to an American radio station in 1969, followed by a tongue-in-cheek article in the Michigan Daily set the world alight, with people searching for clues that one of their beloved Beatles had died.

To this day, people still believe that Paul died in a car crash in 1966 and hundreds of different pieces of 'evidence' have been cited. Many have been debunked, but here are some of our favourites:

Sgt. Pepper's

The complex and eclectic mix of items and characters on the cover of the album gave fans hunting for clues a wealth of material. Here are just a few of the things they picked out:

As well as Paul being the only Beatle playing a black instrument (symbolising death?), he appears to have a hand raised above his head. In certain Eastern societies this is a symbol of death. What is stranger is that a hand appears over Paul's head in seven other photographs included in various Beatles albums.

Many have pointed out that the cover also looks like a funeral scene. The fact that many of the 'mourners' (AKA figures depicted on the cover) are dead, the flowers, the younger version of the band looking down and the priest on the left are all cited as clues that this is a funeral for Paul.

Resting on the Rolling Stones doll on the bottom right is a model of an Aston Martin, the car it is said Paul was driving when he was killed.

The wreath at the bottom right of the album is in the shape of the left-handed bass guitar that Paul played. With some interpretation it can also be seen to spell the word 'Paul'.

A favourite pastime of clue hunters was to listen to Beatles tracks backwards. If you listen hard enough you can hear almost anything, but some tracks that produced interesting results are:

'Revolution 9' produces the words 'turn me on, dead man'

'I'm So Tired' produces 'Paul is dead, man, miss him, miss him'

'Let It Be' produces 'he is dead'

Abbey Road

The cover of *Abbey Road* is again one of the more visually interesting album designs and there's no shortage of theories as to its symbolism:

A popular theory is that the cover depicts a funeral scene, with Ringo as the undertaker (dressed in black), George as the gravedigger (in denim) and John as the preacher (in white). Paul is barefoot and is thought to represent the 'corpse'.

A VW Beetle can be seen in the background of the cover photo, with the last part of the license plate reading '28IF'. Conspiracy theorists say 28 was the age Paul would have been if he were still alive.

Paul is also seen walking across the road with a cigarette in hand, which is unusual for an album cover. A well known slang term for cigarettes is the 'coffin nail'. Could this be another clue?

In the *Magical Mystery Tour* film, Paul is seen wearing a black carnation, something normally associated with funerals, while the rest of the band have red ones. When asked about it, he claimed that they had run out of red ones, despite the fact he is passed a big bunch of them in the same scene...

At the end of the song 'Strawberry Fields', John Lennon is heard muttering in the background. It's not clear what he is saying, but many people have interpreted it as 'I buried Paul'. However, John himself is quoted as saying the words were 'cranberry sauce'.

ALBUM OVERVIEW

Released: 8 May 1970
Producers: George Martin, Phil Spector
Engineers: Glyn Johns, Martin Benge, Ken Scott, Peter Brown, Phil McDonald, Jeff Jarratt

Despite being recorded before *Abbey Road, Let It Be* was the last album to be released by the Beatles. It was a move away from the band's elaborate and intricate studio work and was recorded with a 'back to basics' ethos. In 1969 the band got together at Twickenham Film Studios to work on what they called the 'Get Back' project. They initially planned the project to include one or more live shows, a television show and an album. The sessions began as a rehearsal for a concert which they planned to film.

Enthusiasm in the band was low. They were all exhausted and John Lennon was addicted to heroin. Continual arguments led to George Harrison temporarily leaving the band. On his return he insisted that the idea of a live show was dropped. So they decided to finish their record in the basement of Apple's headquarters in Savile Row, London. They were joined by keyboard player Billy Preston, who they knew from their days in Hamburg. These Apple studio sessions culminated in the famous rooftop performance on 30th January, which would become known as the band's last ever live performance in public.

Once all the album and filming was complete there were hours of recordings to go through. Glyn Johns did this for the band and produced two versions of the album. Both were rejected. In March 1970 Phil Spector began working on it instead, at the invitation of Lennon and Harrison. McCartney and Martin knew nothing about it. Glyn Johns heavily criticised Spector's involvement but it was Spector's version that was finally released.

In 2003 a new version of the recordings was released, called *Let It Be... Naked*. It was produced under McCartney's direction and is meant to sound closer to what the band originally envisioned for the project.

MAY 1970

LET IT BE

TIMELINE: MAY-DECEMBER 1970

June 7, 1970
The Who become the first act to perform rock music at the Metropolitan Opera House, New York

August 26, 1970
The Isle of Wight Festival 1970 begins on East Afton Farm off the coast of England. Some 600,000 people attend the largest rock festival of all time

September 13, 1970
The first New York City Marathon begins

July 21, 1970
The Aswan High Dam in Egypt is completed

June 7, 1970
The Long and Winding Road becomes the Beatles' 20th and final single to reach number one on the US Billboard Hot 100 chart

May 8, 1970
The New York Knicks win their first NBA championship

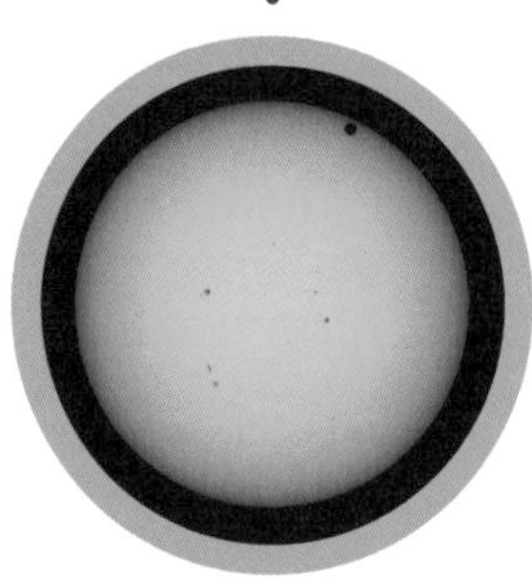

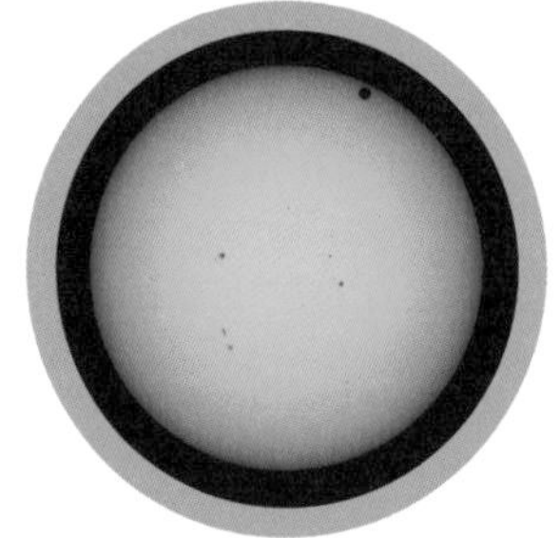

August 17, 1970
Venera 7 is launched toward Venus. It later becomes the first spacecraft to successfully transmit data from the surface of another planet

September 5, 1970
Formula One driver Jochen Rindt is killed in qualifying for the Italian Grand Prix. He becomes World Driving Champion anyhow, the first to earn the honour posthumously

November 17, 1970
The Soviet Union lands Lunokhod 1 on the moon. It is the first roving remote-controlled robot to visit another world

December 31, 1970
The Beatles officially break up after Paul McCartney sues the remaining members in British court

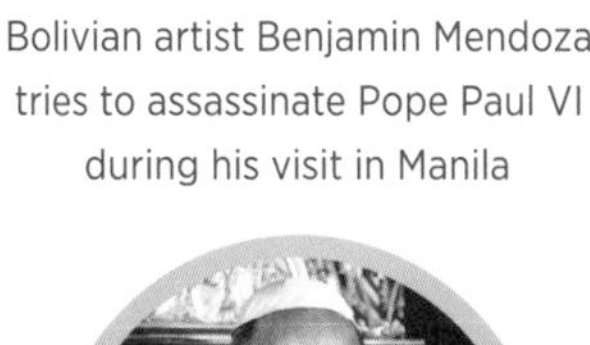

September 20, 1970
Luna 16 lands on the moon and lifts off the next day with samples. It lands on earth September 24

October 2, 1970
Pink Floyd releases *Atom Heart Mother*. It becomes their first number 1 album

November 27, 1970
Bolivian artist Benjamin Mendoza tries to assassinate Pope Paul VI during his visit in Manila

September 18, 1970
American musician Jimi Hendrix dies from an overdose of sleeping pills

November 13, 1970
Bhola tropical cyclone hits the densely populated Ganges Delta region of East Pakistan (now Bangladesh), killing an estimated 500,000 people

December 23, 1970
The North Tower of the World Trade Center is topped out at 1,368 feet (417 m), making it the tallest building in the world

ALBUM COVER DESIGN

Let It Be features portraits of each of the Beatles taken during their recording sessions. Each member was separated by a thick black bar, symbolising the fact they were no longer together.

WE WERE ALL FRAUGHT WITH EACH OTHER AND JUST ABOUT EVERYTHING ELSE. WE WERE PROBABLY ALL ON THE VERGE OF

PAUL MCCARTNEY

1996, ON RECORDING 'LET IT BE'

VOCALS: WHICH BEATLE TOOK THE LEAD?

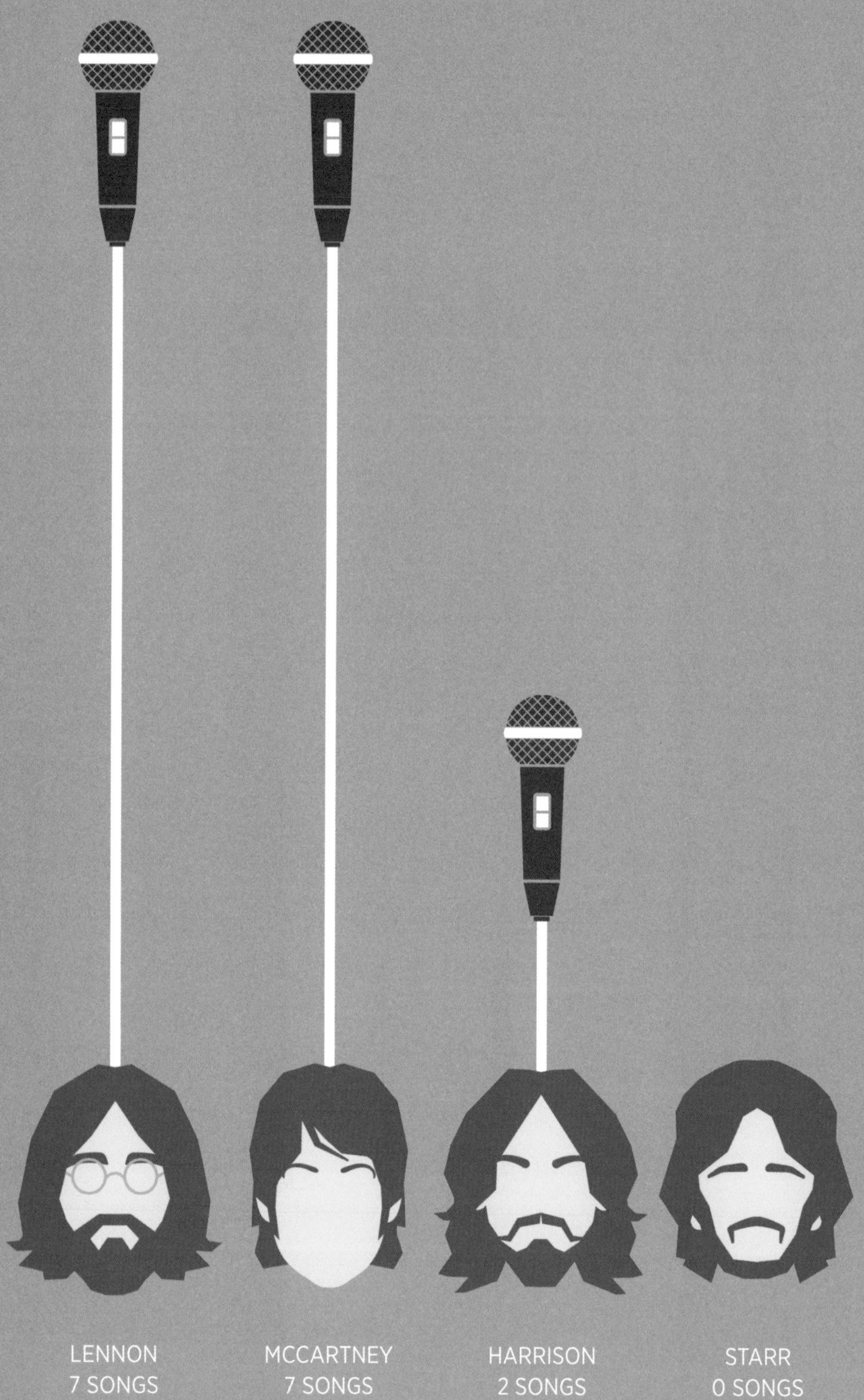

Where band members shared lead vocals both are listed as singing lead vocals (as a result numbers may add up to more than the total number of tracks on the album).

SONG KEYS

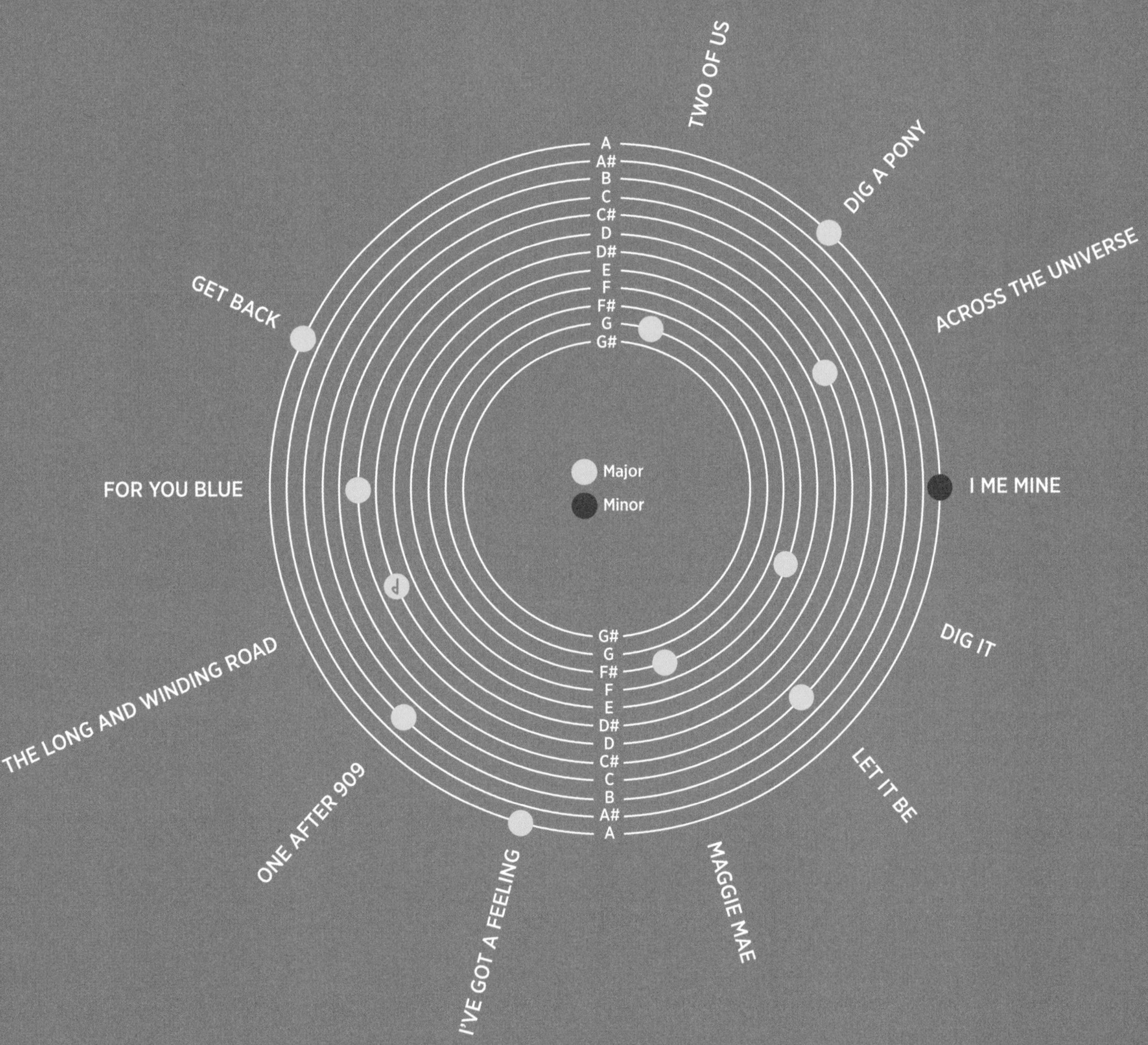

TWO OF US
DIG A PONY
ACROSS THE UNIVERSE
I ME MINE
DIG IT
LET IT BE
MAGGIE MAE
I'VE GOT A FEELING
ONE AFTER 909
THE LONG AND WINDING ROAD
FOR YOU BLUE
GET BACK
A
A#
B
C
C#
D
D#
E
F
F#
G
G#
Major
Minor

SONGWRITING: WHO WROTE WHAT?

*This is an old Liverpool folk song but the Beatles arrangement of it is very different and all four of them worked on it.

Two of Us
Dig a Pony
Across the Universe
I Me Mine
Dig It
Let It Be
I've Got a Feeling
One After 909
The Long and Winding Road
For You Blue
Get Back
Maggie Mae
1 COVER
VS
11 ORIGINALS

LENGTH: TRACKS AND ALBUM

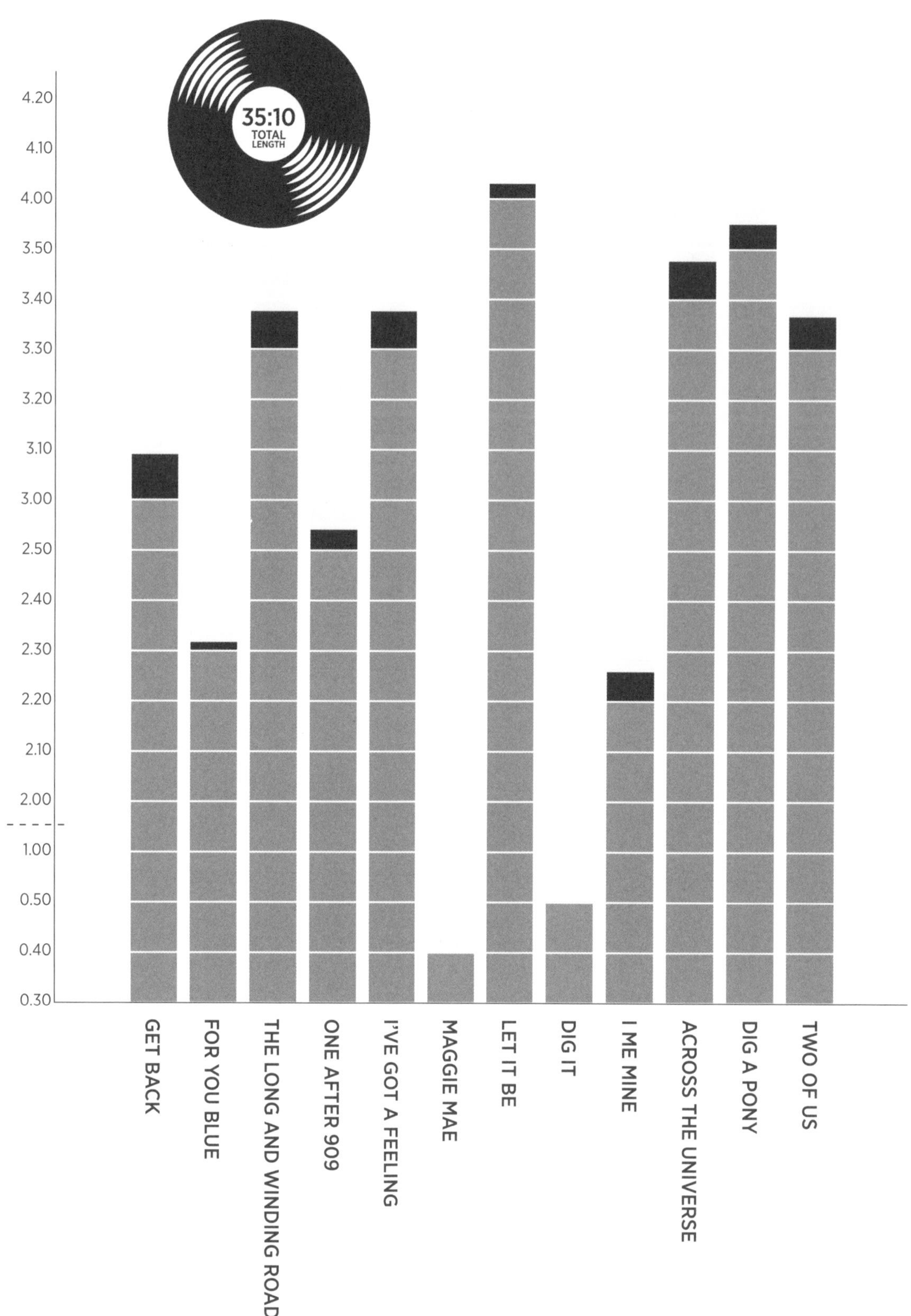

UK SINGLE RELEASES

TWO OF US
DIG A PONY
ACROSS THE UNIVERSE
I ME MINE
DIG IT
LET IT BE
MAGGIE MAE
I'VE GOT A FEELING
ONE AFTER 909
THE LONG AND WINDING ROAD
FOR YOU BLUE
GET BACK

Let It Be was generally badly received. The band had already gone their separate ways and Paul McCartney had released his first solo album a few weeks previously. 'Let It Be', the single, had been released prior to the album on 6 March 1970. 'Get Back' was also released as a single but this version of it, featuring Billy Preston was totally different to the one included in *Let It Be* (hence why it isn't shown here). The album still reached no. 1 but only spent three weeks at the top. In the US, the album had over 3.7 million advance orders, which at the time was the highest number of advanced orders for any album in US history.

ALBUM CHART POSITIONS

UNITED KINGDOM
Number One

GERMANY
Number Three

CANADA
Number One

NETHERLANDS
Number One

JAPAN
Number Two

AUSTRALIA
Number One

UNITED STATES
Number One

NORWAY
Number One

SWEDEN
Number Two

Black circle indicates instruments used for the first time in a Beatles' album

VOLUME AND INTENSITY

A VISUAL REPRESENTATION OF THE VOLUME AND INTENSITY OF EACH TRACK ON THE ALBUM

STYLE

1963
late 1963
mid 1964

late 1964
mid 1965
late 1965
mid 1966

mid 1967
late 1967
late 1968
early 1969
1969

1970

Two days after they had finished recording *Abbey Road*, The Beatles met at John's estate, Tittenhurst Park for what would be their final photo session. Much like the *Abbey Road* shoot, the band chose to dress in the casual, relaxed style they had all become comfortable with, each with an air of individuality.

LEGACY

Hairstyles Over The Years

The Fab Four were always seen as fashion icons, and their hairstyles were as imitated and scrutinised as their outfits. Let's have a look at how their hair changed over the years...

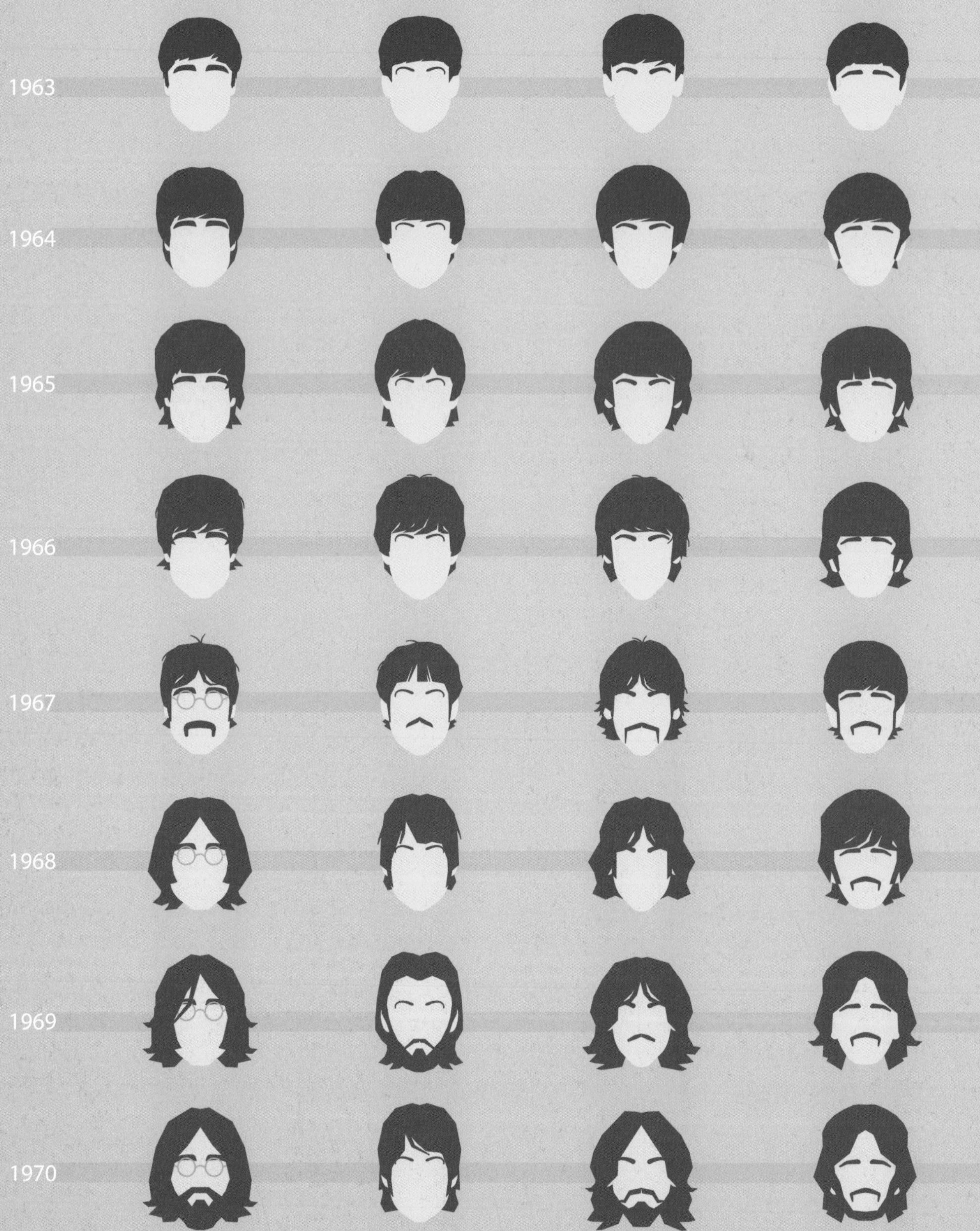

Fab Four Memorabilia Sales

Due to the worldwide appeal of The Beatles, some of the more scarce memorabilia commands huge sums. Here are some of the most expensive Beatles items ever sold at auction:

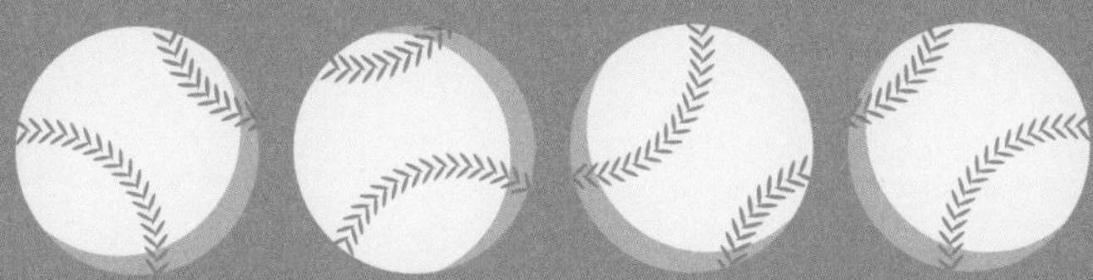

Single baseballs signed by members of the Beatles have sold for as much as $68,000.00

Sgt. Peppers UK Gatefold cover signed by all four members
$290,500.00 (Heritage Auctions 2013)

Bass drum skin used on the Sgt. Pepper cover
£541,250.00
(Christie's 2008)

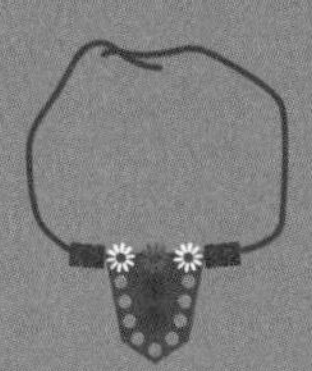

Autographed gnome prop from Sgt. Peppers album cover shoot
$42,500.00
(Heritage Auctions 2015)

John Lennon's leather necklace, worn in 1967-68
£117,250.00
(Christie's 2004)

Handwritten lyrics by John lennon for 'All You Need Is Love'
$1,250,000.00
(Cooper Owen 2005)

John Lennon's 1953 Austin Princess hearse, driven in the 'Imagine' video
Est £185,000.00+
(RM Sotheby 2016)

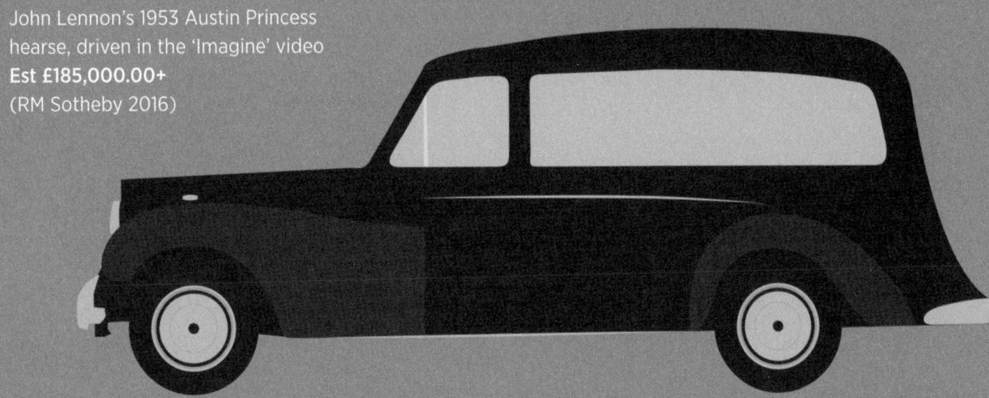

John Lennon's white suit worn for the Abbey Road cover
$46,000.00
(Braswell Galleries 2011)

But the record goes to John Lennon's psychedelic painted Rolls Royce Phantom V, selling for **$2.23 MILLION** **in 1985 to Canadian businessman Jim Pattison, making it the most expensive piece of music memorabilia ever!**

Cover Versions of Beatles Songs

We know the Beatles have always been hugely popular, but just how popular?
Here is everyone to date who has recorded one or more songs originally written by The Beatles...

10cc
7B
801
The 12 cellists of the Berlin Philharmonic
The 5th Dimension
Bryan Adams
Aerosmith
The Aggrolites
Agua De Annique
Air Supply
Monty Alexander
Alice
Alice Donut
Kris Allen
Allister
Herb Alpert & The Tijuana Brass
Alvin and the Chipmunks
Alvin and the Chipmunks and The Chipettes
AM & Tina Dico
Ambrose Slade (pre-Slade)
Ambrosia
Amen Corner
Tori Amos
Ana Gabriel
Anathema
Thomas Anders
Joe Anderson
Marc Anthony
Fiona Apple
The Applejacks
April Wine
David Archuleta
Arctic Monkeys
Arno (Arno Hintjens)
P. P. Arnold
Aritzia
Daniel Ash
Susan Ashton & Gary Chapman
Assagai
Athlete
Atomic Kitten
Jean-Louis Aubert
Emilie Autumn
Ayreon
Pedro Aznar
B5
Babyshambles
Bad Brains
Bad Company
Joan Baez
Bajaga & Instruktori
David Ball
Kenny Ball
Bananarama
Carl Barât
Carl Barât & Pete Doherty
Cris Barber
Sara Bareilles
Barnes & Barnes
Baskin & Copperfield
Shirley Bassey
Bathory
The Beach Boys
Beady Eye
Beastie Boys
Beatallica
BECK
Jeff Beck
Bee Gees
Béla Fleck and the Flecktones
Adrian Belew
Drake Bell
Belle & Sebastian
John Belushi
Pat Benatar
Cliff Bennett and the Rebel Rousers
Cliff Bennett Band
Tony Bennett
David Benoit
George Benson
Cathy Berberian
Matraca Berg
John Berry
Betty
Big Daddy
Big Time Rush
Billie Joe Armstrong
Björk
The Black Crowes
The Black Keys
Black Oak Arkansas
Black Sabbath
Blessid Union of Souls

Blondie
Bloodrock
Blood, Sweat & Tears
James Blunt
Suzy Bogguss & Chet Atkins
Michael Bolton
Gary U.S. Bonds
Bon Jovi
Graham Bonnet
Boney M.
Bono
Booker T. & the M.G.'s
Boris
Alexei Borisov
David Bowie
Boxer
Boyz II Men
Paul Brady
Billy Bragg
Billy Bragg with Cara Tivey
Russell Brand
Eva Braun
Breakfast Club
The Breeders
Brian Bromberg
Herman Brood
Gary Brooker
The Brothers Four
The Brothers Johnson
James Brown
Joe Brown
Michael Bublé
Jeff Buckley
Enrique Bunbury
Los Bunkers
Buranovskiye Babushki
Eric Burdon & War
Chris de Burgh
Jean-Jacques Burnel
George Burns
Sam Bush
Butthole Surfers
Max Bygraves
Junior Campbell
Canadian Brass
Candy Flip
Brandi Carlile
The Carpenters
T. V. Carpio
Vikki Carr
Paul Carrack
Jim Carrey
Waterson–Carthy
Johnny Cash
Rosanne Cash
David Cassidy
Eva Cassidy
Jason Castro
Nick Cave
Nick Cave and the Bad Seeds
Peter Cetera
Eugene Chadbourne
Chapterhouse
Ray Charles
Chayanne
Cheap Trick
Cher
Chicago
Chikezie
Alex Chilton
Chocolate Genius
Wang Chung
Jennifer Cihi
Eric Clapton
Petula Clark
Cloud Cult
Kurt Cobain
Riccardo Cocciante
Bruce Cockburn
Joe Cocker
CoH
Avishai Cohen
Coldplay
Holly Cole
Chris Colfer
Chris Colfer & Lea Michele
Judy Collins
Phil Collins
Shawn Colvin
Perry Como
Les Compagnons de la chanson
Arthur Conley
Sean Connery

Harry Connick, Jr.
Billy Connolly
David Cook
Kristy Lee Cook
Coope Boyes and Simpson
Alice Cooper
Copy
Chick Corea
Chick Corea with Hiromi Uehara
Chris Cornell
Cornershop
Coroner
Andrea Corr
The Corrs
Larry Coryell
Bill Cosby
Elvis Costello
Jonathan Coulton
Count Basie
Counting Crows
Cowboy Junkies
Crash Kings
The Crickets
Bing Crosby
Crosby, Stills & Nash
Sheryl Crow
Crowded House
Celia Cruz
The Cryan' Shames
Dejan Cukić
Jamie Cullum
The Damned
Danger Mouse
Bobby Darin
Dave Matthews Band
Craig David
David and Jonathan
Sammy Davis, Jr.
P.M. Dawn
Danielle Dax
Howie Day
dc Talk
Dead Kennedys
Billy Dean
Deep Purple
Def Leppard
Defunkt
John Denver
The Detroit Emeralds
Neil Diamond
Dillard & Clark
The Dillards
Cara Dillon & Sam Lakeman
Phyllis Dillon
Pat DiNizio
Céline Dion
Divididos
Pete Doherty
Dollar
Plácido Domingo
Fats Domino
Tanya Donelly
The Donnas
Val Doonican
Dream Theater
Dr. Sin
Bob Dylan
Steve Earle and Allison Moorer
Earth, Wind & Fire
Easy Star All-Stars
Easy Star All-Stars ft. Bunny Rugs & U-Roy
Easy Star All-Stars ft. Frankie Paul
Easy Star All-Stars ft. Junior Jazz
Easy Star All-Stars ft. Kirsty Rock
Easy Star All-Stars ft. Luciano
Easy Star All-Stars ft. Matisyahu
Easy Star All-Stars ft. Max Romeo
Easy Star All-Stars ft. Michael Rose and Menny More
Easy Star All-Stars ft. Ranking Roger
Easy Star All-Stars ft. Steel Pulse
Easy Star All-Stars ft. Sugar Minott
Easy Star All-Stars ft. The Mighty Diamonds
Echo & the Bunnymen
Eels
əkoostik hookah
Electric Light Orchestra
Električni Orgazam
Cássia Eller
Andy Ellison
Elmo
Tommy Emmanuel
En Vogue
David Essex

Ethel the Frog
Eurythmics
Extreme
Los Fabulosos Cadillacs (feat. Deborah Harry)
Fairground Attraction
Andy Fairweather-Low
Marianne Faithfull
Falco
Jason Falkner
The Fall
Georgie Fame
Sandy Farina
John Farnham
Father
The Feelies
José Feliciano
Jay Ferguson
Maynard Ferguson
Bryan Ferry
Ferry Aid
The Fiery Furnaces
Neil Finn & Liam Finn
Firewater
Ella Fitzgerald
The Flamin' Groovies
Florence + the Machine
The Flowers
Ben Folds
Foo Fighters
Fool's Garden
Tennessee Ernie Ford
The Format
David Foster with Katharine McPhee
The Fourmost
The Four Seasons
Four Tops
Samantha Fox
Les Fradkin
Nikolai Fraiture
Roddy Frame
Peter Frampton
Aretha Franklin
Franz Ferdinand
The Fray
The Free Design
Russ Freeman
Paul Frees
John Frusciante
Dana Fuchs
Lowell Fulson
Peter Gabriel
Eric Gales Band
Noel Gallagher
James Galway
Garbage
Charly García
Charly García, Pedro Aznar & Gustavo Cerati
Jerry Garcia
Jerry Garcia Band
Art Garfunkel
Marvin Gaye
Gene
Bobbie Gentry
James Genus
George Martin Orchestra
The Georgia Satellites
Ghost
Barry Gibb
Robin Gibb
Seru Giran
GLAY
Glee Cast
Godhead
Godsmack
Golden Earring
Grandaddy
Peter Grant
The Grass Roots
Grateful Dead
Al Green
Green Day
Marcia Griffiths
Paul Griggs
Dave Grohl
Groove Collective
Henry Gross
Dave Grusin
Vince Guaraldi
The Guess Who
Guns N' Roses
Guster
Guys 'n' Dolls
Gyllene Tider

Bill Haley & His Comets
Johnny Hallyday
Herbie Hancock
Hanson
Steve Harley & Cockney Rebel
Ben Harper
Emmylou Harris
Harry J All Stars
Donny Hathaway
Richie Havens
Greg Hawkes
Goldie Hawn
Salma Hayek
Isaac Hayes
Jeff Healey
Heart
The Helio Sequence
Helloween
Jimi Hendrix
The Heptones
David Hernandez
Kristin Hersh
Boo Hewerdine & Eddi Reader
Taylor Hicks
Steve Hillage
The Hobos
Allan Holdsworth
Xaviera Hollander
The Hollies
The Hollyridge Strings
Hoodoo Gurus
The Hooters
The Hour Glass
House of Heroes
Frankie Howerd
Jennifer Hudson
Humble Pie
Hush Sound
Hüsker Dü
Hyde
I Against I
Ibex & Freddie Mercury
The Ides of March
Julio Iglesias
The Impressions
Indexi
James Ingram
The Inmates
Inner Circle
Eddie Izzard
Joe Jackson
Michael Jackson
Willis Jackson
The Jam
Bobby Jameson
Jan and Dean
Al Jarreau
Jefferson Starship
Joan as Police Woman
Billy Joel
Billy Joel with Paul McCartney
John Butler Trio
John's Children
Elton John
Marc Johnson
Syl Johnson
Jonas Brothers
Jonas Brothers and Demi Lovato
Norah Jones
Rickie Lee Jones
Tom Jones
Stanley Jordan
Journey
Laurence Juber
Jump5
Kaiser Chiefs
Kansas
Kasabian
Phil Keaggy & PFR
Keane
Dustin Kensrue
Sammy Kershaw
Alicia Keys
Bob Khaleel
Chaka Khan
Kids Incorporated
The Killers
King Crimson
King Missile
Morgana King
King's Singers
Gershon Kingsley
The Kingsmen